T0024191

Many thanks to the wonderful tourism folks of Michigan for answering my endless questions. My appreciation to the excellent public relations officials and to the Michigan residents and business owners who took the time to share what makes Michigan special.

Gratitude to my Globe Pequot editor Sarah Parke for inviting me to take this treasure-filled trip through Michigan. It has been a delight and a pure pleasure.

This book is dedicated to my family—Kelly Rose; Mike Peters; Sean Rose; Stefanie, Will, Trey, and Arianna Scott; and Logan Peters.

A special remembrance to my husband, Bill Finch, whose spirit goes with me every step of the way through life's journey.

—Jackie Sheckler Finch

OFF THE BEATEN PATH® SERIES

THIRTEENTH EDITION

MICHIGAN

OFF THE BEATEN PATH®

DISCOVER YOUR FUN

JACKIE SHECKLER FINCH

Globe Pequot

Guilford, Connecticut

All the information in this guidebook is subject to change. We recommend that you call ahead to obtain current information before traveling.

Globe Pequot

An imprint of The Rowman & Littlefield Publishing Group, Inc.
4501 Forbes Blvd., Ste. 200
Lanham, MD 20706
www.rowman.com

Distributed by NATIONAL BOOK NETWORK

Copyright © 2021 The Rowman & Littlefield Publishing Group, Inc.
Previous editions written by Jim Dufresne.

Off the Beaten Path is a registered trademark of The Rowman & Littlefield Publishing Group, Inc.

All rights reserved. No part of this book may be reproduced in any form or by any electronic or mechanical means, including information storage and retrieval systems, without written permission from the publisher, except by a reviewer who may quote passages in a review.

British Library Cataloguing in Publication Information available

Library of Congress Cataloging-in-Publication Data available

ISBN 978-1-4930-5359-9 (paper : alk. paper)
ISBN 978-1-4930-5360-5 (electronic)

♾™ The paper used in this publication meets the minimum requirements of American National Standard for Information Sciences—Permanence of Paper for Printed Library Materials, ANSI/NISO Z39.48-1992.

Contents

About the Reviser

Jackie Sheckler Finch has written about a wide array of topics—from birth to death, with all the joy and sorrow in between. An award-winning journalist and photographer, Jackie has done more than a dozen travel guidebooks for Globe Pequot and is a member of the Society of American Travel Writers and the Midwest Travel Journalists Association. She has been named the Mark Twain Travel Writer of the Year a record five times, in 1998, 2001, 2003, 2007, and 2012. One of her greatest joys is taking to the road to find the fascinating people and places that wait over the hill and around the next bend.

Introduction

If you look at a map of the United States or spin a globe, you'll discover that the most prominent state is Michigan. It always stands out, regardless of the size of the map or how obscured the detail.

Michigan is set off from much of the country by water. Four of the five Great Lakes surround it and have turned its borders into 3,200 miles of lakeshore where you can sit in the sand and look out on the watery horizon of the world's largest freshwater seas.

Michigan is inundated with water. It's not only outlined by blue, but its history was shaped by the Great Lakes. Today travelers search the state over for a bit of their own sand and surf, and there is no short supply. Stand anywhere in the state and you are no more than 85 miles from the Great Lakes and only 6 miles from one of the 11,000 sparkling inland lakes or 36,000 miles of streams and rivers. Come winter, Michigan's water turns fluffy and white and gently lands all around, much to the delight of skiers.

Michigan is water, yet beaches and boating, swimming and sunbathing are only part of the state's attractions. To the adventurous traveler, to those who love to swing off the interstates onto the country roads that wander between the woods and the lakes, there are quaint villages to discover and shipwrecks to explore, art fairs and mushroom festivals to enjoy, wine-tasting tours to savor, a stretch of quiet trail to soothe the urban soul.

All you need is time, a good map of Michigan, and this book. The map can be obtained by calling Pure Michigan toll free at (888) 784-7328 or by checking the website michigan.org. The map will lead you away from the six-lane highways to the scenic country roads and then back again when you are ready to return home.

Michigan Off the Beaten Path points out those half-hidden gems that travelers rejoice in discovering, from a lighthouse that has become a country inn to party-fishing boats that let novice anglers stalk and catch the Great Lakes' tastiest offering, the yellow perch. Because addresses, phone numbers, and hours of operation can change from summer to summer, the regional chapters contain a list of tourist associations that can provide the most up-to-date information.

The same holds true for prices. Inflation, with its annual increases in everything from room rates and restaurant prices to entry fees at parks and museums, will quickly outdate anything listed. Therefore, only the prices for substantial items (rooms, meals, and major attractions) have been provided in this book to help readers judge whether a restaurant or hotel is affordable.

Michigan Facts

Nickname: Great Lakes State

Capital: Lansing

Population: 9,986,857, 10th in the country

Area: 96,716 square miles, 11th in the country

Admitted to Union: Michigan became the 26th state when it was admitted on January 26, 1837.

Major Cities: Detroit, population 672,662; Grand Rapids, 200,217; Warren, 134,587; Sterling Heights, 132,964; Flint, 95,943; Lansing, 118,427; Ann Arbor, 121,890; Livonia, 93,971

Famous Residents: Henry Ford, Thomas Edison, Bob Seger, President Gerald Ford, Charles Lindbergh, Diana Ross, Stevie Wonder, Madonna, Magic Johnson, Tom Selleck, and Eminem

National Park Units: Isle Royale National Park, Pictured Rocks National Lakeshore, Sleeping Bear Dunes National Lakeshore

Travel Information: Pure Michigan (300 N. Washington Sq., Lansing 48913; (888) 784-7328; michigan.org) will send you a free travel guide to Michigan along with a road map. The West Michigan Tourist Association (721 D Kenmoor Ave., Grand Rapids 49546; (800) 442-2084 or (616) 245-2217; wmta.org) covers accommodations, attractions, and visitor facilities in the western half of the Lower Peninsula. The Upper Peninsula Travel and Recreation Association (1050 Pyle Dr., Kingsford, 49802; (800) 562-7134 or (906) 774-5480; uptravel.com) covers the Upper Peninsula.

State Parks: For a guide to the Michigan State Park system, contact the Michigan Department of Natural Resources, Parks & Recreation Division, Box 30028, Lansing 48909; (517) 284-6367; michigan.gov/dnr.

Major Newspapers: *Detroit Free Press, Detroit News, Grand Rapids Press, Flint Journal, Lansing State Journal*

Public Transportation: Michigan's major regional air center is Detroit Metro Airport, located in the suburb of Romulus 15 miles southwest of Detroit. The main carrier is Delta Airlines (800-221-1212; delta.com), which uses Detroit as a major hub. Both Greyhound Bus Service (800-231-2222; greyhound.com) and Amtrak (800-872-7245; amtrak.com) maintains service throughout the state.

Climate: Michigan is split in the middle by the 45th Parallel; this northern position means that it has a very temperate, four-season climate. Summers reach the high 90s but rarely break triple digits. Winters can dip to minus 10 or 20 degrees at times in the northern half of the state but usually hover between 10 and 20 degrees in southern Michigan. Thanks to the Great Lakes, Michigan receives an abundance of snow, with some towns like Munising and Calumet totaling more than 250 inches by the end of March. Autumn colors are spectacular in the state, with trees beginning to change in late September in the Upper Peninsula and late October in southern Michigan.

Most of all, more than this book and a map, you need time. Don't short-change Michigan. Don't try to cover half the state in a weekend holiday. You will only be disappointed at the end of your trip. You could spend a summer exploring Michigan and never leave the shoreline. I have spent a lifetime traveling here, yet my never-ending list of places to go and adventures to undertake only grows longer with each journey in the Great Lakes State.

Southeast Michigan

Southeast Michigan, a region of seven counties, revolves around metropolitan Detroit, which sprawls into three of them. And Detroit revolves around automobiles. It's as simple as that.

Known best throughout the country as Motor City, Detroit carries several other titles, including Motown, after the recording company that produced such famous singers as Diana Ross and Stevie Wonder before it fled to Los Angeles from its studio on Woodward Avenue. The city was also home to the nation's oldest state fair (the Michigan State Fair dated to 1849) until it was closed after funding cuts in 2009. On May 30, 2012, it was announced that the Michigan State Fair would be replaced by the Great Lakes Agricultural State Fair, which was held August 31 through September 3, 2012, at the Suburban Collection Showplace in the Detroit suburb of Novi. In 2013, Fifth Third Bank became the sponsor so the name became the Fifth Third Bank Michigan State Fair with a private entity, Michigan State Fair LLC, organizing the annual event. The fair is still held in Novi at the Suburban Collection Showplace. Detroit and its neighboring suburbs wear many faces: some are good, some others are unjustly earned, but the least recognized one is that of a destination for travelers. Detroit is the twenty-fourth

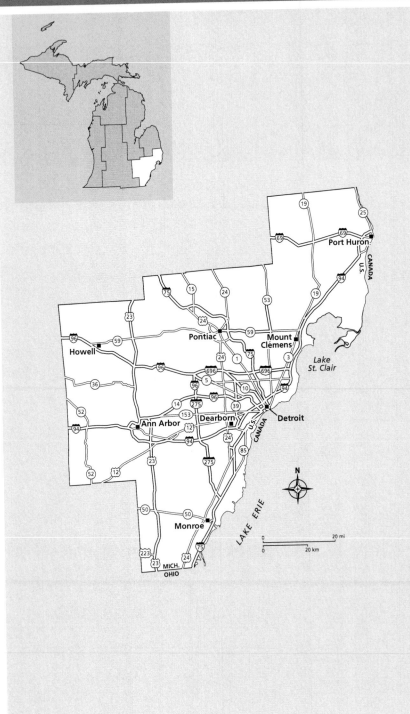

largest city in the country, yet despite its size many tourists consider it very much "off the beaten path." Depart from the city and the rest of Southeast Michigan changes quickly, from the urban sprawl to the rolling hills and lakes of northern Oakland County, the blue water of St. Clair and Port Huron, and the culture and carefree college ways of Ann Arbor, the home of the University of Michigan.

Wayne County

Until the 1870s, **Detroit** was a commercial center for farmers, but at the end of that century the first automobiles appeared, as Ransom E. Olds and Henry Ford began tinkering with "horseless carriages." By 1903, Ford had organized the Ford Motor Company, and when he pioneered the assembly-line method of building cars and introduced the Model T, the vehicle for the common man, Detroit's place as the automobile capital of the world was established.

Cars are a way of life in Detroit. Michigan boasts of having the first mile of concrete rural highway (1909), the first traffic light (1915), and the first urban freeway free of those annoying stoplights (1942). The best-known place to view this history of cars and their immense effect on the American way of life is The Henry Ford, home of Greenfield Village and **Henry Ford Museum** (313-982-6001 or 800-835-5237; thehenryford.org), a 260-acre complex with 100 historic buildings in **Dearborn** that has become the nation's largest indoor and outdoor museum.

A $200 million upgrade of Greenfield Village in 2004 resulted in "America's Greatest Historical Attraction" being extensively redesigned and for the first time open from mid-April through New Year's Eve. Now the streets of the turn-of-the-20th-century village are lined with 331 lampposts, while such famous buildings as Thomas Edison's laboratory from Menlo Park, New Jersey; the Wright Brothers' Ohio cycle workshop; and the Logan County Courthouse where Abraham Lincoln first practiced law are heated for visitors who arrive outside the summer months. The adjacent Henry Ford Museum also features new exhibits, including the bus where in 1955 Rosa Parks refused to give up her seat, thus igniting America's civil rights movement.

So much history, so little time to absorb it all. Keep in mind that the village and the museum are each a separate attraction with a separate admission price, and each requires a good part of a day to view. Car buffs are fascinated by the Henry Ford Museum, especially its main attraction, the Automobile in American Life, an ode to the motorcar culture that is the social history of 20th-century America. Families and children love Greenfield Village.

Henry Ford Museum Home of Priceless American Memorabilia

A glass vial with the dying breath of famed inventor Thomas Edison.

The maroon chair, still bloodstained, where President Abraham Lincoln was assassinated at Ford's Theatre.

A folding camp bed that General George Washington actually slept in during the Revolutionary War.

Henry Ford was a collector. As one of the world's first billionaires, Ford had the money to collect whatever struck his fancy. Instead of expensive works of art or precious gems, however, Ford liked to save pieces of everyday life from the past.

A quote from Ford explains why he was so interested in his unusual collection:

"When I went to our American history books to learn how our forefathers harrowed the land, I discovered that the historians knew nothing about harrows," Ford says. "Yet our country has depended more on harrows than on guns or speeches. I thought that a history which excluded harrows and all the rest of daily life is bunk and I think so yet."

Born July 30, 1863, in Dearborn, Henry Ford was the oldest of six children of first-generation Irish farmers, William and Mary Ford. Not rich, but far from poor, the Fords had a secure homelife. By all rights, Henry probably should have become a farmer. But at 16 and against the wishes of his father, Ford left the farm for Detroit, where he found work as a mechanic's apprentice.

Ford advanced steadily and became chief engineer at the Edison Illuminating Co. At 24, Ford married Clara Bryant, a friend of his sister's. He called his wife "The Believer" because she encouraged his plans to build a horseless carriage from their earliest days together.

In his spare time, Ford tinkered with creating that motorized vehicle. Part of his legacy is that Ford created a mass-produced automobile that was affordable for many common folks. He may have contributed more than any other individual—besides his friend and mentor Thomas Edison—to the reality of the modern world.

Ford also developed an obsessive collection of historical memorabilia and commonplace items like toasters, farm machinery, kerosene lamps, and steam engines. In 1919, the city of Dearborn decided to widen a number of streets. Ford's beloved boyhood home stood directly in the path of development. It seemed ironic that the house was about to be destroyed due to the rush of traffic that Ford helped create.

But Ford found an ideal solution. He moved the entire house and it became the beginning of his Greenfield Village that today contains nearly 100 structures. By 1920, Ford had decided to start a museum that would emphasize industrial history and thereby "give people a true picture of the development of the country."

The best way to create this picture, Ford decided, was to have two parts. An exhibit hall would display inventions and artifacts that recorded man's technological and cultural progress. An adjacent outdoor village of residential, commercial, and industrial architecture would show how those objects were made and used.

He named the entire complex **The Edison Institute**, in honor of the man who encouraged Ford when he was developing his automobile and who embodied, the carmaker believed, practical genius.

Ford greatly admired Edison, who routinely came pretty close to his goal of creating one major invention every six months and a minor one every 10 days. Edison patented 1,097 inventions.

Displayed at the entrance to the museum is a cornerstone with Edison's signature and footprints, along with legendary horticulturist Luther Burbank's spade. It commemorates the dedication of the site on Sept. 27, 1928.

The opening of the new museum and village would take place a year later. Ford decided that Oct. 21, 1929, would be the date since it marked the 50th anniversary of Edison's first successful experiment with a suitable approach to manufacturing an incandescent lamp.

Among the most popular museum exhibits is the one on Presidential Vehicles. It features the Theodore Roosevelt horse-drawn Brougham, Franklin D. Roosevelt Sunshine Special, Dwight D. Eisenhower Bubbletop, and the 1961 Lincoln where JFK was riding when he was assassinated in Dallas on Nov. 22, 1963.

The Reagan presidential limousine is where Ronald Reagan took refuge on March 1, 1981, to escape would-be assassin John Hinckley's gunfire. Going into service under President Nixon, the limo is also the car in which President Ford was riding when an attempt was made on his life. This is the last presidential limo that will be preserved. All presidential cars are now destroyed by the Secret Service for security reasons.

One of the museum's unusual vehicle acquisitions invites visitors to step aboard and sit where Rosa Parks rode on the day she refused to give up her seat. Even years after the 1955 incident shook the country, Montgomery, Alabama, had no clue about the significance of that little bus.

City transit officials took it out of service in 1971 and sold it to a man who threw the seats down a ravine to make more room for his tools. When the vehicle quit running, wild animals eventually moved in and the bus was used for target practice.

Finally, someone realized its historic value and put it on the auction block. The 36-passenger bus was sold in 2001 for $492,000 to the Ford Museum. The museum spent another $318,000 restoring the bus to the way it looked the day Parks boarded it and sparked the modern civil rights movement.

Rosa Parks died in Detroit on Oct. 24, 2005. She and her husband Raymond had moved to Detroit in 1957.

When I visited, an elderly woman sat on the bus and began softly weeping. It was tears of joy, she told me, that the bus had been preserved as an actual witness to an important chapter in American history. Such a remarkable legacy Henry Ford has left to the world.

AUTHOR'S TOP TEN PICKS

Ann Arbor Hands-On Museum
220 E. Ann St.
Ann Arbor
(734) 995-5439
aahom.org

Detroit Institute of Arts
5200 Woodward Ave.
(313) 833-7900
dia.org

Detroit Zoo
8450 W. 10 Mile Rd.
Royal Oak
(248) 541-5717
detroitzoo.org

Eastern Market
Detroit
(313) 833-9300
easternmarket.org

Ford Drive-in
10400 Ford Rd.
Dearborn
(313) 846-6910
forddrivein.com

The Henry Ford
20900 Oakwood Blvd.
Dearborn
(800) 835-5237
thehenryford.org

Motown Museum
2648 W. Grand Blvd.
Detroit
(313) 875-2264
motownmuseum.org

People Mover
Detroit
(313) 224-2160
thepeoplemover.com

River Raisin Battlefield
1403 E. Elm Ave.
Monroe
(734) 243-7136
nps.gov/rira

Wright Museum of African American History
315 E. Warren Ave.
Detroit
(313) 494-5800
thewright.org

The complex is located at 20900 Oakwood Blvd. and reached by following signs from Southfield Freeway. Admission is $25 for adults and $18.75 for children for the museum; $28 for adults and $21 for children for the village.

For a more intimate view of the auto barons themselves, visit one of the many mansions that auto money built and historical societies have since preserved. *Fair Lane,* the Henry Ford estate, is a 56-room mansion located nearby on the *University of Michigan–Dearborn campus.* Built in 1915 at what was then an astronomical $1.8 million, the home is an extension of Ford's ingenuity wrapped up in his love for functionalism. It often hosted such dignitaries as Edison, President Herbert Hoover, and Charles Lindbergh. Underground are the massive turbines and generators that were designed by Ford and his friend Edison in the 6-level powerhouse that made the estate self-sufficient in power, heat, light, and even ice.

From the outside the house looks modest compared with other historic mansions. But inside you'll find such luxuries as a central vacuum cleaner, a 65-extension phone system, and a 1-lane bowling alley. On April 7, 1947, the Rouge River flooded and knocked out the powerhouse. That night, without heat, light, or phone service, Ford suffered a cerebral hemorrhage and died by candlelight.

michigantrivia

Michigan's largest city has the distinction of lying north of the Canadian border. Visitors are often surprised when they learn that to reach Windsor, Ontario, they have to drive south on the Ambassador Bridge or through the Detroit-Windsor Tunnel.

To reach U of M–Dearborn, head west of Southfield Expressway on Michigan Avenue and then north on Greenfield Road, where signs point the way to the small campus. Although the grounds of Fair Lane (313-593-5590; henryfordestate.org) remain open to the public daily from 8 a.m. to 6 p.m., the estate is now closed for renovations. The University of Michigan–Dearborn and the Edsel & Eleanor Ford House in Grosse Pointe Shores, Michigan, have agreed to unite the Henry Ford Estate and Ford House in what they say will become a national model of sustainability. In June 2013, ownership of the Henry Ford Estate was transferred from the university to the Henry Ford Estate, Inc., a new 501(c)(3) corporation to restore and reopen the estate, and no date has been set for reopening. Historic buildings of the estate can be viewed on a limited basis by prearranged group tours. And the grounds remain open year-round for the public to explore and discover. Maps highlighting walking loops are available on-site. Admittance to the grounds and on-site parking are free.

The ultimate experience for many car buffs is the ***Ford Rouge Factory Tour.*** The massive industrial complex is located at the confluence of the Rouge and Detroit Rivers just south of Detroit and began by producing tractors, not cars, in 1921. At its peak in the 1930s, more than 100,000 people worked at the Rouge, and a new car rolled off the line every 49 seconds. The Rouge was so big that 1,500 tons of iron were smelted daily and every month 3,500 mopheads had to be replaced to keep the complex clean.

Today the Ford Rouge Center is still Ford Motor Company's largest single industrial complex, employing 6,000 workers. It is also one of the world's most advanced and flexible manufacturing facilities, capable of building up to 9 different models on 3 vehicle platforms, and features a 10.4-acre "living roof" where thousands of tiny sedum plants help decrease energy consumption and improve air and water quality.

The tour is offered through ***The Henry Ford*** (313-982-6001, 800-835-5237; thehenryford.org) with buses leaving the museum complex in Dearborn every 20 minutes from 9:20 a.m. to 3 p.m. Mon through Sat. It begins with 2 video presentations; the first a historic look at the Rouge, the second a stunning 360-degree IMAX view of how automobiles are made. A trip to an 80-foot-high observation deck for the living roof follows, but for most visitors the best is at the end. From an elevated walkway, the 2-hour tour concludes with a view of the assembly line below and workers putting the final touches on F-150 pickup trucks. The noise and heat of a car factory are not soon forgotten. Because production varies by vehicle demand, the assembly line is not always operating, but visitors can still see it. Check out the website for non-production times. Tickets for the Ford Rouge Factory Tour are $19 for adults and $14.25 for children.

Movie stars and fresh air—you do remember drive-in theaters, don't you? At the ***Ford Drive-in*** in Dearborn, it's hard to forget them. Contrary to the popular belief that drive-ins are cinematic dinosaurs of the bebop era, this motorized movieland in the hometown of Henry Ford is still packing them in.

Ford bills itself as the "largest drive-in theater in the world" because it features 5 theaters—that's right, 5 separate screens, each showing a different movie. Always a double feature, patrons get 2 films for the price of 1.

Ford Drive-in (313-846-6910; forddrivein.com) is reached from I-94 by taking exit 210 and heading north on Wyoming Avenue. Some of the screens are entered from Wyoming Avenue and some from Ford Road. In-car heaters are available.

To most people Detroit is Motor City, but to music lovers it will always be Motown, the birthplace of the famous record company that Berry Gordy Jr. founded in 1958. Gordy started out with $800 and a small recording studio that was built in the back of his Grand Boulevard home. From Studio A emerged the distinct "Motown Sound" and such performers as Marvin Gaye, Smokey Robinson and the Miracles, Gladys Knight and the Pips, the Supremes, the Jackson 5, and a very talented blind singer named Steveland Morris Hardaway, known now as Stevie Wonder. Eventually the famous "Hitsville USA" sign was hung on the front of the home, and Motown expanded into seven additional houses along the street before setting up its Woodward office.

The company continued recording in Studio A until 1972, when it moved its operation to Los Angeles. What remains today at Hitsville USA is the ***Motown Museum,*** a state historic site. The museum is two adjoining houses filled with gold record awards, old album covers, publicity photos, and even some old Temptations costumes that are viewed to the beat of Motown hits played continuously in every room. For most visitors the intriguing part is

TOP ANNUAL EVENTS

JULY

Ann Arbor Street Art Fair
Ann Arbor
(734) 994-5260
artfair.org

Michigan Elvisfest
Ypsilanti
(734) 483-4444
mielvisfest.org

Port Huron to Mackinac Island Yacht Race (Boat Night)
Port Huron
(800) 852-4242
bycmack.com

AUGUST

Woodward Dream Cruise
Birmingham
woodwarddreamcruise.com

LABOR DAY WEEKEND

Ford Arts, Beats & Eats
Royal Oak
(248) 541-7550
artsbeatseats.com

Detroit International Jazz Festival
Downtown Detroit
(313) 447-1248
detroitjazzfest.com

Studio A and its control booth, looking as it did many years ago when Motown was a struggling recording company.

Motown Museum (313-875-2264; motownmuseum.org) is located at 2648 W. Grand Blvd., 2 blocks west of the exit off the Lodge Freeway. The museum is open Wed through Sat 10 a.m. to 6 p.m. and until 8 p.m. on Mon in July and Aug. Admission is $15 for adults, $10 for children ages 5 to 17, free for age 4 and under.

Although Detroit has its mansions and its auto barons, it is known primarily as a blue-collar town, an assembly-line haven that has made it as ethnically diverse as any city in the country. Detroiters love their heritage, ethnic foods, music, and the traditions of an old way of life. The ethnic pride and the love of traditional foods can best be seen at the *Eastern Market* (313-833-9300; easternmarket.org), a farmers' market that, at 43 acres, is said to be the largest of its kind (open to retailers rather than wholesalers) in the country and certainly one of the oldest in the Midwest. It dates back to 1841. Two areas, one open-air, the other enclosed, and both decorated with huge murals on the outside, are the heart of the market with more than 250 independent vendors and merchants covering six blocks. On Sat from 7 a.m. to 5 p.m. they overflow with shoppers, farmers, and vendors bartering for the freshest fruit, vegetables, flowers, meats, and cheeses to be found in the city. Everything from the farm is on sale here, from homemade bratwurst to live rabbits, and the market makes for an enjoyable stroll, even if you don't intend to buy anything. Ringing the market are butcher shops, fish markets, and stores specializing in spices, nuts, and foods imported from around the world. The market is also open every Tues from June through the end of Oct, plus Thanksgiving week, from 9 a.m. to 3 p.m. and every Sun from June through the end of Oct, including Thanksgiving week, 10 a.m. to 4 p.m.

To reach the Eastern Market, head downtown on I-75 and exit east on Mack Avenue. The market is 2 blocks east of the expressway, near Russell Avenue.

Restaurants also reflect the ethnically diverse, hardworking Detroiters who at nightfall put aside their jobs and enjoy themselves immensely with good food served in large portions at very reasonable prices. Coney Island hot dogs and baseball are a summer tradition in the Motor City. Begin with the Detroit Tigers, an American League club that moved into its new stadium, Comerica Park, in 2000; after the ninth inning, head over to **Lafayette Coney Island,** Detroit's premier hot-dog place. Located where Lafayette and Michigan Avenues merge near Kennedy Square downtown at 118 W. Lafayette Blvd., the porcelain white eatery with its male waiters is an institution in Detroit. The fare is Coney dogs (with loads of chopped onions, chili, and mustard), loose burgers (loose hamburger in a hot-dog bun), and bean soup served on Formica counters and tables with paper napkins and truck-stop china. Yet arrive at midnight and you'll see patrons dressed in tuxedos enjoying a late-night hot dog after the symphony, seated next to a couple of rabid baseball fans with a team pennant. Lafayette Coney Island (313-964-8198) is open 24 hours daily with hot dogs and loose burgers priced at around $3. They only accept cash.

A few blocks over at Monroe Street is lively Greektown, where a dozen restaurants, nightclubs, and Greek bakeries make it the liveliest spot in downtown Detroit. My favorite restaurant is **Pegasus Tavernas** (313-964-6800; pegasustavernas.com) at 558 Monroe St., where you can enjoy the Detroit tradition of saganaki—flaming Greek kasseri cheese served to the cry of "Opa!" The best comfort food in Detroit is **Urban Soul** (313-344-9070; urbansoulrestaurant .com) at 1535 E. Lafayette St. It's the place for fried catfish, collard greens, sweet potato pie, even fried corn. Detroit's Polish community is centered around the city of Hamtramck, where Pope John Paul II once performed mass. At the **Polish Village Cafe** (313-874-5726; polishvillagecafe.us) at Yehmans Street and Joseph Campau Avenue, you can dig into stuffed cabbage, pork goulash, and pierogi for less than $8. Great barbecue is easy to find throughout the city but it's hard to pass up the smoked meats and baby back ribs and pulled pork served at **Slows Bar BQ** (313-962-9828; slowsbarbq.com) at 2138 Michigan Ave. in the Corktown District of Detroit.

Dueling Coney Islands

In Michigan a chili dog is called a "Coney Island" in reference to the birthplace of the hot dog. The hot dog itself may be East Coast, but the Coney Island is a Detroit tradition that dates back more than 100 years.

It began in 1917 when Constantine "Gust" Keros, a Greek immigrant to Detroit, opened **American Coney Island** on Lafayette Boulevard. Keros sold his New York–style hot dogs for a nickel and was so successful that he enticed his brother, William, to immigrate from Greece and help with the family business. In 1924, the storefront next door became available and William Keros jumped at the opportunity to start his own shop, **Lafayette Coney Island.** The competition between the two brothers was friendly but fierce, and soon both began slathering their hot dogs with chili to attract customers, leading to Detroit's unique version of a Coney Island. Or so the story goes.

What can't be debated is these two hot dog restaurants, still owned by third generation family members, have been slugging it out for the heart and soul of Detroiters ever since. They are both open 24 hours a day, 7 days a week, serving up a hot dog, covered with a "secret family chili sauce recipe," chopped onions, and yellow mustard on a steamed bun. Your order is called out, usually in a thick accent, by a waiter standing next to your table and arrives almost instantaneously with the toppings piled so high on the hot dog most of your plate is covered with chili and onions. All this for about $5.

In 1989, American Coney Island (313-961-7758; 114 W. Lafayette Blvd.; americanconeyisland.com) moved into an adjacent corner building but Lafayette Coney Island (313-964-8198; 118 W. Lafayette Blvd.) is still housed in the same storefront where the Formica tables, cramped interior, and truck-stop china have changed little since the day it opened. Passion for the Coney Island hot dog is so strong in Detroit that most people have pledged an allegiance to one eatery or the other.

It may not be "off the beaten path," but Detroit's Central Automated Transit System is definitely above the city streets. Better known as the **People Mover,** the mass transit project was opened in 1987 after several years of controversial delays and cost overruns. The 2.9-mile elevated track circles the downtown heart of Detroit. Its automated cars stop every 3 minutes at 13 stations, each decorated with beautiful mosaics and other artwork. The ride costs only 75 cents and lasts 15 minutes, but it gives an excellent overall view of the city from a superb vantage point. The best stretch comes when the cars wind around Cobo Hall and passengers see a panorama of the Detroit River and the skyline of Windsor, the Canadian city to the south. The People Mover (313-224-2160; thepeoplemover.com) operates from 6:30 a.m. to midnight Mon to Thurs, until 2 a.m. Fri, from 9 a.m. to 2 a.m. Sat, and noon to midnight Sun.

The Detroit River, which connects Lake St. Clair with Lake Erie, was the avenue that the city's first residents—the French in 1701—used to arrive in Southeast Michigan. The river remains a focal point of activities for Detroiters, with several parks lining its banks and one—Belle Isle—located in the middle of it. Reached by a bridge at E. Jefferson and Grand Boulevard, the island park features the **Dossin Great Lakes Museum,** which traces the maritime history of Detroit and the Great Lakes in several rooms of displays and hands-on exhibits. Within the museum is the famed hydroplane racer, *Miss Pepsi*, the massive bow anchor of the doomed freighter *Edmund Fitzgerald*, and, from the golden age of steamers of the 1940s, the restored smoking lounge of the SS *City of Detroit III*. Children will love Michigan's largest collection of model ships or stepping up to the steering wheel in the preserved pilothouse of a Great Lakes freighter that actually looks out on the Detroit River.

michigantrivia

Detroit is the birthplace of Vernors, a fizzy ginger drink that many from the Motor City claim was the country's first soft drink, dating back to the 1860s. Pharmacist James Vernor was experimenting with ginger drinks at his drugstore on Woodward Avenue when in 1862 he enlisted in the Union army. Before shipping out for the Civil War, Vernor stored one of his concoctions in an oak cask. When he returned four years later, he discovered to his utter amazement a carbonated drink with delectable taste. For years the Vernors factory on Woodward Avenue was a Detroit icon before it closed when the brand was sold to Cadbury Schweppes Americas Beverages of Texas.

The Dossin Great Lakes Museum (313-833-5538; detroithistorical.org) is open 11 a.m. to 4 p.m. on Sat and Sun. Opened April 2013, a new exhibit titled "Built by the River" traces the settlement that became Detroit. Early history examines Detroit's place at the center of the fur trade and how its geographic placement made it a strategic spot for the French, British, and American armed forces. Later, its location on the river made Detroit a center of industrial development, manufacturing, and marine transportation. The river also serves as an international border and was a factor in Detroit's participation in the Underground Railroad as well as witnessing smuggling activity during the Prohibition era. Today it serves as the busiest international river crossing on the continent. Admission is free.

If the day is nice, you can spend an afternoon at Hart Plaza at the foot of Woodward Avenue overlooking the Detroit River and Windsor. For an even better view of the waterfront, **Diamond Jack's River Tours** (313-843-9376; diamondjack.com) offers 1-hour cruises on the Detroit River that depart from Rivard Plaza at the foot of Rivard Street and Atwater Street and from Bishop on

Wyandotte. The cruises are offered June through Labor Day and run $10 for adults and free for children 3 and under.

Detroit's Cultural Center, clustered around Woodward Avenue and Kirby Street, is dominated by the **Detroit Institute of Arts** (313-833-7900; dia.org) at 5200 Woodward Ave. Thanks to auto baron wealth accumulated in the early 1900s and a $158 million renovation and expansion in 2008, the DIA is the fifth largest art museum in the country and its collection of more than 60,000 pieces is considered one of the best. It is known for its Italian Renaissance, Dutch-Flemish, and German expressionist art, but the most viewed work is probably Diego Rivera's mural *Detroit Industry*, which fills a room and reflects the city's blue-collar work ethic. Hours are 9 a.m. to 4 p.m. Wed through Fri and 10 a.m. to 5 p.m. Sat and Sun. Admission is $14 for adults and $6 for children. Admission is free for residents of Wayne, Oakland, and Macomb Counties.

Within easy walking distance of the DIA at E. Warren Avenue and Brush Street is the **Wright Museum of African American History** (313-494-5800; thewright.org) at 315 E. Warren Ave., the largest such museum in the country; its collection ranges from art to clubs and golf shoes used by Tiger Woods. The museum's popular permanent exhibit is entitled "And Still We Rise." The impressive, $8 million exhibit uses multimedia displays to trace the 400-year history and culture of African Americans. Hours are 9 a.m. to 4 p.m. Thurs through Sat and noon to 5 p.m. Sun. Admission is $10 for adults and $7 for children.

michigantrivia

Michigan's first public whipping post stood at Woodward and Jefferson Avenues in Detroit from 1818 to 1831. At the intersection now is the giant sculptural fist. The controversial statue honors Joe Louis, Detroit's famous son who became world heavyweight boxing champion in 1937.

Also located in the Cultural Center is the **Michigan Science Center** (313-577-8400; mi-sci.org) at 5020 John R St. The center was founded in the early 1970s as the Detroit Science Center and was among the first in the country to feature an IMAX Dome Theater. The Michigan Science Center now runs this Midtown Detroit gem as an entirely new nonprofit organization after purchasing the assets (building, land, and exhibits) of the former Detroit Science Center. Today the museum features 110,000 square feet of scientific exploration with hundreds of hands-on exhibits and 3 live stages where participants have a "hair-raising" good time, along with multiple hands-on lab areas for future scientists. You can still see a more-real-than-life movie in the Chrysler IMAX Dome Theater or gaze at the universe in the Dassault Systemes Planetarium. The Michigan Science Center is often home to large traveling exhibits and even

Detroit's Cool Jazz

There's nothing like spending an evening in nightclubs listening to the local jazz and blues that have always been the foundation of the Detroit music scene. A list of clubs with the type of music they feature can be found in *Metro Times* (metrotimes.com), a free entertainment newspaper.

One of the better-known clubs for jazz is *Baker's Keyboard Lounge* (313-345-6300; theofficialbakerskeyboardlounge.com) at 20510 Livernois Ave. For blues head to *Nancy Whiskey* (313-962-4247; nancywhiskeydetroit.com) at 2644 Harrison St. or *Bert's Jazz Marketplace* (313-567-2030; bertsentertainmentcomplex.com) at 2727 Russell St., a nightclub in the Eastern Market District with sticky menus, small wobbly tables, satisfying soul food, and excellent blues and jazz.

features a discovery space called Kids Town for the youngest explorers. Hours vary so check the center's schedule. Admission is $15 for adults and $12 for children.

In 1882 the Plymouth Iron Windmill Company began to manufacture and give away small BB guns to farmers to encourage them to purchase one of its windmills. Within 4 years, the northwest corner of Wayne County was well "windmilled," but the company kept producing the air rifles. Eventually Plymouth Iron Windmill Company became Daisy Manufacturing Company, and this small town was known as the "air rifle capital of the world" until the operations were moved to Arkansas in 1958.

You can learn about the start of Daisy air rifles and see a collection of the earliest models at the **Plymouth Historical Museum.** The museum also has many other displays, including an impressive Abraham Lincoln exhibit that contains a rare book belonging to Lincoln as a boy and a life mask the president made in 1860. But it is the display of Daisy air rifles that brings back fond memories of tin cans in the backyard to so many of us.

To reach the Plymouth Historical Museum at 155 S. Main St. (734-455-8940; plymouthhistory.org) from I-275, get off at exit 28, head west on Ann Arbor Road, and then turn north on Main Street. Hours are 1 to 4 p.m. Wed, Fri, Sat, and Sun. Admission is $7 for adults and $3 for children.

Monroe County

George Armstrong Custer may have staged his ill-fated "last stand" at the Little Bighorn River in Montana, but he grew up in **Monroe,** Michigan. Custer was actually born in Rumley, Ohio, but spent most of his youth, until he entered a military academy at the age of 16, living with his half sister in this city along Lake Erie. Even after he became a noted brigadier general during the Civil War, Custer continued to return to Monroe, and in 1864 he married Elizabeth Bacon, his boyhood sweetheart, here.

Custer's intriguing life can be traced at the ***Monroe County Historical Museum,*** which features the largest collection of his personal artifacts in the country. The Custer exhibit room occupies a fourth of the museum floor and focuses on his youth in Monroe and his distinguished Civil War career, rather than his well-known days on the western plains. There is an overcoat of buffalo hide that he wore during a winter campaign in 1868 and a buckskin suit that is impressive with its beadwork and porcupine quills. Custer was an avid outdoorsman and also a fine taxidermist. It comes as a surprise to many that Custer enjoyed mounting the game animals he hunted, and housed in the museum along with his favorite Remington buffalo rifle are many mounted game animals.

The museum also has displays on Monroe's early history, which dates back to French missionaries in 1634. But it is the life and tragic death of Custer that most people find fascinating. The Monroe County Historical Museum (734-240-7780; co.monroe.mi.us) is at 126 S. Monroe St. in the heart of the city and is open 10 a.m. to 5 p.m. Thurs through Sat, noon to 5 p.m. Sun. Admission is $5 for adults, $3 for children.

michigantrivia

The center of the University of Michigan campus is the Diag, a parklike opening that extends from State Street to S. University Avenue. The bronze seal in the center was donated by the Class of 1953, and legend has it that any freshman who steps on it before taking his or her first exam at U of M will fail the test.

Nearby on the west side of State Street is the Michigan Union. It was on the steps of this imposing building that John F. Kennedy first announced his vision of the Peace Corps in 1960 while campaigning for the White House.

Unless you are a military buff, you might not realize that the Massacre of the River Raisin was among the largest battles in the War of 1812 and produced more American casualties than any other conflict. But you will because in 2009 the ***River Raisin Battlefield*** was dedicated as one of the country's newest National Park units. At the battlefield and in its fine visitor center, you will retrace what many historians believe was the turning point in the conflict with Great Britain.

After the disastrous opening months of the War of 1812 in which Mackinac Island, Chicago, and Detroit had fallen, two of them without even a shot fired, an elderly Revolutionary War veteran, General James Winchester, was sent to

Michigan with almost 1,000 men. The large American force set up camp on an open field on the north side of the river. But in the predawn darkness of January 22, almost 600 British regulars with 6 cannons and 800 Indians attacked. The fighting raged for 20 minutes and then for Winchester's army turned into a panicked flight for Ohio. Of the 400 Americans who ran, 220 were killed, another 147, including Winchester himself, were captured, and only 33 managed to escape to safety. The next day Indians returned to plunder the homes, scalp the wounded, and toss the bodies into burning homes. More than 60 unarmed Americans were killed, and a nation was horrified. Soon, "Remember the Raisin!" became a battle cry that led US troops to victory in the old Northwest.

All this history has been carefully preserved and clearly presented at the battlefield visitor center. Its most impressive display is a 14-minute fiber-optic map presentation. On 2 wall-size maps, the story of the River Raisin is retold with the Americans, British, and Indians, as colorful lights, maneuvering and taking up positions in front of you. The visitor center (734-243-7136; riverraisinbattlefield.org) is reached from I-75 by taking exit 14 and heading west to 1403 E. Elm Street. The center is open daily from 9 a.m. to 5 p.m. There is no admission charge.

Washtenaw County

Trendy **Ann Arbor,** the cultural capital of Southeast Michigan (and some say the entire state), is the site of the University of Michigan, the "Harvard of the West." The university dominates the city, its buildings and campus entwined in the town's landscape. It provides many of Ann Arbor's top attractions, such as the **Kelsey Museum of Archaeology** at 434 S. State St. (734-764-9304; lsa .umich.edu/kelsey), a renowned collection of art and artifacts, including mummies, from Egyptian, Greek, Roman, and classical Mediterranean cultures. On Saturdays in the fall, Ann Arbor is U of M football; the largest stadium crowds in the country (112,000) gather to cheer on the Wolverines.

But there is another side to this college town, one that children will appreciate, and it begins at the **Ann Arbor Hands-On Museum.** This is no stuffy hall with an endless row of glass-enclosed displays. The entire museum is devoted to participatory exhibits—more than 250 in 9 galleries on 4 floors—and the concept that kids learn by doing. Housed in the classic Central Fire House, the museum was dedicated on September 28, 1982, the 100th anniversary of the building. Inside, the exhibits range from our world—watching dozens of caterpillars feeding on apple leaves and busily spinning their cocoons—to outer space—viewing images from NASA's Hubble Space Telescope that are

Big Leaguers in Motown

Motown is also a die-hard sports town, and its fans have plenty of big-league action to choose from in Southeast Michigan. The **Detroit Pistons** play men's basketball at the Little Caesars Arena (tickets: 248-377-0100; nba.com/pistons). The **Detroit Red Wings** play at Little Caesars Arena (313-983-6606; redwings.nhl.com). The **Detroit Tigers** (313-471-2000; tigers.com), play baseball in impressive Comerica Park, while next door the **Detroit Lions** (800-616-7627; detroitlions.com) play football at Ford Field or they try to. In 2008 the Lions became the first NFL team to go winless in a 16-game season. But Detroiters still love them.

updated daily. All are fun. The bubble capsule is where participants step into a ring of soap film and slowly raise a cylinder bubble around them until it pops. No stuffy science here, yet exhibits are accompanied by an explanation that is appreciated mostly by the parents. The Ann Arbor Hands-On Museum (734-995-5439; aahom.org) is recommended for children 8 years of age and older. It is at 220 E. Ann St. Hours are Mon, Wed, Fri, Sat 10 a.m. to 5 p.m., Tues 9 a.m. to 5 p.m., Thurs 10 a.m. to 8 p.m., and Sun noon to 5 p.m. Admission is $12.50 for adults or children.

There are no mountains in Southeast Michigan, but that doesn't stop the region from being a mecca for mountain biking. In large part because of cycle-crazy Ann Arbor, the trails at *Pinckney State Recreation Area* have been transformed into a playground for off-road cycling. It's estimated that more than 120,000 mountain bikers from Ohio, Indiana, and Illinois as well as Michigan visit the park annually to ride the challenging 17.5-mile Potawatomi Trail, the 5-mile Crooked Lake Trail, or the 2-mile Silver Lake Trail.

The trailhead for all trails is in the park's Silver Lake Day-Use Area, reached from US 23 by taking exit 49 and heading west on N. Territorial Road to Dexter-Townhall Road, then heading north on Dexter-Townhall Road past the park headquarters (734-426-4913) to the day-use area.

Oakland County

It's 4 p.m. in *Birmingham* and you're sipping tea from fine china in a set-ting that includes fresh-cut flowers, silver platters of cakes and other tempting edibles, a fire in a fireplace of imported Italian marble, and a tuxedo-clad piano player, er, excuse me, pianist.

Must be tea at the Townsend. The afternoon ritual, in all its elegance, takes place throughout the week in the *Townsend Hotel,* the most affluent hotel in this ritzy suburb of Detroit. Built in 1988, the hotel has 150 guest rooms plus 9 penthouses and specialty suites on 3 floors, and among its guests have been entertainers such as Madonna, Michael Jackson, Paul McCartney, and New Kids on the Block. (Remember them?) Just about anybody who plays in Detroit stays at the Townsend.

Have afternoon tea here, and who knows? Maybe you'll see Billy Idol stroll in. It has happened before. From Woodward Avenue in downtown Birmingham, turn west onto Townsend Street, and the hotel is reached in 3 blocks at 100 Townsend St. Afternoon tea is offered 7 days a week from noon to 1:30 p.m. The cost is $50 per person, and reservations are required. Contact the Townsend Hotel (248-642-7900; townsendhotel.com) for reservations.

In 1904, George Booth, founder of Booth Newspapers and the publisher of the *Detroit News*, and his wife purchased a run-down farm in Bloomfield Hills with a vision of establishing an educational community that would inspire creativity and excellence. A century later *Cranbrook Schools* have evolved into one of the country's leading centers for art and education as the home to 1,600 students from 17 states and 34 countries. Cranbrook graduates range from presidential candidate Mitt Romney and actress Selma Blair to Sun Microsystems founder Scott McNealy and Michael Kinsley, the first editor of the online magazine *Slate*.

michigantrivia

The country's first shopping mall, Northland, was built in Southfield in Oakland County in 1954.

But visitors are also welcomed to the school's impressive 315-acre campus that was designated a National Historic Landmark in 1989. An afternoon can be spent viewing the *Cranbrook Art Museum*, featuring the work of local, national, and international artists as well as 20 temporary exhibitions a year, or wandering through the 40-acre *Cranbrook House and Gardens,* the home of founders George and Ellen Booth. Kids will be amazed by the displays at the *Cranbrook Institute of Science,* the home of the only *T. Rex* skeleton in Michigan and the Bat Zone that is filled with live bats and other nocturnal creatures.

Cranbrook (248-645-3323; schools.cranbrook.edu) is located at 39221 Woodward Ave. in Bloomfield Hills. Cranbrook Art Museum (248-645-3323; cranbrookartmuseum.org) is open Tues through Sun from 11 a.m. to 5 p.m. Admission is $10 for adults. Cranbrook Institute of Science (248-645-3200; science .cranbrook.edu) is open Wed noon to 5 p.m., Thurs noon to 8 p.m., and Fri through Sun noon to 5 p.m. Admission is $10 for adults and $6 for children. Cranbrook House and Gardens tours (248-645-3147; housegardens.cranbrook .edu) are offered at various times from May through Oct and are $15 for adults, children age 8 and under are free.

Southeast Michigan Drive-ins

The 1950s are alive and well at *Eddie's Drive-in* (586-469-2345; eddies-drive-in .com), a landmark burger place at 36111 Jefferson Ave. in Harrison Township. It's a nightly show in the summer when hip cats and cool chicks show off their hot rods while carhops on roller skates serve you shakes and fries to the bebop music of that golden era. Eddie's is open Tues through Sun from noon to 8 p.m.

With its strong car culture you'd expect many other surviving drive-ins offering curbside service throughout Southeast Michigan and there are. Here a few of the best serving foot-longs, sandwiches called Hammy Sammy, and shakes made with real ice cream:

BERKLEY

A&W
4100 12 Mile Rd.
(248) 547-7126
berkleyaw.com

LIVONIA

Daly Drive-in
31500 Plymouth Rd.
(734) 427-4474
dalyrestaurants.com

YPSILANTI

Bill's Drive-in
1292 E. Michigan Ave.
(734) 485-2831

Chick Inn Drive-in
501 Holmes Rd.
(734) 483-3639

The urban sprawl of Southeast Michigan runs its course to Pontiac, but from there the terrain changes quickly to the rolling hills, lakes, and woods of northern Oakland. A drive of less than an hour from the heart of Detroit can remove you from the city and bring you to the porch steps of a rustic cabin on a small pond in a wooded area where white-tailed deer often pass by. *Holly-Rolston Rustic Cabin* in Holly Recreation Area makes a weekend spent in the woods as comfortable and warm as sitting around the fireplace at night. The cabin is snug and tight, but still rustic and secluded enough to make it seem like an adventure in the woods—even though the car is parked right outside.

Built by the Rolston family as a weekend cottage in 1938–39, the cabin was obtained by the park, which began renting it out in 1984. It's a classic cabin built with walls of logs, polished planked floors, and red-checkered curtains on the windows. There is electricity, and the kitchen features an electric stove and refrigerator as well as a table, benches, and a woodstove. The sleeping room is larger, with a set of bunks and an easy chair facing a fieldstone fireplace. Overlooking the cozy room is a loft, the warmest part of the cabin at night, with 4 more mattresses. Outside you'll find a vault toilet, woodshed, a hand pump for water, and a barbecue grill. Firewood is provided by the park. Visitors need to bring cookware, flashlights, bedding, and anything else needed during the stay. It's necessary to reserve the cabin in advance by calling the park headquarters, and, surprisingly, the most popular time to rent it is during the winter when families arrive to cross-country ski on the unplowed park roads around the lakes. The overnight rate for the cabin is $60 Sun through Thurs, and $100 Fri and Sat. Reservations can be made through the **Michigan Campground Central Reservation System** (800-447-2757; midnrreservations.com). The recreation area is reached by taking Grange Hall Road (exit 101) east off I-75.

Many people exit I-75 at Grange Hall Road and head west to explore the historical town of **Holly.** Established in the early 1800s, Holly was a sleepy little hamlet until 1855, when the Detroit-Milwaukee Railroad reached the town, bringing immediate growth and prosperity with the 25 trains that passed through daily. Martha Street, near the tracks, was the site of the Holly Hotel, many saloons, and frequent brawls. In 1880 an uproar between local rowdies and a traveling circus left so many beaten and bruised that the street became known as **Battle Alley.** The most famous moment in Battle Alley's history was on August 28, 1908, when Carry Nation, the notorious "Kansas Saloon Smasher," arrived in Holly at the request of the local Prohibition committee. The next day Nation, with umbrella in hand and her pro-temperance supporters a step behind her, invaded the saloons, smashing whiskey bottles, clubbing patrons, and preaching about the sins of "demon rum." Nation created the biggest flurry at the hotel, where she entered the "Dispensing Room" and attacked the painting of a nude over the bar.

Battle Alley and its hundred-year-old Victorian buildings have been restored as a string of about 10 specialty shops that include antiques markets both along the alley and on nearby streets.

The **Holly Hotel,** which was built in 1891 and suffered through two devastating fires, the second in 1978, has since been completely restored, including the painting of the nude. It is now listed on the National Register of Historic Places but no longer provides lodging. Instead, the hotel is a fine restaurant, known for both its classic and its creative cuisine, all set in a Victorian tradition that reflects its birth during the railroad era. The main dining room, with its pedestal tables, soft glow of gas lamps, and red velvet wingback chairs, is the stage for such entrees as medallions of beef with morel mushroom sauce, fillet of beef Wellington, and Great Lakes white fish with asiago and garlic panko gratin.

The Holly Hotel (248-634-5208; hollyhotel.com) is open for afternoon tea at 1 p.m. Mon through Sat, and for dinner from 4 to 10 p.m. daily. A Sunday brunch is served from 10:30 a.m. to 2:30 p.m. for $28 for adults, $12 for children. Dinner prices range from $30 to $66, and reservations are recommended.

Visiting the North Pole in Michigan

Our timing was perfect; on the March day we visited the Arctic Ring of Life exhibit at the **Detroit Zoo,** the temperature was in the mid-teens.

At Glacier Overlook we had our hands buried in our pockets and our backs against the wind when suddenly a polar bear appeared, strolled across the pack ice, and then belly flopped into water that was littered with small icebergs.

It looked—and felt—as if we were at the North Pole.

Which is exactly what the officials at the Detroit Zoo were hoping to achieve when they unveiled "the world's largest polar bear exhibit" in 2001.

The $14.9 million Arctic Ring of Life covers 4.2 acres and is designed to simulate a trek through the three environments found north of the Arctic Circle: tundra, open sea, and pack ice.

A one-way path first winds through the tundra, where you can see arctic foxes prance around or a pair of snowy owls blink back at you. From there you descend into the open sea via the Polar Passage.

This passage is a showstopper, a 70-foot-long, acrylic tunnel that takes you through the exhibit's 300,000-gallon sea environment. On one side are a half dozen seals lazily swimming and eyeing you through the transparent walls. On the other side it's possible to watch the powerful elegance of an 800-pound polar bear underwater. It's a fascinating experience watching seals swim over your head.

From the tunnel you venture into the pack ice environment by first entering an ice cave with a howling winter gale and icy walls that are covered with polar bear prints.

From the cave you reemerge outside and follow the path as it leads you past a handful of viewing points of the pack ice where polar bears can be seen swimming among the icebergs in the open water.

The Detroit Zoo (248-541-5717; detroitzoo.org) is open from 9 a.m. to 5 p.m. daily in the summer with shorter hours the rest of the year. Admission is $14 for adults and $10 for children. To reach the zoo from I-696, exit north on Woodward Avenue just west of I-75. There are entrances to the zoo on both Woodward Avenue and Ten Mile Road. The address is 8450 W. Ten Mile Rd.

Stand-up comedians are featured every Fri and Sat at 8:30 p.m. and 10:30 p.m. Cover charge is $15; $12 for dining guests.

Macomb County

In the fall one of the favorite activities in Southeast Michigan is a trip to a cider mill. Parents pack the kids in the car and head out to the edge of the county where a river turns an old wooden waterwheel. The wheel is the source of power for the mill, which crushes apples to extract the dark brown juice and refine it into cider, truly one of Michigan's culinary delights. After viewing the operation, visitors can purchase jugs of cider, cinnamon doughnuts, and sticky caramel apples and then retreat to a place along the river. Here they enjoy a feast in the midst of brilliant fall colors, in the warmth of an Indian summer, and with the fragrance of crushed apples floating by.

Cider mills ring the metropolitan Detroit area, but one of the oldest and most colorful lies right on the border of Oakland and Macomb Counties west of Rochester at 1950 E. Avon Rd. (Twenty-Three Mile Road). **Yates Cider Mill** was built in 1863 along the banks of the Clinton River and began its long history as a gristmill. It has been a water-powered operation ever since, but in 1876 it began making cider, and today the waterwheel still powers the apple elevator, grinders, and press as well as generating electricity for the lights inside. The mill can produce 300 gallons of cider per hour, all of which is needed in the fall to meet the demand of visitors who enjoy their treat around the huge red barn or across the street on the banks of the Clinton River. Yates Cider Mill (248-651-8300; yatescidermill.com) has varying hours of operation so check the website.

You won't find much apple cider to sip, but an equally interesting mill in Macomb County is the focal point at **Wolcott Mill Metropark.** Built in 1847 on the North Branch of the Clinton River, Wolcott Mill was a grist and feed operation for more than a century, commercially milling as late as 1967. Today the mill's grain-grinding machinery is still turning for visitors while exhibits and interpreters provide a glimpse of a bygone era.

The 2,380-acre park also includes several other historical buildings, a short nature trail, and a farm learning center where children can have contact with barnyard animals. Wolcott Mill Metropark (586-749-5997; metroparks.com/wolcott-mill-metropark) is southeast of Romeo, with the mill entrance off Kunstman Road just north of Twenty-Nine Mile Road at 65775 Wolcott Rd. Building hours for the park are 9 a.m. to 5 p.m. daily, with longer weekend hours during the summer and fall. There is a vehicle fee to enter the park.

St. Clair County

This county is often referred to as the Bluewater region of Michigan because it is bounded by Lake St. Clair to the south, Lake Huron to the north, and the St. Clair River to the east. M 29 circles the north side of Lake St. Clair and then follows the river to **Port Huron,** passing small towns and many bait shops, marinas, and shoreline taverns advertising walleye and perch fish fries. The most charming town on the water is *St. Clair,* 15 miles south of Port Huron and a major shipbuilding center in the early 1900s. The city has renovated its downtown section, centering it on *Palmer Park,* which residents claim has one of the longest boardwalks in the world facing freshwater. The favorite activity on the 1,500-foot riverwalk is watching the Great Lakes freighters that glide by exceptionally close, giving land-bound viewers a good look at the massive boats and their crews. The second favorite activity is walleye fishing. The *St. Clair River* is renowned for this fish, and anglers can be seen through-out the summer tossing a line from the riverwalk, trying to entice the walleye with minnows or night crawlers.

Above the walkway is a wide, grassy bank filled with sunbathers, kids playing, and, in mid-June, the arts and crafts booths of the *St. Clair Art Fair,* a popular festival along the river. Call the *St. Clair Art Association* (810-329-9576; stclairart.org) for the exact dates and times.

Port Huron, a city of 30,000, is the site of the *Bluewater Bridge,* the inter-national crossing between Michigan and Sarnia, Ontario. It is also recognized throughout the state as the start of the *Port Huron–Mackinac Sailboat Race* in late July. On the eve of the event, known as *Boat Night,* the downtown area of Water, Lapeer, and Quay Streets, which border the docks on the Black River, becomes congested with block parties. Sailors, local people, and tourists mingle in a festival that spreads throughout the streets, the yacht clubs, and even onto the sailboats themselves.

Port Huron has several museums, and one of the most interesting honors its favorite son; the *Thomas Edison Depot Museum* (810-455-0035; phmu-

michigantrivia

The first underground railroad tunnel in the world was opened between Port Huron and Sarnia, Ontario, in 1891. It is 11,725 feet long with 2,290 feet underground.

seum.org/Thomas-edison-depot-museum) is located under the Bluewater Bridge at 510 Thomas Edison Pkwy. The museum is housed in the historic Fort Gratiot Depot, built in 1858, where Edison picked up the Grand Trunk Railroad train, on which he sold candy and newspapers as a youth. Exhibits portray Edison's younger days and what led him to become the greatest inventor of our times. Outside the depot, a restored baggage car contains Edison's mobile print shop, which he used to publish the *Weekly Herald*, the world's first newspaper to be printed on a moving train. Edison sold the newspaper on the train for 2 cents a copy and eventually had a circulation of more than 400.

The museum is open 11 a.m. to 5 p.m. daily from Memorial Day to Labor Day, and Thurs through Mon from May through Oct. Admission is $10 for adults and $7 for children.

Edison in Port Huron

Port Huron's most famous resident was not its happiest one. Thomas Edison moved to the city with his family when he was 7 years old but quit school after only three days when a teacher wrote that the future inventor was "addled." His mother taught him at home, and Edison, already fascinated with science and chemistry, turned the family basement into his personal laboratory.

To pay for the chemicals and equipment, he took a job selling candy and newspapers on the Grand Trunk Railroad's commute to Detroit and back. The Port Huron Depot that he worked out of is now the *Thomas Edison Depot Museum.*

But Edison left the town as a teen to seek telegraph work and eventually his fortune out east at Menlo Park, New Jersey. "I do not think that any living human being will ever see me there again," he wrote to his father when he was 30 years old and already a well-known inventor. "I don't want you to stay in that hole of a Port Huron, which contains the most despicable remnants of the human race that can be found on earth."

Historians said that over time, Edison softened his views on Port Huron and later in life did return several times, mostly to attend family funerals.

A short walk from the depot museum is the **Port Huron Museum** (810-982-0891; phmuseum.org) at 1115 Sixth St. The museum combines an art gallery with collections of natural history and artifacts from Port Huron's past. Included are bones and displays of the prehistoric mammoths that roamed Michigan's Thumb 10,000 years ago and memorabilia of Thomas Edison's boyhood home, which was located in the city. A popular attraction is the reconstructed pilothouse of a Great Lakes freighter. All the furnishings were taken from various ships, and visitors can work the wheel, signal the alarm horn, and ring the engine bell. All around the pilothouse is a huge mural that gives the impression you are guiding the vessel into Lake Huron. The museum, housed in a 1904 Carnegie library, is open 11 a.m. to 5 p.m. daily. Admission is $10 for adults and $7 for children.

Places to Stay in Southeast Michigan

ANN ARBOR

Ann Arbor Bed & Breakfast
921 E. Huron St.
(734) 994-9100
annarborbedandbreakfast.com

Avalyn Garden Bed and Breakfast
1930 Washtenaw Ave.
(734) 929-5986
avalyngarden.com

Baxter House Bed and Breakfast
719 N. Fourth Ave.
(734) 474-5021
baxterhousebnb.com

Bell Tower Hotel
300 S. Thayer St.
(800) 562-3559
belltowerhotel.com

Burnt Toast Inn
415 W. William St.
(734) 395-4114
burnttoastinn.com

Huron River Guest House
3586 E. Huron River Dr.
(734) 945-8799
huronriverguesthouse.com

Stone Chalet B&B Inn
1917 Washtenaw Ave.
(734) 417-7223
stonechalet.com

Weber's Inn
3050 Jackson Rd.
(734) 769-2500

AUBURN HILLS

Courtyard by Marriott
2550 Aimee Ln.
(248) 373-4100
marriott.com

DEARBORN

Cochrane House
216 Winder St.
(313) 230-0398
thecochranehouse.com

Dearborn Inn
20301 Oakwood Blvd.
(313) 271-2700
marriott.com

Detroit Foundation Hotel
250 W. Larned St.
(313) 800-5500
detroitfoundationhotel.com

Element Detroit at the Metropolitan
33 John R. St.
(313) 306-2400
marriott.com

The Henry
300 Town Center Dr.
(313) 441-2000
behenry.com

York House
1141 N. York
(313) 561-2432
yorkhousedearborn.com

DETROIT

Aloft Detroit at The David Whitney
One Park Ave.
(313) 237-1700
marriott.com

Atheneum Suite Hotel
1000 Brush St.
(313) 962-2323
atheneumsuites.com

The Inn at 97 Winder
97 Winder St.
(313) 832-4348
theinnat97winder.com

Roberts Riverwalk Hotel
1000 River Place
(313) 259-9500
detroitriverwalkhotel.com

Shinola Hotel
1400 Woodward Ave.
(313) 356-1400
shinolahotel.com

The Siren Hotel
1509 Broadway St.
(313) 277-4736
thesirenhotel.com

Westin Book Cadillac Detroit
1114 Washington Blvd.
(313) 442-1600
marriott.com

MONROE

Hotel Sterling
109 W. Front St.
(734) 242-6212
thehotelsterling.com

The Lotus Bed & Breakfast
324 Washington St.
(734) 735-1077

MOUNT CLEMENS

A Victory Inn
1 N. River Rd.
(586) 465-2185
avictoryhotels.com

PORT HURON

Adventure Inn Bed and Breakfast
3650 Shorewood Dr.
(810) 327-6513
adventureinnbedandbreakfast.com

Fairfield Inn
1635 Yeager St.
(810) 982-8500
marriott.com

Pleasant Place Inn
829 Prospect Pl.
(865) 680-3092
ppibnb.com

ROCHESTER

Royal Park Hotel
600 E. University Dr.
(248) 652-2600
royalparkhotel.net

TROY

Detroit Marriott Troy
200 W. Big Beaver Rd.
(248) 680-9797
marriott.com

Drury Inn
575 W. Big Beaver Rd.
(248) 528-3330
druryhotels.com

Somerset Inn
2601 W. Big Beaver Rd.
(248) 643-7800
somersetinn.com

Places to Eat in Southeast Michigan

ANN ARBOR

The Chop House Ann Arbor
322 S. Main St.
(734) 669-9977
thechophouseannarbor
.com
American

The Earle Restaurant
121 W. Washington St.
(734) 994-0211
theearle.com
French-Italian

Gandy Dancer
401 Depot St.
(734) 769-0592
muer.com/gandy-dancer
Seafood

Knight's Steakhouse
2324 Dexter Ave.
(734) 665-8644
knightsrestaurants.com
Steak

Taste Kitchen
521 E. Liberty St.
(734) 369-4241
tastekitchena2.com
American

Zingerman's Delicatessen
422 Detroit St.
(734) 663-3354
zingermansdeli.com
Deli

CLARKSTON

The Fed Community
15 S. Main St.
(248) 297-5833
thefedcommunity.com
American

The Royal Diner
6540 Dixie Hwy.
(248) 620-3333
theroyaldiner.com
American

Union
54 S. Main St.
(248) 620-6100
clarkstonunion.com
American

DEARBORN

Al Ameer
12710 W. Warren Ave.
(313) 582-8185
alameerrestaurant.com
Middle Eastern

Andiamo Dearborn
21400 Michigan Ave.
(313) 359-3300
andiamoitalia.com
Italian

Ford's Garage
21367 Michigan Ave.
(313) 752-3673
fordsgarageusa.com
American

Shatila Bakery and Cafe
14300 W. Warren Ave.
(313) 582-1952
shatila.com
Middle East

TRIA
300 Town Center Dr.
(313) 253-4475
triadearbornrestaurant.com
American

DETROIT

Amore da Roma
3401 Riopelle St.
(313) 831-5940
amoredaroma.com
Italian

The Apparatus Room
250 W. Larned St.
(313) 800-5600
detroitfoundationhotel.com
American

Dakota Inn Rathskeller
17324 John R St.
(313) 867-9722
dakota-inn.com
German

OTHER ATTRACTIONS

Eddy Discovery Center
17030 Bush Rd.
Chelsea
(734) 475-3170

Fox Theatre
2211 Woodward Ave.
Detroit
(317) 471-3200
313presents.com

Holocaust Memorial Center
28123 Orchard Lake Rd.
Farmington Hills
(248) 553-2400
holocaustcenter.org

Meadowbrook Hall
350 Estate Dr.
Rochester
(248) 364-6200
meadowbrookhall.org

U of M Museum of Natural History
1105 N. University Ave.
Ann Arbor
(734) 764-0478
isa.umich.edu/ummnh

U of M Museum of Art
525 S. State St.
Ann Arbor
(734) 764-0478
umma.umich.edu

Yankee Air Museum
47884 D St.
Belleville
(734) 483-4030
yankeeairmuseum.org

Elwood Bar & Grill
300 E. Adams St.
(313) 962-2337
elwoodgrill.com
American

Fishbone's Rhythm Kitchen Cafe
400 Monroe St.
(313) 965-4600
fishbonesusa.com
Cajun

Giovanni's Ristorante
330 Oakwood Blvd.
(313) 841-0122
giovannisrisstorante.com
Italian

Grey Ghost Detroit
47 Watson St.
(313) 262-6534
greyghostdetroit.com
American

Hockeytown Cafe
2301 Woodward Ave.
(313) 471-3400
hockeytowncafe.com
Sports Bar

Lady of the House
1426 Bagley St.
(313) 818-0218
ladyofthehousedetroit.com
American

Marrow
8044 Kercheval Ave.
(313) 652-0200
marrowdetroit.com
International

Traffic Jam and Snug
511 W. Canfield St.
(313) 831-9470
trafficjamdetroit.com
Brewpub

The Whitney
4421 Woodward Ave.
(313) 832-5700
thewhitney.com
Fine Dining

Xochimilco
3409 Bagley Ave.
(313) 843-0179
Mexican

FARMINGTON

Bone Yard Bar-B-Que
31006 Orchard Lake Rd.
(248) 851-7000
theboneyardbbq.com
Barbecue

Peterlins
22004 Farmington Rd.
(248) 426-8822
peterlins.com
American

Rainbow Restaurant
22048 Farmington Rd.
(248) 427-8265
rainbowfarmington.com
Chinese

FERNDALE

Assaggi Bistro
330 W. Nine Mile Rd.
(248) 584-3499
assaggibistro.com
Mediterranean

Howe's Bayou
22848 Woodward Ave.
(248) 691-7145
howesbayouferndale.net
Cajun

MADISON HEIGHTS

The Breakfast Club
30600 John R Rd.
(248) 307-9090
Breakfast

The Masters Restaurant
1775 E. Thirteen Mile Rd.
(248) 588-0915
American

MONROE

Eureka Eatery
3080 N. Monroe St.
(734) 457-4571
eurekaeatery.com
Southern

Public House
138 N. Monroe St.
(734) 242-3010
publichousemonroe.com
American

R Diner
723 S. Monroe St.
(734) 457-9888
rdinermonroe.com
Greek

NORTHVILLE

Genitti's Hole-in-the-Wall
108 E. Main St.
(248) 349-0522
genittis.com
Italian

Table 5
126 E. Main St.
(248) 305-6555
table5.net
American

OAK PARK

Bread Basket Deli
26052 Greenfield Rd.
(248) 968-0022
originalbreadbasketdeli
.com
Deli

Kravings
25270 Greenfield Rd.
(248) 967-1161
kravingsdetroit.com
Deli

La Marra
24700 Greenfield Rd.
(248) 968-0008
lamarraoakpark.com
Middle Eastern

ROYAL OAK

Detroit Eatery
200 Fifth Ave.
(248) 850-8770
detroiteatery.com
American

Inn Season Cafe
500 E. Fourth St.
(248) 547-7916
theinnseasoncafe.com
Vegetarian

**Lily's Seafood Grill &
Brewery**
410 S. Washington Ave.
(248) 591-5459
lilysseafood.com
Seafood

TROY

Eddie V's Prime Seafood
2100 W. Big Beaver Rd.
(248) 649-7319
eddiev.com
Seafood

Melting Pot
888 W. Big Beaver Rd.
(248) 362-2221
meltingpot.com/troy-mi/
Fondue

Pokeworks
716 W. Big Beaver Rd.
(248) 862-6288
pokeworks.com
Sushi, seafood

WATERFORD

Green Apple Restaurant
4780 Dixie Hwy.
(248) 618-7330
greenapplewaterford.com
American

Lion's Den
4444 Highland Rd.
(248) 674-2251
lionsdenrestaurant.com
American

Mexico Lindo
6225 Highland Rd.
(248) 666-3460
mexlindowaterford.com
Mexican

So Thai Restaurant
2553 Elizabeth Lake Rd.
(248) 682-6350
eatsothai.com
Thai

SELECTED CHAMBERS OF COMMERCE & TOURISM BUREAUS

Blue Water Area Convention and Visitors Bureau
(Port Huron and St. Clair)
500 Thomas Edison Pkwy.
Port Huron 48060
(800) 852-4242
bluewater.org

Destination Ann Arbor
315 W. Huron St.
Ann Arbor 48103
(800) 888-9487
annarbor.org

Metropolitan Detroit Convention and Visitors Bureau
211 W. Fort St.
Detroit 48226
(800) 338-7648
visitdetroit.com

Monroe County Convention & Tourism Bureau
333 N. Dixie Hwy.
Monroe 48162
(734) 457-1030
monroeinfo.com

Ypsilanti Area Visitors and Convention Bureau
106 W. Michigan Ave.
Ypsilanti 48197
(734) 483-4444
ypsireal.com

WEST BLOOMFIELD

New Yotsuba Japanese Restaurant
7365 Orchard Lake Rd.
(248) 737-8282
new-yotsuba-japanese-restaurant.business.site
Japanese

Red Coat Tavern
6745 Orchard Lake Rd.
(248) 865-0500
Tavern

The Thumb

Within the mitten that is the Lower Peninsula of Michigan, there is a special area known as "the Thumb." The state's most recognized appendage is shaped by Saginaw Bay to the west and Lake Huron to the east. The bodies of water not only outline the peninsula but also have wrapped it in rural isolation, the Thumb's trademark and the reason it is called "the getaway close to home."

Home is likely to be one of three of the state's largest urban areas: Detroit, Flint, or Saginaw, all less than a two-hour drive from the four counties that compose the region. Yet the Thumb is a world away. In this place where interstates give way to country roads and indistinguishable suburbs turn into distinct villages, the bustle and heartbeat of the city are replaced by the rural charm of the country.

You don't have nightclubs in the Thumb or dominating skylines or symphony orchestras. But you have more than 90 miles of lakeshore to view, small museums to discover, and an easy way of life whose rural pace will soothe the soul and rest a weary urban mind.

Lumber companies opened up the Thumb in the early 1800s, but after the trees were gone and the loggers went

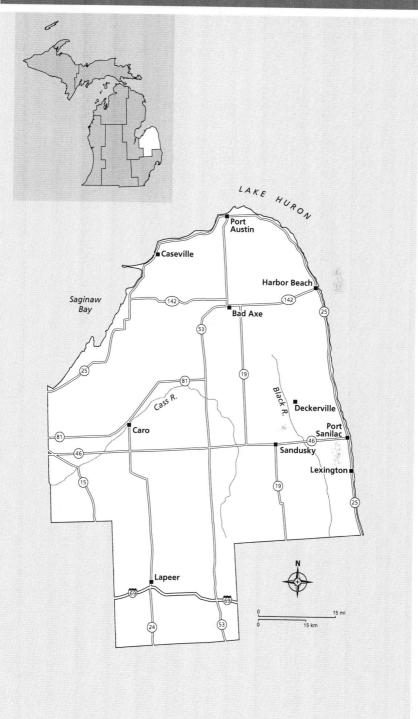

LAKE HURON

Port Austin

■ Caseville

Harbor Beach

Saginaw Bay

142

Bad Axe

142

25

53

19

81

Cass R.

Black R.

■ Deckerville

25

■ Caro

Port Sanilac

81

46

46

Sandusky

15

Lexington

19

25

■ Lapeer

69

69

N

24

53

0   15 mi

0   15 km

north, the region slipped into the small-town realm of agriculture. Today the area is still predominantly a farm belt, and from its rich soil come corn, sugar beets, grains, beans, and the lush grass that supports vast dairy herds and livestock. Huron County produces more navy beans per acre than anyplace else in the world.

In recent years tourist dollars have become a significant part of the economy, but the region will never turn into one of the strips of motels and ice cream stands that characterize much of the Lake Michigan shoreline, the heart of Michigan tourism. The Thumb lies on the other side of the state, away from the mainstream of summer traffic. And many travelers, who come for the fine beaches, country markets, and picturesque lighthouses, leave it cherishing that out-of-the-way character the most.

Lapeer County

A misconception of the Thumb held by many Michigan natives is that the region is flat, without so much as a ripple between the shoreline of Saginaw Bay and the lapping waters of Lake Huron. A drive through Lapeer County dispels that notion immediately. The rolling hills that are the trademark of northern Oakland County continue north through the heart of the peninsula. In southern Lapeer County these hills have an enhancement that makes them unique in Michigan: the distinct white rail fences of horse country. Follow County Road 62 between M 24 and M 53 and dip south along the gravel crossroads of Blood, Garder, or Barber, and you'll pass through one of the greatest concentrations of horse farms in the state. Come in late spring when the grass is green, a new coat of whitewash covers the fences, and the mares and foals are trotting through the fields—and this area could easily be mistaken for the bluegrass region of Kentucky.

The heart of Michigan's horse country is **Metamora,** a village of 565 that lies just east of M 24 and is crowned by the towering steeple of the Pilgrim Church (built in 1878). Settlers first began arriving in the area in 1838, but Metamora earned a spot on the map when it became a stop for a stagecoach route that turned into the Detroit–Bay City Railroad in 1872. North of Metamora along M 24 is **Lapeer,** a town of 8,841. Settlers began arriving in the area in 1828 and borrowed their village name from *la pierre*, the French translation of the Indian name for the Flint River, which lies nearby. Lapeer became the county seat in 1831, and eight years later the county courthouse was built on the town common.

Lapeer is still the center of government, and the **Lapeer County Courthouse** still stands at the corner of Court and Nepessing Streets. It is an

AUTHOR'S TOP TEN PICKS

Be Good to Your Mother-in-Law Bridge
Croswell
(810) 679-2299

Bird Creek County Park
Port Austin
(989) 269-6404

Farm Restaurant
699 Port Crescent Rd.
Port Austin
(989) 874-5700
thefarmrestaurant.com

Frank Murphy Museum
142 S. Huron Ave.
Harbor Beach
(989) 479-6477
harborbeach.com

Huron City Museums
7995 Pioneer Rd.
Huron City
(989) 428-4123
huroncitymuseums.org

Pioneer Log Cabin Village
205 S. Hanselman St.
Bad Axe
(989) 550-2732
thehchs.org

Pointe Aux Barques Lighthouse
7320 Lighthouse Rd.
Port Hope
(586) 243-1838
pointeauxbarqueslighthouse.org

Port Crescent State Park
1775 Port Austin Rd.
Port Austin
(989) 738-8663

Sanilac County Historical Village and Museum
228 S. Ridge Rd.
Port Sanilac
(810) 622-9946
sanilaccountymuseum.org

Sanilac Petroglyphs Historic State Park
8251 Germania Rd.
Cass City
(989) 856-4411

impressive building featuring a Greek Revival style with 4 fluted Doric columns. It's topped by a 3-tiered tower and a Roman dome and is noted as the "oldest courthouse still being used in Michigan today," even though the county has long since built a newer, all-brick building across the street. The old courthouse keeps its title because every summer, the judge, the jury, and a handful of history buffs move to the other side of the street to hear a few cases in the second-floor courtroom of this landmark structure.

The first floor is now the ***Lapeer Historical Society Museum*** (810-245-5808; lapeercountyhistoricalsociety.com), and for a small admission fee, visitors can wander through the turn-of-the-20th-century judge's chambers or the first sheriff's office in the county. The courthouse museum is open from 10 a.m. to 3 p.m. Wed and Sat.

More history and a lot of country charm can be found just up the road from Lapeer at the ***Past Tense Country Store*** (810-664-5559; pasttensecountry

.com). The store is only minutes from downtown Lapeer and can be reached by driving north on M 24 and then turning east on County Road 7 (Daley Road). The first intersection on Daley is Farnsworth Road, and visible to the south from this intersection is one of the most impressive houses in the region. The huge, 23-room home was built by the Farnsworth family, who were part of the first wave of settlers to farm the county. There are several buildings on the old farm, including the original barn that was renovated into the Past Tense Country Store in 1971.

The store is an intriguing place, worth browsing through even if you are not in a buying mood. It is part country store, part antiques shop, and part museum. Walk in on a chilly day and the rush of warm air from the wood-burning stove greets you. Then you'll notice the 100-year-old German barrel piano and the classic red Texaco gasoline pump next to it. The store itself is 4 rooms, each stocked to the rafters with such items as handmade baskets, dried flowers, candles, knickknacks, and children's toys, including one of the most amazing teddy bear collections you'll ever see outside a museum. Upstairs are numerous pieces of antique furniture, while one room is devoted to Christmas, with an old sled in the middle and walls covered with ornaments.

Above every shelf of merchandise, Hiner draws you back into the rural history of Lapeer with small artifacts she has saved. Above the wall of hard candy,

TOP ANNUAL EVENTS

JUNE

Log Cabin Day
Bad Axe
(989) 550-2733

Michigan Sugar Festival
Sebewaing
(989) 883-2150
sebewaingchamber.com

JULY

Farmer's SummerFest
Pigeon
(989) 453-7400
pigeonchamber.com

Maritime Festival
Harbor Beach
(989) 479-3363
themaritimefestival.com

Swinging Bridge Festival
Croswell
(810) 679-2299

AUGUST

Cheeseburger in Caseville Festival
Caseville
(800) 606-1347
casevillechamber.com

Fish Sandwich Festival
Bay Port
(989) 551-9929
visiteastmichigan.com

a requirement in every country store, are rows of cleaning products and cans of food, all from an era long gone. Some you'll recognize, like Oxydol, Quaker Oats, or Calumet Baking Powder, though the packaging hardly resembles the modern-day counterparts. Many you will not (Quick Arrow Soup Chips or Red Moon Early Peas), for they have long since vanished from supermarkets.

The complex has been expanded over the years to include the Cider Mill which offers breakfast, lunch, and dinner. The Cider Mill bakes bread daily and also makes its own pizza dough from scratch. The Country Store is open Thurs through Sun from 10 a.m. to 6 p.m. The Cider Mill is open 11 a.m. to 6 p.m. Thurs through Sun. Winter hours are different so check the website.

Sanilac County

M 25, the state road that leads out of Port Huron, follows the shoreline of Sanilac County and continues along the entire coast of the Thumb, ending in Bay City. While the road does not offer a watery view at every bend, there are more than enough panoramas of Lake Huron and shoreline parks to make it one of the more scenic drives in the Lower Peninsula.

Heading north on M 25, the first town you reach in Sanilac County is *Lexington,* which was incorporated in 1855 and boomed at the turn of the 20th century. Back then the bustling town of 2,400 was a common stop for Great Lakes shipping and boasted an organ factory, a brewery, a flour mill, and 6 saloons. In 1913 the great storm that swept across Lake Huron destroyed the town's docks and virtually isolated it. Lexington slipped into a standstill until the automobile and roads revived it in the 1940s, and today the town of 1,135 has worked harder than any other community in the Thumb to promote its future by preserving its past.

Lexington's streets are lined with turn-of-the-20th-century homes and buildings, including 4 listed on the National Register of Historic Places. One of them is the **Charles H. Moore Public Library** (moorepubliclibrary.org) at Main and Huron Streets next to the village hall at 7239 Huron Ave. The brick building was built in 1859 as the Devine Law Office but somehow passed into the hands of Moore, a local seaman who died in 1901, leaving the building to his three daughters. When a dispute erupted in 1903 as to where to put the town library, the daughters offered the former law office as a permanent site.

It has been the library ever since and today holds nearly 12,000 books, including a rare-book collection. Librarians will tell you that as many people wander through just to view the renovated interior as to check out a book. The wood trim and stained-glass windows have been fully restored inside, as has the graceful wooden banister that leads you past a picture of the "old seaman" to the upstairs. It's hard to imagine a more pleasant place to read than the sunlit room of the second floor, which features desks, tables, and office chairs that were originally used by the law firm.

The Moore Library (810-359-8267) is open Mon and Thurs from 10 a.m. to 7 p.m., Tues, Wed, and Fri from 10 a.m. to 5 p.m., and Sat from 10 a.m. to 1 p.m.

Moore was also responsible for another building in Lexington that is now a National Historic Site. When the seaman built his home in the 1880s, he located it just a block from the lake where he plied his trade. The huge Queen Anne–style home at Simons and Washington Streets was constructed from white pine that loggers were shipping out of the port of Lexington. In 1901, Mary, the youngest daughter, used the house as a backdrop for her marriage to Albert E. Sleeper, a newly elected state senator. When Sleeper's political career led to his election as governor in 1917, the house became an important summer retreat for the couple, who were eager to escape the busy public life in Lansing.

Today the home at 7277 Simons St. is still used as a summer retreat as the *Captain's Quarters Inn* (810-359-2196; captainsbnblex.com), Lexington's first bed-and-breakfast. Guests spend summer evenings much the way the governor and his wife did—on the wraparound porch in wicker rockers (there are 7 now instead of 2), enjoying the cool breezes off Lake Huron. Rooms range from $135 to $225 per night.

From Lexington M 25 continues north along Lake Huron and in 11 miles reaches the next lakeside town, *Port Sanilac.* Like Lexington, Port Sanilac's early history and wealth can be seen in the old homes that border its streets. One is the Loop-Harrison House, a huge Victorian mansion just south of town on M 25 that now serves as the *Sanilac County Historical Village and Museum.* The home was built in 1872 by Dr. Joseph Loop, who arrived in Sanilac in 1854 and began a practice that covered a 40-mile radius. The home

Port Sanilac Lighthouse

Port Sanilac's most distinctive landmark is its lighthouse, a redbrick house and white-washed tower overlooking the town harbor and the watery horizon of Lake Huron. Built in 1886, the 80-foot tower was originally a kerosene-fueled continuous white light. In 1889 it was changed to red, and in 1926 the lighthouse was wired for electricity and changed to a flashing light with a range of 12 to 15 miles. Although the lighthouse is not open to visitors, it's a photographer's delight thanks to its contrasting colors.

The Port Sanilac Lighthouse is on Lake Street, 1 block east of M 25.

Bark Shanty Point

Port Sanilac dates back to the summer of 1830 when a group of lumbermen arrived to peel the bark from the hemlocks in the area for tanning leather. Their accommodations were in a hastily built shanty that was covered in bark. The crude shelter was left standing on the shore after the men departed in the fall, and it quickly became a landmark to sailors who referred to the spot as Bark Shanty Point. Eventually a settlement emerged, and in 1857 the residents decided that the name of a famous Wyandot Indian chief was a little more dignified for their community than Bark Shanty Point.

and its extensive furnishings passed down through three generations of the family until Captain Stanley Harrison, grandson of the good doctor, donated it to the Sanilac Historical Society in 1964.

The Historical Society has kept the home intact, and visitors can wander through 2 floors of rooms that have remained virtually the same since the 1870s, right down to the original carpet, the cooking utensils in the kitchen, and the doctor's instruments in his office. The village includes 7 buildings ranging from the Platt's General Store and a 157-year-old one-room schoolhouse to a pioneer log cabin from 1883, a church from the turn of the 20th century, and what is probably the state's last remaining historic Barn Theater. At 228 N. Ridge St., the Sanilac County Historical Village and Museum (810-622-9946; sanilaccountymuseum.org) is open Memorial Day weekend through Labor Day weekend from noon to 3 p.m. Wed through Sun. Admission is $8 for adults and $5 for students. One child 12 and under may accompany each paid adult for free.

michigantrivia

Michigan's oldest continuously operating hardware store is ***Raymond Hardware*** at 29 S. Ridge St. (810-622-9991; raymond-hardware.com) in downtown Port Sanilac. Founded in 1850 by Uri Raymond, the high-roofed building is a classic hardware store that sells "anything and everything."

The stretch of M 25 from Port Sanilac to Forestville is especially scenic and passes three roadside parks on high bluffs from which you can scramble to the Lake Huron shoreline below. For those who want to explore the center of the Thumb, the Bay City–Forestville Road, the only intersection in tiny Forestville, provides a good excuse to turn off M 25. Head west, through the hamlets of Charleston and Minden, and look for the petroglyphs sign at the corner of Bay City–Forestville and Germania Roads. ***Sanilac Petroglyphs Historic State***

Kayaking at the Tip of the Thumb

You don't have to travel to Alaska or even northern Michigan to join a guided kayak adventure. You don't have to go any farther than the Tip of the Thumb where **Port Austin Kayak & Bike** (989-550-6651; portaustinkayak.com) rents kayaks and offers guided paddles throughout the summer. The cost of a guided tour is the price of a 3-hour rental ($30) plus $75 for the guide for up to 8 people. The cost for the guide is the same whether there is 1 person or 8. Port Austin Kayak also rents mountain bikes and children's bikes for $5 an hour and offers stand-up paddleboards for lessons and to rent at $15 an hour.

Park is located just south on Germania and marked by a large Department of Natural Resources sign. Situated in the wooded heart of the Thumb, the park features a large slab of stone with petroglyphs, Indian carvings that archaeologists believe to be between 300 and 1,000 years old and the only ones in the Lower Peninsula. The department has erected a large pavilion over the rock, which contains dozens of carvings. The most prominent one features a bowman with a single long line depicting his arm and arrow. A short trail leads from the parking lot a few hundred yards inland to the pavilion and then continues beyond as a 1.5-mile interpretive trail.

There is no entrance fee. The park and the trail system are open year-round. But the petroglyphs pavilion is only open late May through early Sept Wed through Sun from 10 a.m. to 5 p.m. Contact the *Michigan Department of Natural Resources* (989-856-4411; michigan.gov/dnr).

Another reason to head inland in summer and fall is to pick berries—sweet, juicy, and backbreakingly close to the ground. Next to the town of Croswell is the *Croswell Berry Farm* (810-679-3273) at 33 Black River Rd. This farm features strawberries in early July, then extends the picking season with blueberries, and finishes up the year with raspberries that are harvested as late as November. The last person goes out in the field at 3 p.m. Hours are 8 a.m. to 3 p.m. daily.

One final reason to head inland to Croswell is to get some advice for keeping your marriage intact from a bridge that Dear Abby would appreciate. In the middle of this Sanilac County village is the *Be Good to Your Mother-in-Law Bridge,* which was first constructed in 1905 and has been rebuilt three times since then with David Weis, a local businessman, assisting in the effort.

Best known in town for offering sage advice to newlyweds, it was Weis who hung a sign at one end of the bridge that advises them to be good to their mothers-in-law and at the other end one that admonishes them to love one another. It's such good advice that the bridge has become something of a ritual with both newlyweds and longtime married couples, who are photographed under the black-and-white sign and then walk hand in hand across the structure.

They hold hands partly out of devotion to each other and partly to keep their balance. The 139-foot suspension footbridge is held up by 4 thick cables that make you bounce with each step across. The wooden slats sway, jiggle, and dip toward the Black River, coming within 8 feet of its murky surface. Some people are even more nervous about crossing the 4-foot-wide swinging bridge than strolling up to the altar. Small tree-lined parks are at each end of the bridge. The bridge is open daily from dawn to dusk.

Huron County

The country charm of M 25 continues into Huron County as it winds north toward Port Austin on the Tip of the Thumb. Along the way it passes several museums, including two in **Harbor Beach,** a quiet rural town of 1,657 residents.

Frank Murphy Museum preserves the birthplace of Governor Frank Murphy, best known for refusing to use the National Guard to end the 1937 Flint Sit-Down Strike at General Motors. By pushing for collective bargaining, Murphy, in effect, paved the way for the United Auto Workers and unionization of the auto industry. Murphy also served as mayor of Detroit, US attorney general, and a US Supreme Court justice from 1940 to his death in 1949. The house is packed with historical artifacts relating to one of Michigan's most influential residents.

Frank Murphy Museum is at 142 S. Huron Ave. next door to the Harbor Beach Visitor Center (989-479-6477; harborbeach.com) in downtown Harbor Beach. Tours are offered Memorial Day through Labor Day, Tues through Fri noon to 4 p.m., Sat and Sun 10 a.m. to 4 p.m. Adults $2, children $1. Just north of town on M 25 at the Harbor Beach Marina is **Grice House Museum.** The Gothic-style home was built in 1875 and still contains 19th-century furnishings along with displays on the early history of Harbor Beach. Outside there is a one-room schoolhouse and a barn full of farm tools from days gone by. Both museums are open from Memorial Day to Labor Day 8 a.m. to 4 p.m. on Wed through Sat, and noon to 4 p.m. on Sun. Weekends in Sept Sat 8 a.m. to 4 p.m. and Sun noon to 4 p.m. Admission is $2 for adults and $1 for children.

Another small museum along M 25 is at **Lighthouse County Park,** 15 miles north of Harbor Beach. The museum is on the first floor of the classic **Pointe Aux Barques Lighthouse** (pointeauxbarqueslighthouse.org), which was built in 1857 and is still used by the US Coast Guard. The lighthouse actually overlooks 2 parks; the county park around it features 74 campsites with electricity for recreational vehicles, a swimming beach, a boat launch, and a picnic area. Out in Lake Huron is an underwater park, the Thumb Area Bottomland Preserve, which the state set up in 1985 to protect the 9 known shipwrecks that lie offshore. Many of the relics that are gathered from the wrecks are stored in the Lighthouse Museum, which is open daily from 10 a.m. to 6 p.m. from Memorial Day through Oct 15. There is no admission charge for the park (989-428-4749) or the museum.

Where Lighthouse Road loops back to M 25 is the Thumb's most impressive attraction, **Huron City Museums.** The town was founded in the mid-1850s by lumberman Langdon Hubbard, who needed a port for his 29,000-acre tract of timberland, which included most of northern Huron County. It quickly became the largest town in the county, with several hundred residents and two sawmills that produced 80,000 feet of lumber a day. After the Great Fire of 1881 that swept across the Thumb devastated Hubbard's logging efforts, he sold his land to immigrant farmers (after opening a bank to lend them the money), and for a while Huron City hung on as a farming community.

michigantrivia

A historical marker at a rest area along M 25 is dedicated to the Storm of November 1913, another deadly disaster in the history of the Thumb. The devastating storm blew in with little warning, sinking more than 40 ships, killing 235 sailors, and destroying almost every dock along Michigan's Lake Huron shoreline.

By the early 1900s, Huron City had withered away to a ghost town when it experienced a revival—a religious awakening, you might say. One of Hubbard's daughters had married William Lyon Phelps, a Yale professor and an

The Fires of 1881

What began as small fires in the middle of a hot, dry summer turned into the Thumb's worst disaster when on September 5, 1881, a gale swept in from the southwest. The high winds turned the fires into an inferno that raged for three days and burned more than a million acres in Sanilac and Huron Counties alone.

The fire put a sudden end to the logging era in the region while killing 125 people and leaving thousands more destitute. Aid to victims was the first disaster relief effort by the new American Red Cross. Its prompt response quickly won the support of the country.

Grindstone Capital of the World

Where M 25 begins to curve around the top of the Thumb, you can take Pointe Aux Barques Road to Grindstone City. Amazingly, this tiny village was once the world's leading producer of natural sandstone grinding wheels. Sandstone was first quarried in 1834 by Captain Aaron G. Peer, who shipped it to Detroit, where it was used to pave the intersection of Woodward and Jefferson Avenues. Two years later the first grindstone wheel was turned out, and for nearly a century Grindstone City grind-stones were shipped all over the world. Today you can still see many of the huge grindstones, some 6 feet in diameter, on the beach and around the village's boat harbor.

ordained minister, and each summer the couple returned to Huron City and stayed at Seven Gables, the rambling Hubbard home. Eventually Dr. Phelps began preaching in the nearby church on Sunday. Local people soon discovered the magic of his oratory: simple solutions and relief from the problems of everyday life. The church, which originally held 250, was quickly enlarged to 1,000 in the 1920s as people throughout Michigan heard of the preacher and began finding their way to Huron City for his Sunday afternoon service.

Dr. Phelps died in 1937, but Huron City survived when the granddaughter of the founder preserved the community as a museum town. Twelve buildings are on the site, nine of them furnished and open to the public. They include a country store, a church, a lifesaving station, a settler's cabin, the old inn, a barn with antique farm equipment, and the Phelps Museum, which was built in honor of the minister in the early 1950s. Huron City Museums (989-428-4123; huroncitymuseums.org) is open July and Aug from 11 a.m. to 4 p.m. on Fri and Sat. Admission is $10 for adults and $5 for children over 12.

Where Lake Huron and Saginaw Bay meet is ***Port Austin,*** the town at the Tip of the Thumb. M 25 winds through the center of Port Austin and near its two busiest spots in the summer, the city marina and, just east of the marina's breakwall, delightful ***Bird Creek County Park***. This 7-acre park includes a beautiful sandy beach and a half-mile boardwalk where people fish during the day and gather nightly to watch the sunset over Saginaw Bay.

In keeping with the restored atmosphere of Port Austin, there is the ***Bank 1884 Restaurant*** for, unquestionably, the finest dining in town. Built in 1884 as the Winsorsnover Bank on the corner of Lake and State Streets at 8646 Lake St., the red-washed, brick building ceased being a place of financial business in 1957. In 1982 extensive renovation of the historic structure began, and two years later it reopened as a restaurant. The interior features stained glass over the classic stand-up bar, a teller's cage on the first floor, and walls of oversize photographs depicting early Huron County. The changing menu usually has prime rib of beef au jus and that Michigan summertime favorite: lightly battered lake perch. Hours vary, so check the website. Prices for entrees range from $26 to $39, and reservations (989-738-5353; thebank1884.com) are strongly recommended for the weekends.

West of Port Austin, M 25 begins to follow the shoreline of Saginaw Bay and is especially scenic in its 19-mile stretch to Caseville. It passes many views of the bay and its islands, numerous roadside parks, and the finest beaches in the Thumb. One of the parks is **Port Crescent State Park,** popular with sunbathers and swimmers for the long stretches of sandy shoreline. Located at 1775 Port Austin Rd., the park also offers opportunities and facilities for camping, hiking, and fishing, and it contains the Thumb's only set of dunes, a unique place for beachcombers to explore. There is an entrance fee to Port Crescent State Park (989-738-8663; enr.state.mi.us) and a $30 charge to camp overnight, $33 for full hookup. A cabin is also available for $52 to $110.

michigantrivia

Huron County accounts for more than 90 percent of the country's production of navy beans.

Even more than for sand and sun, Saginaw Bay has always been known as a boater's destination for great sightseeing tours and scuba diving. **Explorer Tours** (989-550-1234; explorercharters.com) offers sunset and sightseeing tours aboard its 56-passenger *Lady of the Lake*. Times and fees vary so contact Explorer Tours for more information.

To enjoy your perch without having to put a minnow on your hook, stay on M 25 as it curves southwest toward Bay Port. From the 1880s until the late 1940s, this sleepy village was known as the "largest freshwater fishing port in the world," as tons of perch, whitefish, walleye, and herring were shipped as far away as New York City in refrigerated railroad cars. Today it honors its fishing past on the first Fri, Sat, and Sun in August with its annual **Bay Port Fish Sandwich Festival** (989-551-9929; bayportchamber.com). The small festival includes arts and crafts, a petting zoo, fireworks, live music, and lots of sandwiches—close to 8,000 are served during the event.

A small commercial fishery is still operating in Bay Port, a place to go for fresh walleye, perch, whitefish, and herring. From the center of town, head for the waterfront docks of the **Bay Port Fish Company** (989-656-2121; bayport fish.com) at 1008 First St. for the catch of the day or to watch fishermen work on the boats or nets in the evening from Apr through Nov, depending on the

Dining Down on the Farm

You're in the heart of the Thumb, might as well head to a farmhouse for a hearty home-cooked meal of country goodness and straight-from-the-fields freshness. There are two wonderful restaurants in Huron County that make you feel like your aunt still lives on a farm, if for no other reason than they're surrounded by cornfields and faded red barns.

The first is just outside of Port Austin, a short drive in the country to a converted farmhouse at 699 Port Crescent Rd. What else could you possibly name this place but *The Farm Restaurant* (989-874-5700; thefarmrestaurant.com)?

The restaurant was originally the Old Homestead and was known for fried chicken and homemade pies when Jeff and Pam Gabriel purchased it in 1993. The owner and chef is now Mary Gabriel-Roth. Favorites include farmers'-style Hungarian meatballs with smoky paprika–sour cream brown sauce, served with roasted garlic mashed potatoes and seasonal vegetables, and chicken schnitzel, panko-crusted chicken breast with lemon caper sauce, roasted garlic mashed potatoes, creamed cabbage, and seasonal vegetables.

The dessert menu is also impressive, and many diners opt for the warm seasonal cobbler topped with vanilla ice cream. There are just some things people expect when eating dinner at a farmhouse.

Hours vary, so check the Farm schedule. Entrees range in price from $25 to $40.

More wholesome cooking can be found 3 miles south of Harbor Beach on M 25 at *Williams Inn* (989-479-3361) where a huge sign outside says Let's Eat Here! Let's, because this farmhouse restaurant with its green awning is too inviting to pass up.

In the huge enclosed porch of Williams Inn, diners can feast on such traditional favorites as country fried steak, grilled ham steaks topped with a sweet pineapple ring, or roast beef, slow roasted to be extra tender and juicy. But the best time to come is on Sunday morning for the inn's breakfast buffet, when you can load your plate up with 3 types of homemade sausage, ham, eggs, waffles, hash browns and thick-cut potatoes, and hot-from-the-oven biscuits that can be topped with sausage gravy.

During the summer Williams Inn is open from 8 a.m. to 9 p.m. Mon through Thurs, 7 a.m. to 10 p.m. Fri and Sat, and 7 a.m. to 7 p.m. on Sun. In the winter, Williams Inn is open from 8 a.m. to 8 p.m. Thurs, 8 a.m. to 9 p.m. Fri, 7 a.m. to 9 p.m. Sat, and 7 a.m. to 8 p.m. Sun.

weather. The company, which is open from 9 a.m. to 3 p.m. daily, sells whitefish, perch, salmon, catfish, walleye, and smoked fish.

In the heart of Huron County is *Bad Axe,* the county seat and a city of 2,945 residents. The town's most interesting attraction is *Pioneer Log Cabin Village* (989-712-0050; thehchs.org). This unique outdoor museum features a home, blacksmith shop, chapel, general store, barn, and one-room

One Bad Axe

Rudolph Papst is credited by many with giving Bad Axe its name. While surveying for a new road across the heart of Huron County in 1861, he discovered a "bad axe" near his campsite one night and labeled the spot Bad Axe Corners on his map.

In 1872 county supervisors wanted the government moved from Port Austin to a more central location in the county and chose Bad Axe Corners, which in reality was little more than a junction in a dense forest. But 5 acres were quickly cleared, and in 1873 a courthouse was built. Since then Bad Axe has grown to be Huron County's largest city while its residents have resisted several attempts to give it a more dignified name.

schoolhouse. All the buildings are log cabins that were built in Huron and moved to Bad Axe. The cabins are fully furnished to reflect the pioneer lifestyle of the 19th century and often are staffed during the summer by guides in period costumes.

The village is located in Bad Axe City Park at 210 S. Hanselman St. and is open Sun from 2 to 4 p.m. from Memorial Day through Labor Day. There is no admission fee.

Places to Stay in The Thumb

BAD AXE

Franklin Inn
1070 E. Huron St.
(989) 269-9951 or
(800) 645-0211
franklininnmi.com

CASEVILLE

Bella Vista Inn
6024 Port Austin Rd.
(989) 856-2650
bella-caseville.com

Crew's Lakeside Resort
4750 Port Austin Rd.
(989) 856-2786
crewslakesideresort.com

Lake Street Manor B&B
8569 Lake St.
(989) 738-7720
lakestreetmanor.com

The Lodge at Oak Pointe
5857 Port Austin Rd.
(989) 856-3055
oakpointelodge.com

HARBOR BEACH

State Street Inn
646 State St.
(989) 479-3388
thestatestreetinn.com

Train Station Motel
2044 N. Lakeshore Rd.
(989) 479-3215

LEXINGTON

A Night to Remember Bed & Breakfast
5712 Main St.
(810) 359-7134
anighttorememberbandb
.com

Butler Bed & Breakfast
5774 Main St.
(810) 359-5910
butlerphotosbb.com

Cadillac House Inn & Tavern
5502 Main St.
(810) 359-7201
thecadillachouse.com

Captain's Quarters Inn
7277 Simons St.
(810) 359-2196
cqilex.com

Inn the Garden Bed and Breakfast
7156 Huron Ave.
(810) 359-8966
inngarden.com

Lex on the Lake Lodges
5795 Main St.
(810) 359-7910

Powell House Bed & Breakfast
5076 Lakeshore Rd.
(810) 359-5533
powellhouselex.com

PORT AUSTIN

Garfield Inn
8544 Lake St.
(989) 738-5254
thegarfieldinn.com

Krebs Cottages
3478 Port Austin Rd.
(989) 550-7363
krebscottages.com

Lakeside Motor Lodge
8654 Lake St.
(989) 738-5201
lakesideportaustin.com

Lake Vista Resort
168 W. Spring St.
(989) 738-8612
lakevistaresort.com

PORT SANILAC

Bellaire Motel & Lodge
120 S. Ridge St.
(810) 622-9981
bellairemotelandlodge.com

Holland's Little House in the Country
1995 N. Huron View Rd.
(810) 622-9739

Raymond House Inn
111 S. Ridge St.
(810) 622-8800
theraymondhouseinn.com

Places to Eat in The Thumb

BAD AXE

Franklin Inn
1070 E. Huron St.
(989) 269-9951 or
(800) 645-0211
franklininnbadaxe.com
American

Peppermill Restaurant
685 N. Port Crescent St.
(989) 269-9347
peppermillba.com
American

Rachel's
754 N. Van Dyke Rd.
(989) 269-5000
rachelsofbadaxe.com
Sushi, Asian

OTHER ATTRACTIONS

Albert E. Sleeper State Park
6573 State Park Rd.
Caseville
(989) 856-4411
michigan.gov.dnr

Luckhard Museum
590 E. Bay St.
Sebewaing
(989) 883-2539

Pigeon Historical Museum
59 S. Main St.
Pigeon
(989) 453-3242
pigeonhistoricalsociety.com

46

SELECTED CHAMBERS OF COMMERCE & TOURISM BUREAUS

Bad Axe Chamber of Commerce
300 E. Huron Ave.
Bad Axe 48413
(969) 269-9351

Caseville Chamber of Commerce
6632 Main St.
Caseville 48725
(989) 856-3818
casevillechamber.com

Harbor Beach Chamber of Commerce
146 S. Huron Ave.
Harbor Beach 48441
(989) 479-6477
harborbeachchamber.com

Huron County Visitors Bureau
250 E. Huron Ave.
Bad Axe 48413
(989) 269-8463

Port Austin Chamber of Commerce
2 W. Spring St.
Port Austin 48467
(989) 738-7600
portaustinarea.com

CASEVILLE

Hersel's on the Bay
6024 Port Austin
(989) 856-2500
bella-caseville.com
Fine Dining

Lefty's Diner
6937 Main St.
(989) 856-8899
leftysdinermi.com
American

HARBOR BEACH

Hooks Waterfront Resort
2044 N. Lakeshore Rd.
(989) 479-3215
American

Williams Inn
1724 S. Lakeshore Rd.
(989) 479-3361
williamsinn.org
American

METAMORA

White Horse Inn
1 E. High St.
(810) 678-2276
thewhitehorseinn.com
American

PORT AUSTIN

Bank 1884
8646 Lake St.
(989) 738-5353
thebank1884.com
Fine Dining

Bird Creek Farms
282 Grindstone Rd.
(989) 553-6444
American

Farm Restaurant
699 Port Crescent
(989) 874-5700
thefarmrestaurant.com
American

Lighthouse Cafe
44 W. Spring St.
(989) 738-5239
lighthouse-café.com
American

Pak's Backyard
119 E. Spring St.
(989) 551-0444
paksbackyard.com
American

PORT SANILAC

Mary's Diner
14 N. Ridge St.
(810) 622-9377
American

Stone Lodge
156 S. Ridge Rd.
(810) 622-6200
thestonelodgerestaurant
.com
American

The Heartland

By the 1830s "Michigan Fever" had become an epidemic. Scores of pioneer families from the East Coast floated through the Erie Canal, made their way to Detroit, and then took to the newly completed Detroit-Chicago Road, which cut across the southern half of the Lower Peninsula. They soon discovered the rolling prairies of Michigan, where the soil was very rich and the land very cheap—the federal government was selling it for only $1.25 an acre.

From this onrush of settlers between 1825 and 1855, some of the state's largest cities emerged: Kalamazoo, Lansing, Battle Creek, Jackson, and Grand Rapids, all in this central region. But the Heartland of Michigan, the only area without direct links to the Great Lakes, is still an agricultural breadbasket. It is faded red barns and rolling fields of oats, the birthplace of Kellogg's Corn Flakes, and the home of a village antiques dealer who scours area farms for the furniture and knickknacks that fill her store.

The vibrant cities, each with a distinct downtown that never sleeps, are popular destinations for travelers who can zip from one to the next on interstates six lanes wide. But the unique nature of this region is found by rambling along its

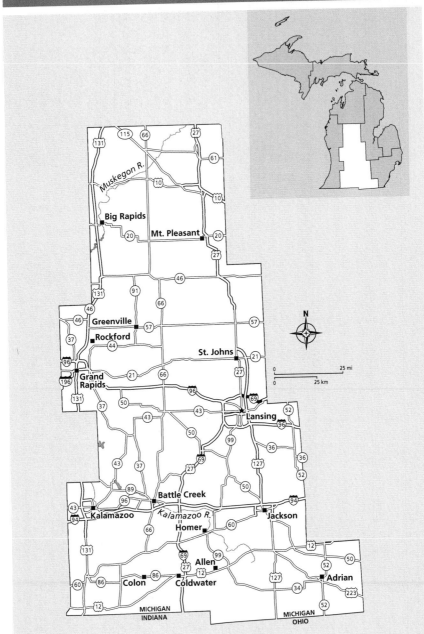

AUTHOR'S TOP TEN PICKS

Abbott's Magic Co.
124 St. Joseph St.
Colon
(269) 432-3235
abbottmagic.com

Air Zoo Aerospace & Science Museum
6151 Portage Rd.
Portage
(269) 382-6555
airzoo.org

Allen Antique Mall
9011 W. Chicago Rd.
Allen
(517) 869-2788
allenantiquebarn.com

Frederik Meijer Gardens
1000 E. Beltline Ave. NE
Grand Rapids
(888) 957-1580
meijergardens.org

Gerald R. Ford Museum
303 Pearl St. NW
Grand Rapids
(616) 254-0400
fordlibrarymuseum.gov

Gilmore Car Museum
6865 W. Hickory Rd.
Hickory Corners
(269) 671-5089
gilmorecarmuseum.org

Grand Rapids Public Museum
272 Pearl St. NW
Grand Rapids
(616) 929-1700
grpm.org

Hidden Lake Gardens
6214 Monroe Rd.
Tipton
(517) 431-2060
canr.msu.edu

Michigan Library and Historical Center
702 W. Kalamazoo St.
Lansing
(517) 335-1477
michigan.gov/libraryofmichigan

State Capitol Tours
100 N. Capitol Ave.
Lansing
(517) 373-2353
capitol.michigan.gov

two-lane county roads, which take you past the horse-drawn carriages of Amish country, down main streets of small villages, and along roadside stands loaded with the summer's harvest. In these out-of-the-way places, you can sample the fruits of Michigan's Heartland.

Lenawee County

At the northern edge of Lenawee County are the famed *Irish Hills,* an area of green rolling hills with intermittent lakes and ponds. US 12 cuts through the middle of this popular area and has become an avenue of manufactured tourist attractions: miniature golf courses and go-kart tracks, a dinosaur amusement park, another park called Stagecoach Stop USA, motels, gift shops, and even an international speedway that holds Indy car races. So overwhelming are these modern-day sights that it's easy to pass by one of the most interesting attractions and probably the only one that is free, ***Walker Tavern.***

Located in ***Cambridge Junction Historic State Park,*** the white clapboard tavern overlooks US 12, and rightfully so. The highway was originally an Indian trail and then became a stagecoach route known as the Detroit-Chicago Road. The stagecoach era lasted from 1835 to 1855, and on these rickety wagons, passengers traveled 50 miles a day with the hope of reaching Chicago in five days. The string of frontier taverns along the way was a crucial part of the system. They provided not only overnight accommodations (two or three travelers would share a bed for 25 cents a night) but also meals for the weary passengers who had just spent the day bouncing along the rough dirt road.

By the 1830s Walker Tavern had a reputation as a fine place to dine. Proprietor Sylvester Walker ran not only the inn but a small farm as well, while his wife, Lucy, performed miracles baking in the stone fireplace. A typical supper at Walker Tavern might include stewed chicken, biscuits, corn bread, and applesauce cake or pumpkin pie. The tavern still stands on its original site, and the pub, sitting room, and kitchen have been renovated. Next to the tavern is a reconstructed wheelwright shop, featuring the tools used to build and repair the fragile wooden wheels as well as the covered wagons and carriages of the era. Visitors begin the self-guided walking tour at the Interpretive Center with a film in its theater and an exhibit on the settling of Michigan.

Cambridge Junction Historic State Park (517-467-4401; michigan.gov/dnr) is at US 12 and M 50, 25 miles south of Jackson. The tavern complex is open from Memorial Day through Labor Day and for special events. Times vary so check the website or call.

Also located in the Irish Hills is Lenawee County's other outstanding attraction, ***Hidden Lake Gardens.*** Glaciers were responsible for the rolling terrain of the gardens, and when the ice sheet finally melted away, it left a topography of prominent knolls, ridges, valleys, and funnel-like depressions. Harry A. Fee was responsible for preserving it. The Adrian businessman fell in love with the scenic land formations and in 1926 purchased 226 acres, including its namesake lake. He began developing the landscape and supervising its early plantings before giving the gardens to Michigan State University in 1945. The visitor center was added in 1966, the plant conservatory four years later, and today Hidden Lake Gardens covers 670 acres with 6 miles of picturesque, winding, one-way roads, 5 miles of hiking trails to its remote corners, and more than 2,500 introduced species of plants.

Upon entering the gardens, most people head for the visitor center, which includes an orientation and information area, a gift shop, and a walk-through exhibit concourse. Next door is the plant conservatory, where 8,000 square feet of glass houses plants from around the world. Along with the kumquats and vanilla plants in the tropical house and the old-man cacti in the arid dome, there is the 80- by 36-foot temperate house used to display unusual houseplants and seasonal flowers. From the conservatory visitors can follow a winding drive around Hidden Lake and then ascend through a unique forest carpeted in ivy before topping out at Gobblers Knob with a view of the surrounding ridges and hardwood trees below. The network of one-way roads also leads visitors past a glacial pothole, through an oak upland forest, and around an open meadow, and ends, of course, at a picnic area.

The entrance to the gardens (517-431-2060; canr.msu.edu) is located on M 50, 2 miles west of Tipton or 7 miles west of Tecumseh at 6214 Monroe Rd. The gardens, visitor center, and plant conservatory are open daily from 9 a.m. to 7 p.m. Apr through Oct and 9 a.m. to 4 p.m. Nov through Mar. Admission is $5 per person.

TOP ANNUAL EVENTS

MARCH

Clare Irish Festival
Clare
(989) 386-2442
claremichigan.com

MAY

Alma Highland Festival and Games
Alma
(989) 463-8979
almahighlandfestival.com

JUNE

World's Longest Breakfast Table
Battle Creek
(800) 397-2240
bcfestivals.com

JULY

Common Ground Music Festival
Lansing
(577) 267-1502
commongroundfest.com

AUGUST

Abbott's Magic Get Together
Colon
(269) 432-3235
magicgettogether.com

Civil War Muster
Jackson
(517) 788-4320
civilwarmuster.org

Great Lakes Folk Festival
East Lansing

SEPTEMBER

Historic Homes Tour
Marshall
(269) 781-8544
marshallhistoricalsociety.org

Paw Paw Wine and Harvest Festival
Paw Paw
(269) 655-1111
wineandharvestfestival.com

michigantrivia

Adrian's *Croswell Opera House* at 129 E. Maumee St. is the third oldest continuously operated theater in the country. The Opera House (517-263-6868; croswell .org) dates back to 1866 and today still features live theater productions.

There are many mansions-turned-restaurants in Michigan, but few evoke an aura of gracious living and fine dining the way the **Hathaway House** does. A National Historic Site, the home was built by David Carpenter, who arrived in Blissfield in 1836 as a 21-year-old with $25. Seventeen years later, Carpenter was a wealthy merchant, and he decided to build a home that would reflect his position as one of the county's most prominent residents. The 18-room Hathaway House resembles a southern mansion. Inside guests are seated in 6 distinctively decorated rooms that were previously the east and west parlors, the card room, and the library, among others. In this restaurant you can still run your hand along the original cherry banister of the sweeping staircase, be warmed during the winter by one of 5 fireplaces, and admire the classic woodwork.

Afterward you can drop in at the Main Street Stable. What used to be the carriage house in the back of Carpenter's mansion is now a lively little pub that still features a rustic interior of hand-hewn beams, wooden benches, and lanterns hanging from the ceiling.

The Hathaway House (517-486-2141 or 888-937-4284; hathawayhouse .com) is reached from US 23 by taking exit 5 and heading 10 miles west on US 223 to 424 W. Adrian St. Hours are 5 to 9 p.m. Fri and Sat and noon to 7 p.m. Sun. Dinner entrees range from $25 to $35.

Hillsdale County

In 1827 a surveying crew from the Detroit-Chicago Road was working in the fertile prairie of the St. Joseph Valley when one crew member, Captain Moses Allen, fell in love with the area. His homestead led to a small hamlet of homes and shops known as Allen's Prairie, the first white settlement west of Tecumseh. This is the birthplace of Hillsdale County, but today **Allen** is better known as the Antiques Capital of Michigan.

It began as a weekend flea market in the late 1960s and soon drew crowds of antiques hunters from several states to the junction of US 12 and M 49. Eventually some of the antiques dealers who rented the summer stalls began to set up permanent businesses in Allen. Today this quaint village of 190 residents supports a half-dozen antiques malls, shops, and auction houses scattered in the downtown area and to the west along US 12. Some of the shops are in old homes or weathered barns that are packed with large furniture and other odds and ends. One of the malls is so large it houses more than 300 dealers.

The **Tristate Corner** in Hillsdale County is hardly a major tourist attraction. But there is enough interest in this geographical oddity that the Hillsdale County Historical Association maintains a stone monument dedicated to where three states—Michigan, Indiana, and Ohio—come together, the only such spot in the Midwest that doesn't involve a river.

The monument is actually in Michigan, but it explains exactly where the corner is (130 feet to the south) because when you reach this obscure spot, a farm field on a county dirt road, you want to make sure you're standing in all three states at the same time.

It's not as famous as Four Corners, the spot where Arizona, New Mexico, Colorado, and Utah come together, but on the other hand, as the locals say, it won't burn two weeks of your vacation to visit.

From Camden, in the southwest corner of Hillsdale County, head south on M 49 and then west on Territorial Road. In less than 3 miles, turn south on Cope Road and look for the stone monument on the left-hand side of the road.

> ## michigantrivia
>
> Somerset Center's **McCourtie Park,** located in the northeast corner of Hillsdale County, was once the Prohibition-era playground of cement mogul William McCourtie and features 17 sculpted cement bridges across a winding stream.

St. Joseph County

Michigan is known for many things, but to the average tourist, magicians and magic are not generally among them. Yet Harry Houdini died in Michigan, and the state has deep roots in the art of illusion and the related conjuring culture. One of the most famous American magicians in the 1920s, Harry Blackstone, toured the country with his act. At one time he passed through the village of **Colon** and then returned in 1926 and purchased property. Blackstone toured in the winter but spent his summers in Colon creating new illusions and rehearsing his show. One summer Australian magician Percy Abbott came to Colon to visit Blackstone and fell in love with a local girl and the quiet area. Abbott, eager to end his days of traveling, moved to Michigan and formed a partnership with Blackstone to begin a magic-apparatus manufacturing company.

The partnership went sour after only eight months, but the Australian magician went ahead with his plans and in 1933 set up **Abbott's Magic Co.** Today this sleepy farming village is the home of the world's largest magic company, an interesting stop even if you've never done a card trick. The walls inside are plastered with posters and photographs of magicians, for all the famous performers, from Doug Henning to David Copperfield, have done business with this company. A display room in the factory, an all-black brick building, has cases and shelves filled with a portion of the 2,000 tricks and gadgets Abbott's Magic builds. And there is always a resident magician on hand to show you how they work.

A year after beginning his company, Abbott also instituted an open house for magicians as a sales incentive, and that quickly evolved into Colon's annual festival, the *Abbott's Magical Get Together.* Every August more than a thousand amateur and professional magicians flood the village for a series of shows at the high school auditorium. Abbott's Magic Company (269-432-3235; abbottmagic.com) is at 124 St. Joseph St., 1 block off M 86, and is open 9 a.m. to 5 p.m. Mon through Fri and 10 a.m. to 4 p.m. on Sat.

More magic memorabilia can be viewed at the *Colon Community Museum* (269-432-3806), which is housed in an 1893 church at 219 N. Blackstone Rd. Although many artifacts deal with the town's first pioneer families, one area is devoted to the personal items and photographs of Blackstone and Abbott. The museum is open Tues, Thurs, and Sun from 2 to 4:30 p.m. from June 1 to Labor Day and the rest of the year by appointment.

Jackson County

The Lower Peninsula lacks the waterfalls that grace the countryside in the Upper Peninsula, but in Jackson there are the *Cascades.* Billed as the largest constructed waterfalls in North America, the Cascades were a creation of "Captain" William Sparks, a well-known Jackson industrialist and philanthropist. They date to the early 1930s, when Sparks was developing a 450-acre park as a gift to the city and wanted it to showcase something different, something no other Michigan city had.

What he developed were the Cascades, a series of 18 waterfalls with water dancing down the side of a hill from one to the next. Six fountains, varying in height and patterns, supply more than 3,000 gallons per minute, while 1,200 colored lights turn the attraction into a nightly event of constantly changing light, color, and music. The total length of the falls is 500 feet, and energetic viewers climb the 129 steps that run along each side of the Cascades, dodging the spray along the way. Others prefer to sit in the amphitheater seats to watch the water and light show that takes place nightly from 8 to 11 p.m. Wed through Sun, Memorial Day to Labor Day.

The Cascades (517-768-2901, co.jackson.mi.us/departments/parks/cascades_falls) can be reached from I-94 by taking exit 138 and heading south for 3 miles to 1401 S. Brown St. Signs point the way to the falls. Admission is $5 per person and $7 per person on nights when there is a fireworks show. Children 4 to 12 are $3 and $5 on nights when there is a fireworks show.

Ten miles southwest of Jackson is the Victorian town of Concord, the proper setting for the **Mann House,** a Michigan historical museum. The three-story house was built in 1883 by Daniel and Ellen Mann, two of the earliest settlers in the area. They raised two daughters, Jessie and Mary Ida, who continued to live in the house and maintained the original furnishings, most dating to the 1870s. The younger daughter died in

michigantrivia

The longest of Michigan's handful of remaining covered bridges is just north of Centreville along Covered Bridge Road. Built in 1887, the **Langley Covered Bridge** is 282 feet long and uses three spans to cross the St. Joseph River.

The Parlour

Late one night, when **The Parlour** is humming with people, ice cream dishes clanging, and waitresses hustling orders from the kitchen, a woman screams and no one takes notice. It's her first trip to the landmark ice cream parlor, and a waitress has just placed in front of her the largest Black Cow she has ever seen. The fountain glass itself is 12 inches high, and still the rich mixture of root beer and ice cream is cascading over the top, because at the Parlour, they put 5 scoops of vanilla—count 'em, 5—in their Black Cow.

"Oh my goodness," says the woman, in a near state of calorie shock. "All I asked for was a root beer float, and look what they brought me."

If you're a die-hard ice cream lover, then the Parlour is heaven on earth, or at the very least a parfait paradise. Operated by the Jackson Dairy, this hot fudge haven is basically 4 U-shaped lunch counters plus a handful of booths for those of us who like to pig out anonymously. Everybody else has to sit across from total strangers and indulge in 5 scoops of cherry ripple drowning in a sea of marshmallow syrup. Then again, maybe it's better they are strangers.

Or else, who cares? When you enter the Parlour, you have momentarily forgotten about your waistband if you ever thought about it to begin with. The most popular item is the Deluxe Pecan Combo: 3 scoops of ice cream smothered in hot fudge and hot caramel, sprinkled with pecans, and buried in real whipped cream. You don't eat this sundae, you attack it, using your spoon like a shovel to remove large portions from the sides before it avalanches onto your place mat.

The Parlour (517-783-1581) is off Wildwood Avenue at 1401 Daniel St. in Jackson and reached from I-94 by taking exit 137. Head south on Lawrence and then east on Wildwood Avenue.

michigantrivia

The Republican Party was born on the corner of Second and Franklin Streets in Jackson. The hall where the founders had originally planned to meet on July 6, 1854, was too small for the 1,500 people who arrived to form a new political party. So the crowd walked 8 blocks to an oak grove and met there "under the oaks."

1969 but bequeathed the historic house and all its contents to the people of Michigan through the Michigan Historical Commission.

The house can be toured today, and its 8 rooms are a well-preserved trip back to life in the 1880s. The table is set in the dining room; a chess game waits to be played in the parlor; toys, books, and knickknacks fill the children's rooms. As soon as you walk through the wrought-iron gate at the street, you enter an era gone by. The Mann House (517-524-8943; michigan.gov/mannhouse) at 205 Hanover St. in Concord is open from 9 a.m. to 4 p.m. Mon through Sat from Memorial Day to Labor Day. There is no admission fee.

Deer hunting is not just an outdoor sport in Michigan, it's a passion. Every November more than 750,000 hunters participate in the 16-day firearm deer

Michigan's Oldest Restaurant & Hotel

Detroit's *Amore da Roma* (313-831-5940; amoredaroma.com) near the Eastern Market is the oldest restaurant in the state. The cafe began as a boardinghouse in 1890, offering a bed and meals to farmers who arrived to sell their produce and goods at the market. By the 1920s the boarding portion of the business was closed but the restaurant remained, serving fine Italian meals at the corner of Riopelle and Erskine Streets at 3401 Riopelle St. for more than 130 years.

Michigan's oldest hotel is the *National House Inn* (269-781-7374; nationalhouseinn .com) overlooking Marshall's picturesque Fountain Circle at 102 Parkview. The inn was built in 1835 with bricks that were molded and fired on the site, making it the oldest brick building in Calhoun County. It was located two dusty days and nights by stagecoach from Detroit and served as a welcome halfway stop for early travelers on the way to Chicago.

When the Michigan Central Railroad arrived in Marshall in 1844, the inn catered to railroad passengers then closed its doors as a hotel in 1878, the victim of dining cars and Pullman sleepers. At that time the building was converted to a factory for producing windmills and farm wagons. But it returned to being a place of fine lodging when in 1976 the National House Inn was restored as a bed-and-breakfast with 16 rooms as part of a community bicentennial project. Today it is listed as a state historical site and on the National Register of Historic Places.

Sojourner Truth Museum Exhibit

The **Kimball House Museum** is a restored 1886 Victorian home furnished with antiques and devoted to the history of Battle Creek. But by far the most interesting exhibit is dedicated to **Sojourner Truth.** This famous antislavery reformer was born into slavery in Hurley, New York, in 1797 but was freed when the state emancipated slaves in 1829. A mystic who believed she heard God's voice, Truth began to preach in the streets of New York City in 1829 and then along the Eastern Seaboard after embracing the abolitionist movement in 1843. She added women's rights to her causes a few years later, and in 1864 she was received by President Abraham Lincoln at the White House.

Eventually Truth relocated to Battle Creek but continued to stump the country on speaking tours, advocating women's rights. Illiterate all her life, Truth was nevertheless a charismatic speaker who drew large crowds to her lectures and quickly became Battle Creek's first nationally known figure.

The second-floor exhibit at the Kimball House Museum features a handful of Truth's mementos, including her crude attempt to write her name. The museum (269-965-2613) is at 196 Capital Ave., 3 blocks north of Michigan Avenue. Self-guided and guided tours are offered on request. Open to the public on 1st and 3rd Sundays of Apr to Dec. Otherwise, schedule an appointment. Admission is $5 for adults and $3 for children ages 12 and under.

-season. Add in the people who participate in the archery and muzzle-loading deer seasons, and the number tops a million.

These hunters' shrine is the **Michigan Whitetail Hall of Fame Museum,** just off I-94 near Jackson. At this unusual "hall of fame," you can feed live deer, or, if you are around on June 1, see newborn fawns. Inside the hall is a gallery of more than 100 trophy racks including 50 Boone and Crockett world-record buck racks and Michigan's record buck. This is the stuff that deer hunters dream about while sitting in their blinds every November.

The Michigan Whitetail Hall of Fame Museum (517-937-0533; Michigan-whitetail-hall-of-fame-museum.business.site) is at 4220 Willis Rd. and reached by taking exit 150 at Grass Lake and following the signs. Hours are 10 a.m. to 6:30 p.m. daily; winter hours 11 a.m. to 5:30 p.m. Admission is $6 for adults and $2 for children.

Calhoun County

Homer is a small town in the southeast corner of the county, and its most impressive structure is a century-old gristmill on the banks of the Kalamazoo

River. The US government once wanted to turn the mill's black walnut beams into propellers for World War I airplanes. Another historic building in town, though considerably smaller, is the **Homer Fire Museum** (517-568-4311). The redbrick structure with its arched windows and decorative cornice was built in 1876, 5 years after Homer was incorporated as a village. It has always been the classic fire hall on the main street, but in its early days it also served as a jail, town hall, and place for public meetings and local theater performances. It's the oldest building in town, and when Homer residents decided to replace it, they preserved the old fire hall by attaching the new fire station to it.

In 1983 it was set up as a museum, with suits and equipment donated by former firefighters. By far the most impressive item on display had always been there, a horse-pulled steam pumper built in 1887. Homer bought it from Union City in 1904 for $1,200 and placed it in the fire hall, where it has been

Strange as it Sounds

It looked so plain when the woman behind the counter handed it to me, wrapped in waxed paper and placed in a brown paper bag. But there it is: a buttered turkey sandwich, slices of moist meat on a bun, topped with mayonnaise. It's the kind of sandwich you'd make after Thanksgiving dinner with the leftover rolls and that platter of turkey still sitting in the kitchen.

But here at a place they call *Turkeyville, USA,* you don't have to wait until Uncle Harry and the kids go home. You can order one year-round because this simple sandwich—turkey, butter, mayonnaise on soft white bread—is the foundation of a multimillion-dollar company. Cornwell's Turkeyville, USA has been called "the oldest, best-known, and possibly largest all-turkey specialty restaurant in North America."

The Cornwells have done to the turkey what the Zehner family has done to the chicken in Frankenmuth: turned a meal into a tourist attraction. Today the restaurant is an entertainment complex serving an average of 1,000 people a day, grossing more than $2 million annually, and feeding more than 400 busloads a summer—and pretty much does it all on the backs of 15,000, 30-pound toms a year. In 1985, when a photo of founders Wayne and Marjorie Cornwell was featured in *People* magazine with an item proclaiming their buttered bun "the world's best turkey sandwich," people around here knew the Cornwells had hit the big time.

After you've had your fill of turkey, you can wander into Cornwell's Ice Cream Parlour or the huge gift shop. Also among the attractions is a dinner theater, plus craft shows, bazaars, and other events throughout the year.

From I-94, take I-69 north to exit 42 and then head west on N. Drive North, also known as Turkeyville Road. The restaurant is reached in a half mile at 18935 15½ Mile Rd. Cornwell's Turkeyville, USA (269-781-4293; turkeyville.com) is open from 11 a.m. to 7 p.m. daily year-round.

ever since. The museum does not have regular hours, but those who are passing through can go to the Homer City Offices (517-568-4321) next to the fire station at 130 E. Main St., and an employee will open up the museum for you. There is no admission fee.

Battle Creek is best known as the Cereal Bowl of America, dating back to 1876 when Dr. John Harvey Kellogg joined the staff of the Battle Creek Sanitarium. A Seventh-day Adventist at the time, Kellogg spent 25 years developing the sanitarium into an institution recognized around the world for its "health building and training" based on the church's principles of a vegetarian diet, abstinence from alcohol and tobacco, and a regimen of exercise. Along the way he found a way to process grains into appetizing breakfast food as an alternative to the standard breakfast of eggs and meat. Cornflakes and other cereals quickly revolutionized the eating habits of people everywhere, and by the early 1900s more than 40 cereal manufacturers were based in Battle Creek, including Kellogg's.

The best place to learn about Dr. Kellogg and the birth of cereal is at the **Dr. John Harvey Kellogg Discovery Center,** one of 8 buildings within **Historic Adventist Village.** On the second floor of the center are interactive exhibits focused on the health treatments and practices that made the Battle Creek Sanitarium world famous a century ago. The rest of the re-created 19th-century village is devoted to the history of the Seventh-day Adventist Church and includes a log cabin, one-room schoolhouse, and the houses of the Adventist pioneers who settled in the west end of Battle Creek in 1855.

The Historic Adventist Village (269-965-3000; adventistheritage.org) is just west of Battle Creek at 480 W. Van Buren St. It is open from Apr 1 to Oct 31, Sun through Fri from 10 a.m. to 5 p.m., and 2 to 5 p.m. on Sat. In the winter, the village is open Sun through Fri from 10 a.m. to 4 p.m., and Sat from 2 to 4 p.m. Call for an appointment in the winter. Admission by donation.

Not every attraction in Battle Creek is wrapped around sugar-frosted flakes. Just south of the city in a wooded area along Harper Creek is **Binder Park Zoo,** one of Michigan's most unusual displays of fauna and flora. Instead of a series of cages and animal houses in the middle of a city, Binder Park is a walk through the woods along boardwalks, brick walkways, and wood-chip trails, passing animal exhibits that have been designed around the existing flora and terrain.

The most impressive is Wild Africa, where you can view gazelles, zebras, or one of the largest giraffe herds in the country. In other areas you will see giant tortoises, Chinese red pandas, snow leopards, or wallabies from Australia, but the section kids love the most is Binder's zoo within a zoo. Miller Children's Zoo is the largest animal-contact area in the state and provides children an opportunity to feed and touch dozens of animals, including donkeys, rabbits, pygmy goats, draft horses, and pigs. Constructed around these contact stations are intriguing play areas. There's the Pig Pen, with models of pigs that children can play on; the dinosaur area, with a 100-foot-long brachiosaurus and a fossil-find pit; a giant spider web to climb; and a farm area with a silo slide and cow climber.

Binder Park Zoo (269-979-1351; binderparkzoo.org) is reached from I-94 by taking exit 100 south along Beadle Lake Road and following the signs to the entrance at 7400 Division Dr. The zoo is open from mid-Apr to mid-Oct from 9 a.m. to 5 p.m. Mon through Fri, 9 a.m. to 6 p.m. Sat, and 11 a.m. to 6 p.m. Sun. Admission is $14.50 for adults and $12.50 for children. Children under age 2 are free.

Battle Creek is also home to one of the most unusual county parks in Michigan. The focus of **Historic Bridge Park** is the preservation of turn-of-the-20th-century truss bridges, making it the first of its kind in the country. Truss bridges that need to be replaced elsewhere are relocated over Dickinson Creek within the park and then restored for their historic and aesthetic value. There are currently 5 metal truss bridges and a stone arch bridge in the park, but eventually there will be up to 15, providing walkers, picnickers, and cyclists a unique way to cross the stream.

After being closed for over a year due to an oil spill from a broken Enbridge pipeline upstream from the park, Historic Bridge Park reopened on June 5, 2012, following a cleanup and renovations. Enbridge also paid for improved restroom facilities, parking lots, and a new playground, as well as an improved stairway up to the Charlotte Highway Bridge. Enbridge has funded an endowment for maintenance of the new park features.

To reach the park from I-94, depart at exit 104 and head south on 11 Mile Road. Turn right on F Drive North and left on Wattles Road where the entrance is posted. Historic Bridge Park (269-781-0784; historicbridges.org) is open year-round from 8 a.m. to 8 p.m., and there are no entry fees.

Kalamazoo County

Is it a museum or a theme park? You decide—but what can't be debated is the fact that the **Air Zoo Aerospace & Science Museum** has been gradually expanded until today it's the 10th largest nongovernment aviation museum in the nation. Officially the Air Zoo is dedicated to the aircraft of World War II and the role they played in the Allies' success. It's a "living museum" that not only displays many planes in its hangars at the southeast corner of the Kalamazoo/Battle Creek International Airport but also restores them to working condition.

Inside there are more than 80 planes and historical crafts on display, including a Curtiss P-40 "Flying Tiger" and 3 Grumman cats: "Wildcat," "Hellcat," and "Bearcat," thus the reason for the Air Zoo's name.

But at the Air Zoo you can also join a space walk and discover how walking in space is different from walking on earth, fly a bi-plane complete with wind in your hair, experience weightlessness just like an astronaut on a Zero Gravity ride, or view a WWII bombing mission in a unique 4-dimensional, 180-degree theater (3-D film plus live actors). The Air Zoo (866-524-7966; airzoo.org) is at 6151 Portage Rd. and open Mon through Sat 9 a.m. to 5 p.m., and noon to 5 p.m. on Sun. Admission is $15.95 for adults and $14.95 for children ages 5 to 18; it's free for children under 5.

michigantrivia

The city of Kalamazoo dates back to 1829 when Titus Bronson arrived and founded a settlement that was first called Bronson. The only known speech Abraham Lincoln gave in Michigan was in Kalamazoo.

Also on the edge of Kalamazoo is the *Celery Flats Interpretive Center.* This is a truly unique facility that teaches the history of the efforts of Dutch immigrants to convert wetlands into one of the most productive celery-growing areas in the world. From the 1890s through the 1930s, fields of green-tipped celery covered Portage, Comstock, and Kalamazoo; the celery was touted as "fresh as dew from Kalamazoo."

The historic area offers an 1856 one-room schoolhouse, a 1931 grain elevator, and historical displays on celery, as well as an opportunity to rent canoes to explore the surrounding wetlands. Celery Flats (269-329-4522; portagemi .gov) is open from June through Aug from 10 a.m. to 3 p.m. Mon through Fri and noon to 5 p.m. Sat and Sun. From I-94 take exit 76A and head south 2.5 miles on S. Westedge Avenue and then east 0.5 mile on Garden Lane to 7335 Garden Ln. Free admission.

Barry County

In 1962 Donald Gilmore, the son-in-law of Dr. W. E. Upjohn, founder of one of the nation's leading pharmaceutical firms, was restoring a 1920 Pierce-Arrow touring car in the driveway of his Gull Lake summer home. The project dragged on into the fall, and by the time it was finished, Gilmore had to erect a tent around the car and light a kerosene heater. This was no way to work on a classic car. So Gilmore purchased three farms north of his home and then scouted the countryside for old wooden barns, which he had dismantled and moved.

The wooden structures held his growing collection, and in 1966 Gilmore opened his barn doors to the public on 90 acres of rolling farmland. The Classic Car Club of America added its collection to what had become the Hickory Corners Museum in 1984, and today the **Gilmore Car Museum** forms a complex of 22 barns displaying 200 vintage automobiles in mint condition. The car that attracts the most attention is a 1929 Duesenberg. Some visitors, however, are fascinated with Rolls-Royces, and the museum contains 15 of them, including 8 in one barn, ranging from a 1910 Silver Ghost to a 1938 Phantom III.

There is also a 1927 Bugatti Grand Sport Roadster, the "Gnome-Mobile" from the Disney movie of the same name, as well as other transportation displays, including a replica of the Wright Brothers' Kitty Hawk flier. Those intrigued by hood ornaments can view a collection of more than 1,500—the largest such collection in North America—that captures everything from a windblown angel to an archer taking aim at the road ahead. They come from as far away as the former Soviet Union and include leaded-glass ornaments from France.

Dedicated in May 2012, the **Automotive Heritage Center** is a state-of-the-art $5 million, 32,000-square-foot attraction. Fashioned after an early 1900s factory, the center is the museum's largest expansion to date. The center connects to one of the museum's historic barns, which leads to 5 additional exhibit galleries as well as the vintage Franklin Auto Dealership.

The center features a large exhibit gallery, a multimedia theater, and an expansive research library and archives, as well as educational and interactive areas, a museum store, offices, and artifact storage facility.

The complex (269-671-5089; gilmorecarmuseum.org) is located at M 43 and Hickory Road, 7 miles north of Richland. From I-94, take exit 80 and head north to M 43 to 6865 W. Hickory Rd. The museum is open year-round from 9 a.m. to 5 p.m. Mon through Fri, and 9 a.m. to 6 p.m. Sat and Sun. Admission is $16 for adults and $11 for children ages 11 to 17; free for ages 10 and under.

Ingham County

One of the best urban park developments in Michigan is **Lansing River Trail** (lansingrivertrail.org). The 6-mile-long park is a greenbelt that stretches on both sides of the Grand River from Kalamazoo Avenue just north of I-496 to North Street, 3 miles downstream. A riverwalk, made of long sections of boardwalk near or on the river, runs along the entire east side of the park, with bridges that lead to more walkways on the west side. Interesting attractions are found throughout the park, and you could easily spend an entire day walking from one to the next.

At the south end at 240 Museum Dr. is the **R. E. Olds Transportation Museum** (517-372-0529; reoldsmuseum.org), dedicated to the history of transportation in Lansing, where at one time or another 15 makes of automobile were manufactured. More than 50 vehicles, from the first Oldsmobile, built in 1897, to an Indy 500 pace car, fill the old City Bus Garage along with old motoring apparel and other memorabilia. The museum is open Tues through Sat from 10 a.m. to 5 p.m, Sun from noon to 5 p.m. Admission is $7 for adults, $5 for children, and $15 for families.

Right next door at 200 Museum Dr. you'll find the **Impression 5 Science Center** (517-485-8116; impression5.org), which is described as an "exploratorium" for children and their parents, stressing hands-on exhibits. The 240 exhibits on several floors range from a music room, filled with unusual instruments to be played, to a bubble room where children can be totally encased in a bubble. Impression 5 is open 10 a.m. to 5 p.m. Tues to Sat and noon to 5 p.m. Sun. Admission is $8.50 for adults or children.

Continuing north along the east side, you'll walk under Michigan Avenue and past views of the state capitol, around Sun Bowl Amphitheater and reach the **Brenke River Sculpture and Fish Ladder.** The structure is a swirl of steps and stone benches leading down to the fish ladder that curves its way

Planet Walk

For most children one of the most enjoyable aspects of the River Trail is the **Planet Walk**, a cleverly simple but thoroughly enjoyable trek through our solar system. It is also very enlightening. Most maps of our solar system have condensed the distances to fit the sun and the orbiting planets on the same page. You learn the names of the planets, but distances in the universe, the 93 million miles from the sun to Earth or the 3.7 billion miles to Pluto (recently downgraded to a dwarf planet), are simply too large for children to comprehend from textbooks.

That's the idea behind the Planet Walk. The one-way walk of 2 miles is strung out along River Front Park, beginning and ending at two of Lansing's most enjoyable attractions: the Impression 5 Science Center and Potter Park Zoo. In between it's a 45- to 60-minute walk from the sun to Pluto, a hike in which every step represents a million miles.

Not only are the distances properly scaled but so are the size and mass of the sun and each planet. The sun, located near the entrance to the Impression 5 Science Center, is a 20-inch golden sphere looking like an overinflated basketball.

From there it's a few quick steps to reach Mercury, the size of a pencil eraser. The first 4 planets are reached within a few hundred feet. But the rest are spread out, and it's probably three-quarters of a mile between Saturn and Uranus alone.

around scenic North Lansing Dam. Come mid-September you can watch salmon and steelhead trout leap from one water ledge of the ladder to the next on the way to their spawning grounds.

There are two great ways to explore Lansing's River Trail and the Grand River: by land and by water.

You can rent bicycles, tandems, even child trailers for the back of the bike at **Riverfront Cycle** (517-482-8585; riverfrontcycle.com) near the trail at 507 E. Shiawassee St. The bike shop is open Mon through Fri 10 a.m. to 6 p.m. and Sat 10 a.m. to 5 p.m.

You can also cruise the Grand River aboard the triple-deck **Michigan Princess** (517-627-2154; michiganprincess.com) on a variety of outings, including dinner cruises, color tours, and evening trips that feature music, dancing, or a murder mystery theater. Located at 3004 W. Main St., the paddle-wheeler is operated year-round, thanks to heated cabins, with most tours priced between $25 and $60 per adult.

For a closer look at Michigan's most famous government building, join a **State Capitol Tour** and be prepared for the building's stunning interior. In 1992 a major renovation of the century-old capitol was completed at a cost of more than $45 million. When the building was originally dedicated on January 1, 1879, it was one of the first state capitols to emulate the dome and wings of the US Capitol in Washington, DC, and today it is considered by most as an outstanding example of Victorian craftsmanship. All tours begin in the rotunda, where visitors stand on the floor of glass tiles imported from England and stare at the stars in the top of the dome 172 feet above. In between are portraits of governors on the second level and, on the main floor, flags carried by Michigan regiments during battles from as long ago as the Civil War. Tours also include a look into the restored state Senate and House of Representative chambers as well as other offices and rooms, each accompanied by bits and pieces of Michigan's history.

To reach the state capitol from I-96, follow I-496 through Lansing and take the Walnut exit to 115 W. Allegan St. STATE CAPITOL signs point the way to the building and parking nearby. Capitol Tour Guide Service (517-373-2353) offers the tours every half hour Mon through Fri from 9 a.m. to 4 p.m. Self-guided tours can be taken Mon through Fri from 8 a.m. to 5 p.m. Visits by groups of more than 10 must be scheduled in advance. There is no charge for tours.

Almost as impressive as the state capitol is the **Michigan Library and Historical Center,** which opened in 1988. Nationally recognized for its architectural design, the 312,000-square-foot center houses the Michigan Historical Museum, the State Archives, and the Library of Michigan, the second largest state library in the country.

Chocolate Cheese & Other Attractions at MSU

You don't have to be enrolled at Michigan State University to enjoy its campus. In fact it's better if you're not . . . who needs to pay tuition?

MSU is loaded with attractions that are open to the public, and many of them will be of interest to adults, such as the *Eli and Edythe Broad Art Museum* (517-884-4800; broadmuseum.msu.edu), opened in 2012, or the *Wharton Center for Performing Arts* (517-353-1982; whartoncenter.com). But most are geared for children, and families can have a great time at MSU.

In the heart of the campus is the *Michigan State University Museum* (517-355-2370; museum.msu.edu) where you can explore 3 floors devoted to natural history, from mounted skeletons of the great Jurassic dinosaurs allosaurus and stegosaurus to Habitat Hall where life-size dioramas depict the environments of North America—forests, grasslands, deserts, tropics, and tundra. The MSU Museum is open from 9 a.m. to 5 p.m. Mon through Fri, 10 a.m. to 5 p.m. Sat, and 1 to 5 p.m. Sun.

The *Michigan 4H Children's Garden* (517-355-5191; 4hgardencowplex.com) is designed especially for children with its maze entrance, Magic Bubble Fountain, and pizza garden and open from sunup to sundown daily. Things get icky at *Michigan State University Bug House* (517-355-4662; ent.msu.edu/bughouse) as kids will learn that a cricket's ears are on its knees and a fly has taste buds on its feet. They will also be able to view an extensive collection of pinned bugs or have the opportunity to get up close and personal with a whole room of creepy crawlers. The Bug House is in room 147 of the Natural Science building and open during open houses and by appointment.

But the best place to visit, whether you're a kid or not, is the *Michigan State University Dairy Store* (517-355-8466; canr.msu.edu/dairystore) in Anthony Hall on Farm Lane at 474 S. Shaw Ln. At the store there is an observation deck to watch workers process milk and cream and a multimedia presentation about how the MSU Dairy Plant makes cheese and ice cream. Or you can skip all that and just order a double dip of some the creamiest ice cream you'll ever taste. There are 32 flavors to choose from. Even better, try the store's most unusual offering: chocolate cheese. The dessert cheese is made of cocoa, sugar, and peanuts that are mixed into cheddar and other cheeses. Its fudge-like taste and consistency have MSU alumni ordering it online from around the country long after they graduate.

The MSU Dairy Store is open 9 a.m. to 6 p.m. Mon through Fri and noon to 8 p.m. Sat and Sun. Everything, from the Bug House to the museum, is free unless you're tempted to order a scoop of Badger Cherry Cheesecake or Final Four Fudge Dribble.

Most people, however, visit the center to see the museum. The Michigan Historical Museum features 12 permanent galleries displaying facades of a lumber baron's mansion and the state's first territorial capitol, a walk-through copper mine tunnel, and an impressive woodland diorama. Other rooms feature a working sawmill, historic cars, a stake fort, and many other exhibits relating to the history of the Great Lakes State. To view the museum and the capitol is a full day for most families.

The Michigan Library and Historical Center (517-335-2573; michigan.gov/mhc) is at 702 W. Kalamazoo St., within easy walking distance of the capitol. Hours are 9 a.m. to 5 p.m. Mon through Fri; 10 a.m. to 4 p.m. Sat; and Sun 1 to 5 p.m. Admission is $6 for adults and $2 for children 6 to 17. Sunday admission is free.

Ionia County

When autumn arrives in Michigan and the leaves begin turning shades of red, yellow, and orange, many people instinctively head north to view the fall colors. But the southern portions of the state also enjoy their share of autumn brilliance, and one of the best drives is a 15-mile route that is lined by hardwood forests and rolling farm fields and crosses three covered bridges, including the oldest one in Michigan, *White's Covered Bridge.*

Nestled in a wooded area and spanning the Flat River, White's Covered Bridge was built in 1867 by J. N. Brazee for $1,700 and has faithfully served the public ever since. It is a classic covered bridge, its trusses hand-hewn and secured with wooden pegs and hand-cut square nails. The bridge is 14 feet wide and 116 feet long, and you can still drive a car across it; most travelers park on the other side and return on foot for a closer inspection. The bridge is reached by driving to the hamlet of Smyrna in Ionia County (5 miles southwest of Belding) and then heading south on White's Bridge Road.

The Roadside Table

For those who like obscure historical sites, Ionia County has one of the best in the state. Located at Morrison Lake Road and Grand River Avenue, south of the town of Saranac, is the place known simply as the *Roadside Table.* It was at this very spot that in 1929 county engineer Allen Williams used a stack of leftover guardrail planks to build a table, the first public picnic table ever placed on a highway right-of-way. Today, of course, there are roadside tables and rest areas in all 50 states, and the only sights more common on our nation's highways are billboards and McDonald's restaurants. Along the road, the site is marked only by a small white historical sign, but a green state historic site plaque detailing the story has been erected next to the tables. The state still maintains the tables and garbage barrels, even though most of the traffic now flows along I-94 to the south.

Continue south on White's Bridge Road for 4 miles, and turn west (left) onto Potters Road for a short distance to Fallasburg Bridge Road, which will lead you over another covered bridge in Fallasburg County Park just inside Kent County. Brazee and his construction company also built the **Fallasburg Covered Bridge.** Its design is similar to White's bridge, and it was built with the same high standards that have allowed both these structures to exist for more than a century. Above both entrances to the Fallasburg Bridge is a stern warning: $5 fine for riding or driving on this

michigantrivia

Grand Rapids entered the national furniture market with exhibits at the Philadelphia Centennial Exposition in 1876. Today the city still accounts for 40 percent of the business and office furniture market.

bridge faster than a walk. The county park is a pleasant stretch of picnic tables and grills on the grassy slopes of the Flat River.

From the park, take Lincoln Lake Avenue south into the town of Lowell and head west on M 21 along the Grand River until you finally cross it into the town of Ada, where signs will point the way to the **Ada Covered Bridge.** The original bridge that crossed the Thornapple River was built in 1867 by Will Holmes but was destroyed by fire in 1980. The residents of Ada immediately opened their hearts (and their wallets), and the bridge was quickly rebuilt and restored. The Ada Bridge is open to pedestrian traffic only.

Kent County

The favorite son of **Grand Rapids** is Gerald R. Ford, a local congressman who eventually became the 38th president of the United States. In 1981 the **Gerald R. Ford Presidential Museum** opened, and today the center, dedicated to Ford's life and his days in office, is one of the city's top attractions.

The museum still features a full-scale reproduction of the Oval Office as it appeared in Ford's administration and a Watergate gallery that includes a 6-minute, multiscreen history of the 1972 break-in along with the actual burglary tools, but now has several new galleries that feature hands-on and computerized exhibits. Among them is a TelePrompTer that allows you to give a Ford speech and an interactive Cabinet Room that allows you to take part in presidential decision-making. President Ford died in 2006 and his Presidential Burial Site is also on the museum grounds and open to the public.

The Gerald R. Ford Presidential Museum (616-254-0400; fordlibrarymuseum .gov) is at 303 Pearl St. NW on the west bank of the Grand River and reached by

Gerald Ford Presidential Museum Brings History to Life

The nation's 38th president was born in Omaha in 1913 and named Leslie Lynch King Jr. If that name doesn't ring a bell, it's because his name was soon changed. Shortly after his birth, his mother moved to Grand Rapids. Following a divorce, his mother married a man named Gerald R. Ford. His mother then changed her son's name to Gerald R. Ford Jr.

That interesting tidbit, along with much more, is shared at the Gerald R. Ford Presidential Museum in Grand Rapids. Opened in 1981, the museum is organized in chronological order. The museum starts with Ford's birth and ends with his death and legacy.

The museum is a treasure trove of personal items, old photographs, newsclips, music, gifts, scholarly papers, tape recordings, and interesting information. Instead of just showing history to visitors, the museum tries to put people right in the middle of it. The result is a conglomeration of sights and sounds that does a good job of taking visitors back in time to a decade when many museum visitors hadn't even been born.

On display are the tiny booties the president wore as a baby, the lucky penny his wife Betty kept in her shoe at their wedding, the gun a Manson follower used in an assassination attempt on Ford's life and the actual Saigon staircase used by thousands of people in the final days of the evacuation of Saigon in April 1975. People climbed to the roof of the American Embassy to escape aboard helicopters.

Known as "Junior," Ford was an outstanding athlete and an Eagle Scout. He was a good enough football player that he earned a scholarship at the University of Michigan in 1931. He was voted the team's most valuable player in 1934.

Then Ford arrived at a crossroads. Ford had a chance to play pro football after college, but instead he entered Yale University and earned a law degree.

His career was put on hold when World War II broke out. Ford joined the US Naval Reserve and served in the South Pacific aboard an aircraft carrier. Ironically, it wasn't the enemy's mortar that almost took his life—it was a force of nature. During a terrible typhoon in December 1944, Ford was almost swept overboard.

After the war, Ford returned to Grand Rapids and became a lawyer. He entered politics and was elected to Congress in 1948. He was reelected 12 times. October of 1948 also saw Ford and Betty Bloomer become husband and wife.

exiting US 131 at Pearl Street. Hours are 9 a.m. to 5 p.m. Mon through Sat, noon to 5 p.m. on Sun. Admission is $10 for adults and $4 for children ages 6 to 18.

Long before the presidential seal was stamped on this portion of Kent County, Grand Rapids was known as the City of Furniture. In 1853 it was a small frontier town surrounded by forests with a seemingly endless supply of lumber and situated on the banks of the Grand River, which provided power for

Ford quickly climbed the political ladder. After Vice President Spiro Agnew resigned his office in late 1973, President Nixon chose Ford. Then the scandal escalated that cost Nixon his office and gave Ford his. At the museum, you can see the original tools used in the June 1972 Watergate break-in. A presentation traces the history of America's notorious political scandal.

The result, of course, was that Congress charged Nixon in 1974 with obstruction of justice and misusing the power of his office. Nixon had a choice either to resign or be impeached.

On Aug. 9, 1974, Nixon resigned the presidency. At the same time, Vice President Ford was sworn in as the nation's 38th president. One month later, Ford pardoned Nixon for "crimes he committed or may have committed."

President Ford gave the pardon so that the country could move on. He believed America needed to stop discussing Watergate and work on other problems at hand.

But many Americans were angry about the pardon and that may be a prime reason why Ford wasn't elected when his two years as Nixon's replacement were up. Jimmy Carter beat him in the election.

The museum itself could take hours to tour if you want to read, hear, and view all the materials presented. Some of the galleries bring back memories for anyone who lived the 1970s. Video and sound bites recall various news events, plus displays feature such 1970s memorabilia as platform shoes, tie-dyed garments, bell-bottom jeans, love beads, eight-track tapes, and MIA bracelets.

A recreated Oval Office lets visitors feel as though they are peeking in on a day in Ford's presidency. Another display spotlights First Lady Betty Ford and her battle with breast cancer.

Probably the most disturbing items on display can be easily overlooked. Mounted behind a glass frame is a .45 caliber pistol taken from Charles Manson follower Squeaky Fromme after her assassination attempt on September 6, 1975. A little over two weeks later, Sara Jane Moore tried to kill the president in San Francisco.

On display is a letter Moore wrote to Ford from prison saying she was glad she didn't kill the president because she has "an abhorrence of violence, particularly murder."

Both Gerald Ford and his wife Betty chose to be buried on museum grounds. Gerald died December 26, 2006. Betty died July 8, 2011.

the mills. In this setting William "Deacon" Haldane opened a cabinet shop and soon was building not only cupboards but also cradles, coffins, and tables and chairs. By the end of the decade, there were several shops, and soon "Grand Rapids–Made Furniture" became the standard of excellence.

As impressive as the Ford Museum is, it now has a rival practically next door. In 1994 the **_Grand Rapids Public Museum_** opened to the public.

Sculpture Park Features "Bigger Than Life" Art

Frederik Meijer once said, "All art is bigger than life." So he created a huge unusual open-air museum for his outstanding art collection. This is the same Fred Meijer of supermarket fame. Meijer Inc. is one of the nation's largest family-owned retailers. But Meijer wasn't born into the lap of luxury. The son of Dutch immigrants, Meijer grew up on a farm in the small community of Greenville, 25 miles northeast of Grand Rapids. Money was tight, and Meijer did whatever odd jobs he could find. For a while, he sold eggs at 10 cents a dozen from a pony and cart.

Even in the hardest of times, Meijer says his parents made sure their children learned about culture. Meijer children took music lessons and Frederik played the violin for 15 years—even if finding money for music lessons was often difficult. When his dad opened the family's first grocery story on June 30, 1934, the 14-year-old Meijer was there as a bag boy. Throughout his years at Greenville High School, Meijer put in about 40 hours a week at the family business. He never went to college but continued working with his father until Hendrik died in 1964 at age 80.

In 1951, Meijer and his wife Lena moved to Grand Rapids but kept close ties to their hometown of Greenville. Then in 1983, the Meijers sponsored a project that would change their lives forever. That year, the Meijers funded the creation of a public work by Detroit sculptor Marshall Fredericks based on the classic Danish children's tale, *The Ugly Duckling* by Hans Christian Andersen. Meijer fell in love with the art of sculpture and began buying works by Fredericks. Before long, he had a wealth of sculptures in storage.

When he was approached in 1990 by the West Michigan Horticultural Society to help create a new botanical garden, Meijer saw a natural fit. He could combine his wife's love of gardens and flowers with his own desire to build and share a significant sculpture collection. That's how the **Frederik Meijer Gardens & Sculpture Park** was born. In his initial gift, Meijer donated 70 acres of land, operational and foundation support, and more

The $40 million structure is on the Grand River, and overlooking the water is its centerpiece, a glass pavilion housing a working 1928 carousel with hand-carved horses and a Wurlitzer organ. Rides are $1, and it's debatable who has more fun—children or their parents.

Other exhibits in the 3-story building include a replica of a Union Depot waiting room, a 76-foot finback whale suspended from the ceiling, an entire street from Grand Rapids in the 1890s, a high-tech planetarium, and many interactive and hands-on exhibits that focus on natural science and the unique western Michigan environment.

The Grand Rapids Public Museum (616-929-1700; grpm.org) is at 272 Pearl, just east of the Pearl exit off US 131. Hours are 9 a.m. to 8 p.m. Tues, 9 a.m.

than 60 sculptures from his extensive collection. The Frederik Meijer Gardens opened on April 20, 1995. Now 132 acres, the gardens feature the largest tropical conservatory in Michigan, indoor specialty gardens, outdoor gardens, nature trails, boardwalk, and indoor sculpture galleries for changing exhibitions. Then came the 30-acre sculpture garden in 2002.

Sculptures are set among trees, streams, waterfalls, hills, and meadows offering views from many different vantage points. The park has a 16-foot waterfall with winding stream and landscaped natural areas called Nature's Niches, the Meditation Garden, the Gallery, the Meadow, the Hollow, the Commons, and the Wedding Garden. Each is uniquely different, and all are connected by more than 1.5 miles of sculptured pathway.

The sculpture garden has more than two dozen pieces in bronze, iron, stainless steel, marble, industrial porcelain, and painted aluminum. It features modern as well as abstract and nonobjective styles. Each sculpture setting was designed to blend harmoniously with nature. In many instances, the artists themselves were involved in the placement and in the development of the site.

You can see works by giants like Rodin and Aristide Maillol, Jacques Lipchitz, Louise Nevelson, and Henry Moore. Of course, one of the biggest headliners of the Sculpture Park is the 24-foot bronze monument, *The American Horse,* created by Nina Akamu in homage to Leonardo da Vinci. At the turn of the 16th century, the legendary Italian Renaissance artist whose great works include *The Last Supper* and the *Mona Lisa* was commissioned to create the world's largest horse sculpture. A full-scale clay model was as far as da Vinci's plans got. The model was destroyed when invading French troops used it for target practice.

Da Vinci's 500-year-old dream became reality when the 15-ton statue was unveiled in Grand Rapids. Its twin resides in Milan, Italy. At three stories tall, it is the largest equine sculpture in the world. Stand at its feet and look up at one huge uplifted hoof to appreciate its immense size. Contact Frederik Meijer Gardens & Sculpture Park at (888) 957-1580 or visit meijergardens.org.

to 5 p.m. Wed through Sat, and noon to 5 p.m. Sun. There is an admission fee of $15 for adults and $10 for children ages 3 to 17.

When the state began stocking salmon in the Great Lakes in the 1960s, the fish would spawn up the Grand River but had problems getting beyond the Sixth Street Dam in Grand Rapids. The solution was the **Fish Ladder Sculpture,** a unique sculptured viewing area designed by local artist Joseph Kinnebrew. Located at 560 Front Ave. Northwest, just on the north side of I-196, the ladder is a series of 7 small ledges on the west bank of the river that let the salmon easily leap around the dam. The rest of the sculpture is a platform above the ladder that provides a close view of the large fish as they jump completely out of the water from one ledge to the next.

The first salmon begin arriving in early September, and the run is over in October. Local people say the third week of September is when you'll see the major portion of the spawning run. Spectators won't be the only ones there, however, as the river will be filled with anglers trying to interest the fish in a lure, a spectacle in itself.

Fred Meijer, founder of the chain of Meijer's stores, is also responsible for *Frederik Meijer Gardens,* the largest tropical conservatory in the state. Meijer funded the project after members of West Michigan Horticultural Society pointed out to him that their side of the state had no large public gardens.

Opened in 1995, the 132-acre complex features plants from around the world, waterfalls, streams, and more than 60 bronze sculptures by Marshall Fredericks and other renowned artists. Along with the main conservatory are smaller garden areas including Arid Gardens, Victorian Garden, and Gardener's Corner where specialty plants are sold. Winding through the complex is the "magnificent mile," a system of barrier-free nature trails and boardwalks that overlook wetlands, ponds, and meadows.

The gardens (888-957-1580; meijergardens.org) are northeast of Grand Rapids. From I-96 take exit 38 and head north on E. Beltline Road and then

Hot Dog Hall of Fame (No Kidding!)

To travelers passing through Rockford, the *Corner Bar* appears from the outside to be just that, a small-town tavern on the corner of Main Street and Northland at 31 N. Main St. Once you step inside, though, you soon realize that this pub, decorated in brass nameplates, sports memorabilia, and newspaper clippings, is packed with history and hot dog legends. For starters, the Corner Bar is the oldest brick building in Rockford. Built in 1873, it survived several fires, including the Great Main Street Fire of 1896, and today is exceeded in age only by a wood-frame house behind the railroad depot.

At one time the building was a dry goods store, then a hardware store, and finally, at the turn of the 20th century, its most enduring business moved in. It became a saloon noted for its hot dogs. People came from all around to enjoy hot dogs served in steamed buns and topped with special sauce, a good heaping of relish, and chopped onions. Among the patrons one night in 1967 were several members of the Detroit Lions football team who amazed their waitress when they challenged each other to eat 12 hot dogs apiece. By the following year owner Donald R. Berg had turned that 12-dog challenge into the Hot Dog Hall of Fame, Michigan's most unusual hall of fame, where 12 hot dogs at $2 apiece can immortalize your appetite with a brass nameplate on the wall. The present record of 43.5 hot dogs was set in March 2006 by Tim Janus. The bar (616-866-9866; rockfordcornerbar.com) is open daily 11 a.m. to 8 p.m.

east on Bradford Street to reach the gardens at 1000 E. Beltline Ave. Northeast. Hours are 9 a.m. to 5 p.m. Mon and Wed through Sat, 9 a.m. to 9 p.m. Tues, and 11 a.m. to 5 p.m. Sun. Admission is $14.50 for adults, $7 for children ages 5 to 13, and $4 for children ages 3 and 4.

Just 15 miles north of Grand Rapids is the small town of *Rockford,* which dates back to the 1840s when a dam and sawmill were built along the Rogue River. Soon a railroad line passed through Rockford, and the town became a trading center with warehouses, a train depot, mills, and a bean-processing plant built along the river. What connected them on land was an unnamed alley that eventually became known as Squires Street. In 1970, the bean plant was renovated into the Old Mill, a cider mill and restaurant. This led to more historical buildings being bought and turned into a strip of specialized shops and stores.

Today *Squires Street Square* is the heart of Rockford, a charming 3-block section of more than 40 shops and restaurants. You'll find stores in old warehouses, barns, a former shoe factory, a carriage house, even in railroad cars. The *Rockford Area Historical Museum* (616-866-2235; rockfordmuseum.org) occupies the Power House at 11 E. Bridge St., which sits on the banks of the Rogue River and at one time was a generator plant for a local factory. The museum is open Tues, Wed, Fri, and Sun from 1 to 4 p.m., Thurs 10 a.m. to 4 p.m., and Sat noon to 4 p.m. Admission is free. All the businesses are within walking distance of each other, and most are open Mon through Sat. Rockford can be reached from US 131 by taking exit 97 and following Ten Mile Road east a short way.

Places to Stay in The Heartland

BATTLE CREEK

Greencrest Manor
6174 Halbert Rd.
(269) 962-8633
greencrestmanor.com

Hampton Inn
1150 Riverside Dr.
(269) 979-5577
hilton.com

COLDWATER

Best Western Plus
630 E. Chicago St.
(517) 279-0900
bestwestern.com

EAST LANSING

Kellogg Hotel
on the Michigan State campus
219 S. Harrison Rd.
(517) 432-4000
kelloggcenter.com

Marriott East Lansing
300 M.A.C. Ave.
(517) 337-4440
marriott.com

Wild Goose Inn
512 Albert St.
(517) 333-3334
wildgooseinn.com

GRAND RAPIDS

Amway Grand Plaza Hotel
187 Monroe Ave. NW
(616) 774-2000
amwaygrand.com

The Brauhaus Inn
611 Madison Ave. SE
(616) 328-0804
thebrauhausinn.com

Courtyard by Marriott
11 Monroe Ave. NW
(616) 242-6000
marriott.com

Holiday Inn Downtown
310 Pearl St. NW
(616) 235-7611
ihg.com

The Lafayette House Bed & Breakfast
135 Lafayette Ave. NE
(616) 214-8655
thelafayettehousebb.com

The Leonard at Logan House
440 Logan St. SE
(616) 308-6585
leonardatlogan.com

The Parsonage Inn
423 Madison Ave. SE
(616) 481-4434
parsonageinn.org

JONESVILLE

Munro House Bed & Breakfast
202 Maumee St.
(517) 849-9292
munrohouse.com

The Rooms at Grayfield
310 W. Chicago St.
(517) 849-9580
roomsatgrayfield.com

KALAMAZOO

Country Inn
1912 E. Kilgore Rd.
(269) 382-2303
radissonhotels.com

Festive West Bed & BreakFest
435 Stuart Ave.
(269) 366-4505
festivewestbnb.com

Henderson Castle
100 Monroe St.
(269) 344-1827
hendersoncastle.com

Kalamazoo House
447 W. South St.
(269) 382-0880
thekalamazoohouse.com

Kara's Kottages
837 W. Main St.
(269) 491-0765
karaskottages.com

Radisson Plaza Hotel
100 W. Michigan Ave.
(269) 343-3333
radissonhotels.com

Stuart Avenue Inn
229 Stuart Ave.
(269) 342-0230
stuartavenueinn.com

LANSING

Radisson Hotel
111 N. Grand Ave.
(517) 482-0188
radissonhotels.com

Red Roof Inn
3615 Dunckel Rd.
(517) 332-2575
redroof.com

MARSHALL

Arbor Inn
15435 W. Michigan Ave.
(269) 781-7772
arborinnmarshall.com

National House Inn
102 S. Parkview Ave.
(269) 781-7374
nationalhouseinn.com

Villa on Verona
1110 Verona St.
(269) 832-1796
villaonverona.com

Places to Eat in The Heartland

BATTLE CREEK

Clara's on the River
44 N. McCamly St.
(269) 963-0966
claras.com
Fine Dining

Pancake House
185 Capital Ave.
(269) 964-6790
Breakfast

Sakura Sushi Bar & Grill
5285 Beckley Rd.
(269) 979-0200
sakurabattlecreek.com
Japanese

Shwe Mandalay Burmese Cuisine
451 W. Michigan Ave.
(269) 753-1702
Mandalese

Torti Taco
5275 Beckley Rd.
(269) 224-6941
tortitaco.com
Mexican

Umami Ramen
66-80 Calhoun St.
(269) 224-3264
umamiramenbc.com
Pan Asian

EAST LANSING

Altu's Ethiopian Cuisine
1312 E. Michigan Ave.
(517) 333-6295
eataltus.com
Ethiopian

Beggar's Banquet
218 Abbott Rd.
(517) 351-4540
beggarsbanquet.com
American

El Azteco
225 Ann St.
(517) 351-9111
elazteco.net
Mexican

Harpers
131 Albert St.
(517) 333-4040
harpersbrewpub.com
Brewpub

Sansu Sushi and Cocktails
4750 Hagadorn Rd., #100
(517) 333-1933
sansu-sushi.com
Japanese

GRAND RAPIDS

Bistro Bella Vita
44 Grandville Ave. SW
(616) 222-4600
bistrobellavita.com
Italian

The Cottage Bar & Restaurant
18 LaGrave Ave. SE
(616) 454-9088
cottagebar.biz
American

Grand Rapids Brewing Company
1 Iona Ave. SW
(616) 458-7000
grbrewingcompany.com
Brewpub

SELECTED CHAMBERS OF COMMERCE & TOURISM BUREAUS

Calhoun County Visitors Bureau
34 W. Jackson St.
Battle Creek 49017
(800) 397-2240
battlecreekvisitors.org

Experience Grand Rapids
171 Monroe Ave. NW, Ste. 545
Grand Rapids 49503
(800) 678-9859
experiencegr.com

Greater Lansing Convention and Visitors Bureau
500 E. Michigan Ave., Ste. 180
Lansing 48906
(888) 252-6746
lansing.org

Jackson Convention and Visitors Bureau
134 W. Michigan Ave.
Jackson 49201
(571) 764-4440
experiencejackson.com

Kalamazoo County Convention and Visitors Bureau
240 W. Michigan Ave.
Kalamazoo 49007
(800) 888-0509
discoverkalamazoo.com

OTHER ATTRACTIONS

Grand Rapids Art Museum
101 Monroe Center St. NW
Grand Rapids
(616) 831-1000
artmuseumgr.org

Grand Rapids Children's Museum
11 Sheldon Ave. NE
Grand Rapids
(616) 235-4726
grcm.org

Honolulu House Museum
107 N. Kalamazoo Ave.
Marshall
(269) 781-8544

John Ball Zoo
1300 Fulton W.
Grand Rapids
(616) 336-4300
jbzoo.org

Kalamazoo Nature Center
7000 N. Westnedge Ave.
Kalamazoo
(269) 381-1574
naturecenter.org

Kalamazoo Valley Museum
230 N. Rose St.
Kalamazoo
(269) 373-7990
kalamazoomuseum.org

Kellogg Bird Sanctuary
12685 E. C Ave.
Augusta
(269) 671-2510
birdsanctuary.kbs.msu.edu

Kingman Museum of Natural History
175 Limit St.
Battle Creek
(269) 965-5117
kingmanmuseum.org

Leila Arboretum
928 W. Michigan Ave.
Battle Creek
(269) 969-0270
lasgarden.org

Michigan Supreme Court Learning Center
925 W. Ottawa St.
Lansing
(571) 373-7171
courts.michigan.gov

Michigan Women's Historical Center & Hall of Fame
105 W. Allegen St.
Lansing
(517) 853-5890
miwf.org

Potter Park Zoo
1301 S. Pennsylvania Ave.
Lansing
(517) 483-4222
potterparkzoo.org

Graydon's Crossing
1223 Plainfield Ave. NE
(616) 726-8260
graydonscrossing.com
Global

Heritage Restaurant
151 Fountain St. NE
(616) 234-3700
grcc.edu
American

Leo's Seafood Restaurant & Bar
60 Ottawa Ave. NW
(616) 454-6700
leosrestaurant.com
Seafood

Paddock Place
1033 Lake Dr. SE
(616) 742-0600
thegilmorecollection.com
Italian

JACKSON

Bella Notte Ristorante
137 W. Michigan Ave.
(517) 782-5727
bellanotteristorante.com
Italian

Crazy Cowboy
215 S. Mechanic St.
(517) 817-1910
thecrazycowboy.com
Mexican

**Ichiban Japanese
Steakhouse Jackson**
915 N. Wisner St.
(517) 315-4970
ichibanrestaurants.com
Japanese

**West Texas Barbeque
Co.**
2190 Brooklyn Rd.
(517) 784-0510
westexbbq.com
Barbecue

JONESVILLE

Olivia's Chop House
205 E. Chicago St.
(517) 849-3663
olivaschophouse.com
American

Rosalie's Roadhouse
417 W. Chicago St.
(517) 849-2120
rosaliesroadhouse.com
American

**Spangler's Family
Restaurant**
601 E. Chicago St.
(517) 849-2900
spanglersfamilyrestaurants
.com
American

The Udder Side
121 W. Chicago St.
(517) 849-9666
American

KALAMAZOO

Bell's Eccentric Cafe
355 E. Kalamazoo Ave.
(269) 382-2332
bellsbeer.com
Brewpub

Central City Tap House
359 S. Kalamazoo Mall
(269) 492-0100
American

Principle Food and Drink
230 S. Kalamazoo Mall
(269) 743-6563
principlekzoo.com
American

Rustica
236 S. Kalamazoo Mall
(269) 492-0247
rusticakzoo.com
Modern European

Saffron Indian Cuisine
1710 W. Main St.
(269) 381-9898
saffronkzoo.com
Indian

Theo & Stacy's
234 W. Michigan Ave.
(269) 388-5025
theoandstacys.com
Greek

LANSING

Bowdies Chophouse
320 E. Michigan Ave.
(517) 580-4792
bowdieschophouse.com

Capital Prime
2324 Showtime Dr.
(517) 377-7463
capitalprimelansing.com

**Green Door Blues Bar &
Grill**
2005 E. Michigan Ave.
(517) 482-6376
greendoorlive.com
American

Mitchell's Fish Market
2975 Preyde Blvd.
(517) 482-3474
mitchellsfishmarket.com
Seafood

Nuthouse Sports Grill
420 E. Michigan Ave.
(517) 484-6887
nuthousesportsgrill.com
American

MARSHALL

Grand River Brewery
101 W. Michigan Ave.
(269) 727-9311
grandriverbrewery.com
American

**Outside the Box Wellness
Café**
136 W. Michigan Ave.
(269) 558-4054
obx.cafe
American

**Schuler's Restaurant &
Pub**
115 S. Eagle St.
(616) 781-0600
schulersrestaurant.com
American

Lake Huron Region

The Lake Huron shoreline, the eastern side of Michigan, is a region that has come full circle in its history and its appearance. The first inhabitants of the area were Indians who traveled lightly through the woods and lived off the land but rarely disfigured it. When Europeans arrived, they were awed by what was perceived as an endless forest, woods so thick with towering white pines that the sun rarely reached the forest floor.

All that changed in the mid-1800s. Lumbering companies that had exhausted the forests in Maine were looking for pine to cut for new settlements on the Great Plains, which were desperate for wood in their treeless region. Michigan met those needs as the greatest lumber-producing state in the nation between 1850 and 1910, with an estimated 700 logging camps and more than 2,000 mills. Massive log drives filled the Saginaw and Au Sable Rivers, which were avenues to the sawmill towns on Lake Huron. In mill towns like Saginaw and Bay City, sawmills lined the riverbanks, and huge mansions lined the streets as more wealth was made off Michigan's white pine than by miners in the Klondike gold rush.

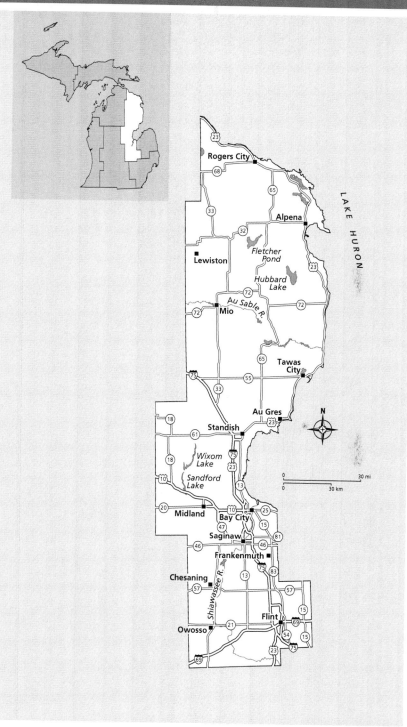

By the turn of the 20th century, all that was left were the stumps. The lumbering era had devastated the region, turning it into treeless areas that were wastelands of soil erosion. The Huron National Forest was established in 1909 along the Au Sable River, the first of many such preserves, in an effort to repair and manage the land. Lake Huron entered a new era in which terms such as reforestation, conservation, and renewable resources replaced the lumber lingo of log drives, river rats, and clear-cuts.

Almost a century later the northeastern portion of the Lower Peninsula is once again a forested region. The trees are of a different generation and often a different species, but the effect on visitors is the same as when the first Europeans wandered through. To walk quietly among the towering pines in a forest padded by needles while listening to the gentle rustling of a cold-water trout stream is as much an attraction in this part of the state as sandy beaches or a cottage on the lake.

Shiawassee County

In the early 1900s a young writer was tracking a grizzly bear he had shot in British Columbia when suddenly the wounded animal appeared and trapped the man on a narrow mountain ledge. As the author would write later, "Sudden death seemed the hunter's inevitable fate. Then the huge bruin turned away, leaving the hunter unharmed. But not unchanged—the man packed away his guns and never hunted for sport again."

Instead *James Oliver Curwood* used the experience in his best-selling novel *The Grizzly King*, which was published in 1916. In 1989, when the book served as the basis of the movie *The Bear*, **Owosso**'s favorite son—and one of its best-kept secrets—was finally exposed to the rest of the country. Curwood was born in the Shiawassee County town of Owosso in 1878 and returned with his family in 1891. After attending the University of Michigan for two years and working on a newspaper in Detroit, Curwood resigned to pursue literary work entirely in 1907.

He wrote 33 novels, most of them fast-paced tales set predominantly in northwest Canada, or "God's country," as the author called it. They were best sellers worldwide and, between royalties and movie deals, made Curwood a millionaire and allowed him to build **Curwood Castle** along the banks of the Shiawassee River in Owosso in 1922. Built solely as a writing studio, the castle features a great room on the first floor, where the author entertained guests; a twisting staircase leads to his work area upstairs. Today the castle is a museum devoted to the author, featuring memorabilia from Curwood's life, including his original writing desk, which is used in the reception center.

The castle, a replica of a French chateau, is part of the city's historical area, which also includes the first cabin built in Owosso. The museum (989-725-0597; owossohistory.org) is at 224 Curwood Castle Dr., which is reached from M 52 south of the Shiawassee River. The castle is open from 1 to 5 p.m. daily except Mon. It is closed the month of January. Admission is $5 for adults, $2 for children under the age of 10.

Another reason to make tracks to Owosso is to see the tracks and what steamed across them at the ***Steam Railroading Institute.*** The 7-acre museum is packed with railroad memorabilia and exhibits, but its star attraction is Père Marquette No. 1225, the steam locomotive that was built in 1941 and used to develop the train images for the movie *Polar Express.* Various excursions are offered throughout the year on this famous train with the most popular one staged during the holidays. On weekends from Thanksgiving to late Dec, the Père Marquette No. 1225 makes a special 4-hour North Pole Express trip, stopping at the Village of Ashley's Country Christmas.

AUTHOR'S TOP TEN PICKS

Curwood Castle
Owosso
224 Curwood Castle Dr.
(989) 725-0597
owossohistory.org

Dow Gardens
Midland
1809 Eastman Ave.
(989) 631-2677
dowgardens.org

Elk Viewing Sleigh Ride Dinner
Hillman
27800 M 32
(800) 729-9375
thunderbayresort.com

Frankenmuth
(989) 652-6106
frankenmuth.org

Kirtland's Warbler Tour
Okemos
(517) 580-7364
michiganaudubon.org

Lumbermen's Monument
Oscoda
5401 Monument Rd.
(989) 362-8961
fs.usda.gov

Negwegon State Park
Harrisville
(989) 724-5126

Ocqueoc Falls
Onaway
(989) 739-7322

Shiawassee National Wildlife Refuge
Saginaw
6975 Mower Rd.
(989) 777-5930
fws.gov/refuge/shiawassee

Steam Railroading Institute
Owosso
405 S. Washington St.
(989) 725-9464
michigansteamtrain.com

TOP ANNUAL EVENTS

FEBRUARY

Perchville USA
Tawas City
(989) 362-8643
tawas.com

JUNE

Bavarian Festival
Frankenmuth
(877) 879-8919
bavarianfestival.org

Curwood Festival
Owosso
(989) 723-2161
curwoodfestival.com

JULY

Auburn Corn Fest
Auburn
(989) 662-4001

Michigan Brown Trout Festival
Alpena
(989) 590-2480
browntroutfestival.com

AUGUST

Nautical City Festival
Rogers City
(989) 734-4656

OCTOBER

Blues & Brews Festival
Adrian
(517) 260-0934
blues-n-brews.com

Also on-site is a gift shop with engineer caps, shirts, movie posters, and, of course, copies of the book *Polar Express.* The museum (989-725-9464; michigansteamtrain.com) is at 405 S. Washington St. and open from various hours. Check the website for hours. Admission is $6 per person, and the North Pole Express trip is $35 in economy, $55 in coach, and $75 for Cocoa Coach. The entire Baggage Train which seats up to 12 people can be rented for $1,500.

More railroading lore is just a short drive south of Owosso at **Durand.** At the turn of the 20th century, Durand was what Detroit's Metro Airport or Chicago's O'Hare is today—the transportation hub of the Midwest. The first railroad, the Detroit-Milwaukee Line, arrived at the small town in 1865 because of Durand's central location, and by 1907 there were seven lines, promoting the construction of **Union Station,** a massive depot 239 feet long and costing $60,000 to build. It burned down two years later but was quickly rebuilt by Grand Trunk Railroad as the age of railroading and the town of Durand entered their golden eras. Almost half of the town's population of 2,500 worked for Grand Trunk, and more people changed trains in Durand than there were residents living there!

Union Station (989-288-3561; durandstation.org), often called the "most photographed depot in the country," was designated the Michigan Railroad History Museum and Information Center. Visitors can wander through the station and view a gallery of railroading artifacts, including handcars, engine lights, rolltop desks, and other furnishings of a 1900-era depot.

Durand can be reached from I-69 by heading south at exit 116. Union Station is on the south side of Main Street at 200 S. Railroad St., and its museum is open Tues through Fri 1 to 5 p.m., Sat 11 a.m. to 5 p.m., Sun 1 to 5 p.m.

Genesee County

The heart of Genesee County is *Flint,* Michigan's fourth largest city and the home of the Buick Division of General Motors.

The automobile industry and cars are a major part of Flint's livelihood, and both have been well preserved in the city's *Sloan Museum.* The most dramatic chapter in Flint's history is the Great Sit-Down Strike of 1937, which is retold in the museum's permanent 10,000-square-foot exhibit entitled "Flint and the American Dream." The 44-day ordeal ended when General Motors agreed to sign its first contract with the United Auto Workers. It was a bitter struggle that led to the unionization of all American autoworkers and changed the course of history in Michigan, if not the entire country.

Sloan Museum, however, is probably best known for its classic car collection. More than 60 cars are on display in 2 buildings and range from the oldest production-model Chevrolet in existence and a 1910 Buick "Bug" raced by Louis Chevrolet to prototype vehicles that never made it into production.

The museum (810-237-3450; sloanlongway.org) is located at 4190 E. Court St. Hours are 10 a.m. to 5 p.m. Mon through Sat, and noon to 5 p.m. Sun. Admission is $9 for adults and $6 for children.

Flint also has many interesting nonautomotive attractions, including its delightful *Flint Children's Museum.* Described by its staff as a "touchable discovery center," the museum was proposed in 1980, and after six years of collecting donated materials, the center opened in 1986. Unlike other hands-on museums in Ann Arbor and Lansing, the exhibits here are not complex demonstrations in science or physics. They're

michigantrivia

The largest planetarium in Michigan is the **Longway Planetarium** (810-237-3400; sloanlongway.org) at 1310 E. Kearsley St. in Flint, which features a 60-foot domed screen.

simply everyday items that children can touch, ride, climb, and make believe with.

Among the museum's 40 hands-on exhibits is Mr. Bones, who will take your kids on a bicycle ride to show them how their skeletons work. At Our Town, children shop for groceries or visit Fractions Pizza Parlor, while at Recycled Rhythms they can bang, toot, and hum on a variety of unconventional musical instruments. Most of the displays are recommended for children ages 3 to 10 years old, but the Tot Spot is a cleverly designed area with activities for even younger visitors.

The museum (810-767-5437; flintchildrensmuseum.org) is located at 1602 W. University Ave. Take I-75 to I-475 and then exit 8A to head west on Robert T. Longway Road, which turns into Fifth Avenue. Turn south on Grand Traverse Street and then west on University Avenue. The center is open year-round from 10 a.m. to 5 p.m. Tues through Sat, and noon to 4 p.m. Sun. Admission is $6 per person.

There are only two natural waterfalls in the Lower Peninsula, so many cities have created their own, including Flint. **Stepping Stone Falls** is an artificial cascade of water over an intricate patchwork of steps and levels and one of the most picturesque spots in Genesee County. A scenic, winding path leads visitors to an overlook of the falls, and in the evening underwater lighting creates multicolored patterns on the rushing waters.

Stepping Stone Falls (800-648-7275) is located at the foot of Mott Lake at 5161 Branch Rd., across from the historic attraction of Crossroads Village. Hours are 8 a.m. to 11 p.m. Sun through Thurs and 8 a.m. to midnight Fri and Sat from May 1 through Sept 1. From Sept 2 through Dec 31, the falls are open 8 a.m. to dusk daily. Admission is free.

Departing from Stepping Stone Falls is the **Genesee Belle Paddlewheel Riverboat** at 6140 N. Bray Rd., a replica of the riverboats that once traveled down the Mississippi River. From July to Sept, the *Genesee Belle* (810-736-7100; geneseecountyparks.org) takes passengers on a scenic 45-minute cruise through Mott Lake on Sun evening, departing at 7 p.m. Tickets are $7 for adults and children. A great—and affordable—way to beat the heat in the middle of summer. Lunch cruises in October are $23.95 for a one-hour cruise with lunch. Check the website for dates.

Saginaw County

The only Michigan county without a natural lake, Saginaw County still has plenty of water, as the Saginaw, Tittabawassee, Bad, Cass, Shiawassee, and Flint Rivers make it the largest river basin in the state, with 160 miles of waterway. It was these natural avenues and the vast forests bordering them that allowed the area to boom with loggers and sawmills in the mid-1800s. By the early 1900s the trees and loggers were gone, but reminders of the immense wealth they produced are seen throughout the county in magnificent mansions, especially along Washington Boulevard in Saginaw. Among them at 1581 S. Washington Blvd. is *Montague Inn* (989-752-3939; montagueinn.com), an elegant Georgian mansion turned urban bed-and-breakfast with parklike grounds and cozy fireplaces. The rooms and suites at the inn range from $85 to $225.

But to learn about the lumbering era, head to Saginaw's eclectic *Castle Museum* at 500 Federal Ave. Built in 1898, at the height of Saginaw's golden era as a lumbering center, the 60,000-square-foot castle wasn't the home of a rich lumber baron but a post office designed in the style of a French chateau. Today the Historical Society of Saginaw County occupies the castle and its collection includes a lumbering exhibit that retraces the half-century when Saginaw produced more lumber than anywhere in the country.

Castle Museum (989-752-2861; castlemuseum.org) is open Mon through Wed and Fri and Sat 10 a.m. to 4:30 p.m., Thurs 10 a.m. to 7 p.m., and Sun 1 to 4:30 p.m. Admission is $1 for adults and 50 cents for children.

Also in Saginaw, near the Anderson Water Slide, is the city's *Japanese Cultural Center and Tea House.* The house was actually built by Japanese artisans, who used no nails, only intricate traditional hand tools. Today the center is the only facility in the country where visitors can observe the classic formal tea ceremony.

The Polka Hotel

Frankenmuth is of German descent so you'll find both home-brewed ales and home-grown polka. The town's most favorite son and most famous accordionist is Marv Herzog, who was renowned for his Bavarian-American polka music. The bandleader performed for years throughout the country and even the world but always managed to return to his hometown for polka festivals, playing such favorites as "In Heaven There is No Beer" and "Red Raven Polka."

After Herzog died in 2002, his friend Bob Drury, owner of the Drury Hotel chain, built the hotel in Frankenmuth in honor of the late polka king. The 38-room *Marv Herzog Hotel* opened in 2007 on the banks of the Cass River within walking distance of a Zehnder's chicken dinner. Inside you'll find Herzog's accordion on display in the lobby along with his lederhosen and many awards while each guest room celebrates a year of his life with a collage of memorabilia.

Marv Herzog Hotel (877-400-4210; marvherzoghotel.com) is at 501 Main St. and rooms range from $119 to $154 per night.

The house is open from noon to 4 p.m. Tues through Sat, Apr through Oct. The symbolic tea ritual is performed and interpreted on the second Sat of each month, except for Dec, beginning at 2 p.m. There is a $5 fee. The tea ceremony is $10. The house (989-759-1648; japaneseculturalcenter.org) and its tranquil gardens are located in Saginaw's Celebration Square, just north of M 46 at 527 Ezra Rust Dr.

World's Largest Year-round Christmas Store

Wally Bronner found his calling when he was still in high school. Or rather, it found him.

He was painting signs in his basement for local farmers when someone asked if he could design some Christmas signs for streets. That gave him the idea of opening a Christmas store in 1945.

And what a Christmas store it turned out to be. Today, *Bronner's CHRISTmas Wonderland* in Frankenmuth, Michigan, is the world's largest year-round Christmas store with 2.2 acres (1.7 football fields) of showroom at its 27-acre complex. More than 2 million guests visit annually from around the world.

On my trip to Bronner's, I thought one hour would be more than adequate to browse through the store. I was wrong. I should have caught on when a saleslady handed me a store map as I entered the facility. A map definitely comes in handy.

"We allow a whole morning or a whole afternoon when we come to Bronner's," said Ellen Carruthers, on a girlfriends getaway with four friends from Detroit. "If you haven't been here before, you have no idea how big it is."

The Detroit woman certainly was right. Not only does Bronner's have more Christmas decorations than you can imagine, it also has a small museum honoring founder Wally Bronner. A permanent fixture in the store until his death of cancer at age 81 in 2008, Bronner liked to say he only worked on days "that end on Y."

Bronner's also has a cafe called Season's Eatings, many outdoor displays, a ½-mile Christmas Lane glowing with lights each night from dusk until midnight, and a lovely Silent Night Memorial Chapel that tells the story of the popular Christmas carol. When I walked down the quiet lane to the stained-glass-windowed chapel, not another person was there. The sounds of "Silent Night" echoed inside and out.

Plaques in more than 300 languages share the words of the song that was sung for the first time in a tiny Austrian village on Christmas Eve 1818. It was written by a young pastor, Joseph Mohr, and organist Franz Gruber.

Outside the chapel is a life-size Nativity scene. That is one thing I noticed right away at Bronner's—the Bronner family keeps Christ in Christmas, as evidenced by the company motto: "Enjoy CHRISTmas, it's HIS birthday. Enjoy LIFE, it's HIS way."

Generally recognized as Michigan's number one attraction is the German town of *Frankenmuth.* "Little Bavaria" is famous for homestyle chicken dinners served at one of two huge restaurants, *Zehnder's* and the *Bavarian Inn,* which face each other on Main Street. The restaurants were founded by the Zehnder brothers, whose family arrived in Frankenmuth from Bavaria in 1846. Each restaurant is a sprawling complex of a dozen German-themed dining rooms, gift shops, bakeries, and candy shops. More than 700 tons of chicken are served annually in the restaurants along with buttery noodles, savory dressing, giblet gravy, salads, and homemade breads in an all-you-can-eat affair.

The Bavarian Inn (989-652-9985; bavarianinn.com) is at 713 S. Main St., and Zehnder's (800-863-7999; zehnders.com) is at 730 S. Main St. Check the websites for hours of operation.

What could be better with a chicken dinner than a mug of dark German beer? Frankenmuth is the home of the state's oldest brewery, *Frankenmuth Brewery,* which is located near the corner of Tuscola and Main Streets at 425 S. Main St. It began making beer in 1862 as the Cass River Brewery and then became Geyer Brewing in 1874. The company was temporarily shut down in 1976 and again in 2007 but has such a loyal following in this German town that it has managed to reopen each time. A state historic site, Frankenmuth Brewery (989-262-8300; frankenmuthbrewery.com) now doubles as a brewery and a fine restaurant and offers informal tours of its beer-making facility year-round. After seeing how the beer is made, how can you not grab a table and order a pint . . . or even a pitcher?

You can enjoy a stein of the local brew in almost every restaurant and bar in town, but the most intriguing place is *Tiffany's Food & Spirits* just north of Zehnder's restaurant on S. Main Street. The lumbermen's saloon is on the first floor of the Hotel Goetz, which was built in 1895, when Frankenmuth was one of the leading logging communities in the Saginaw Valley. The tavern picks up its name from its 18 Tiffany chandeliers, made in the 1930s. It is also adorned by a beautiful wooden bar, the original tin ceiling, inlaid tile floor, and leaded stained glass. Tiffany's (989-652-6881; tiffanysfoodandspirits.com) is open 11 a.m. to midnight daily.

Christmas in July? Only in Frankenmuth, where *Bronner's CHRISTmas Wonderland* is home of the world's largest year-round display of holiday ornaments, decorations, trimmings, and gifts. More than 50,000 items are stocked in the 230,000-square-foot building that houses the store's showroom, warehouse, and offices. The business can be traced back to 1945, when Wally Bronner operated Bronner's Displays and Signs out of his parents' home and was approached by Bay City officials to decorate the city streets for the upcoming holiday.

Bronner created and built lamppost panels for the city, leading to more requests by other towns and eventually to his present business providing Christmas decorations to businesses, communities, and private homes. The store is an amazing trip into the spirit of the holiday, especially its religious aspect. Inside you will find more than 500 kinds of nativity scenes, figures from 1 inch tall to life-size; 260 Christmas trees decorated in such themes as sports and wildlife; and more than 6,000 ornaments from around the world. There are music boxes, every model of Hummel figurine ever produced, and, in the store's Nutcracker Suite, 200 styles of wooden characters imported from Austria, Switzerland, and Germany.

You can't miss the store—outside it is surrounded by 15 acres of painted snowflakes, twinkling lights, and the same kind of lamppost Bronner designed

Shiawassee National Wildlife Refuge

When the fall migration peaks in late October or early November, more than 25,000 Canada geese and 30,000 ducks are often at the *Shiawassee National Wildlife Refuge.* The view of so many birds gathered at one time is nothing short of spectacular, making this one of the great wildlife sightings in Michigan.

One of two federal wildlife refuges in Michigan, Shiawassee encompasses 9,042 acres on the doorstep of Saginaw and includes the confluence of four major rivers, the Flint, Cass, Shiawassee, and Tittabawassee. When combined with the Shiawassee River State Game Area, which borders it to the west, this goose management area exceeds 20,000 acres and is larger than any state park in the Lower Peninsula.

The Ferguson Bayou Trail, a 5-mile loop from the Curtis Road parking area, is the best trail for seeing birds any time of the year but especially during the fall migration. The trail is a network of gravel roads, two-tracks, and paths along the dikes that leads to an observation tower in the heart of the refuge. Most visitors walk to the tower, but the easiest way to explore the park is on a hybrid or mountain bike.

From the tower in the fall, small flocks of geese can be seen arriving by late afternoon. By evening it's practically pandemonium with hundreds of birds coming and going. Stick around for the sunset and your day will end with the most memorable sight at the refuge: flights of geese silhouetted against a red-orange sky.

The Shiawassee National Wildlife Refuge is 7 miles south of M 46 in Saginaw and reached from M 13 by turning west on Curtis Road. Within a mile is the refuge headquarters (989-777-5930, fws.gov/refuge/shiawassee) where trail maps and bird checklists are available. The Ferguson Bayou Trail is 3 miles beyond the headquarters near the end of Curtis Road. Office hours are Mon through Fri from 7:30 a.m. to 4 p.m.

Shopping at Birch Run

In the early 1980s, Birch Run was a sleepy little village at the Frankenmuth exit of I-75. Today it's the discount shopping capital of Michigan, thanks to **Birch Run Premium Outlets** (989-624-6226, premiumoutlet.com). The 140 stores form the largest manufacturers' mall in the state and include everything from Ann Taylor to Lane Bryant and Eddie Bauer to J. Crew. The mall is right off I-75, exit 136, at 12240 S. Beyer Rd., and most shops are open from 10 a.m. to 9 p.m. Mon through Sat, and 10 a.m. to 7 p.m. Sun. This place can be unbearably crowded on the weekends with travelers dropping in for a little shopping on their way up north. The best time to shop is 3 to 6 p.m. in the middle of the week.

more than 70 years ago for Bay City. Bronner's CHRISTmas Wonderland (989-652-9931; bronners.com) is at the south end of town just off Main Street (M 83) at 25 Christmas Ln. Check the website for hours.

Midland County

To most people the city of **Midland** is Dow Chemical Corporation, the place where Herbert Dow founded the company in 1897 that today gives us everything from Ziploc sandwich bags and Saran Wrap to much of the aspirin used in the country. The **H. H. Dow Museum** (989-631-5930) tells the story of the young chemist and features replicas of the gristmill and brine well that he built to launch his famous company as well as the 1890 lab where he perfected his bromine-extracting process. The museum is reached from downtown Midland by heading west on Main Street for 1.2 miles and then turning north on Cook Road to 3200 Cook Rd. The museum is free during Hands-On Weekends. Otherwise, check for fees, hours, and dates.

Another interesting museum is the **Alden B. Dow Museum of Science and Art** in the Midland Center for the Arts. The science, history, and art museum reopened in 1994 after a $3 million face-lift, and it is 4 floors of hands-on displays and exhibits. Staff members estimate that 340 topics are covered in the new exhibits and a person who pushed every button, viewed every screen, and took part in every interactive display would spend more than 20 hours in the hall.

A 500-pound life-size mastodon skeleton greets visitors, and from there the topics range from how an Olympic skater does a triple axel to viewing a replica of Midland's famed Frolic Theater (complete with the aroma of popcorn). The hall (989-631-5930; mcfta.org) is at Eastman Avenue and West Street and open

10 a.m. to 4 p.m. Wed, Fri, and Sat and 10 a.m. to 8 p.m. Thurs. Admission is $15 for adults and $12 for children 4 to 14.

Midland is also a city of parks, with 2,700 acres in 74 parks scattered throughout the community. The most famous of these is *Dow Gardens,* 110 acres of streams, waterfalls, small bridges, and beautifully manicured landscaping next to Discovery Square, home of the *Midland Center for the Arts.*

What began as Herbert Dow's backyard in 1899 was eventually extended and shaped in the 1970s by his son, Alden Dow, a noted architect and a student of Frank Lloyd Wright. It was the younger Dow who installed the "jungle walk" through a thicket, the sensory trail, and various waterfalls.

The gardens (989-631-2677; dowgardens.org) are just northwest of downtown Midland off Business US 10 (Eastman Road to 1809 Eastman Ave.), next to the Midland Center for the Arts. Hours are 9 a.m. to 8:30 p.m. daily from mid-Apr to Labor Day with shorter hours the rest of the year. Admission is $10 for adults and $2 for children 6 to 17.

Another intriguing park is *Chippewassee,* site of the *Tridge,* the only three-way footbridge in the world, city officials proudly claim. The unusual bridge was built in 1981 over the confluence of the Tittabawassee and Chippewa Rivers, and its wooden spans connect three shorelines. In the middle they form a hub where benches overlook the merging currents of two rivers. The Tridge and the nearby riverfront area form the center of activity in downtown

Père Marquette Rail-Trail

Departing from the Tridge is the *Père Marquette Rail-Trail,* a perfectly paved path without so much as a ripple, much less a hill. Originally a line for the Flint and Père Marquette Railroad, the rail-trail extends from Midland to Clare, 32 miles.

It's open to a variety of nonmotorized users, including runners, walkers, and cyclists. But in the first 3 miles, from the Tridge to Dublin Road, the most popular form of transportation is in-line skates. The Père Marquette is well designed for that. At the street crossings are locator maps, benches, and, most important, large red posts to stop skaters from flying across the intersections.

This stretch is also very scenic. From the Tridge you skirt the Tittabawassee River for more than a mile, passing fishing docks, the historic Upper Bridge, and one of the original cement mile markers that told railroad engineers how far it was to Saginaw. The trail also passes the H. H. Dow Museum, which has installed interpretive displays along the way.

For more information call the Midland County Parks and Recreation Commission at (989) 832-6874.

Midland. Tunes by the Tridge free concerts are presented for 10 nights in June, July, and August.

During the third week of July, the annual Riverdays festival (989-839-9661; riverdaysmidland.com) is held in downtown Midland for 4 days. Festivities include a milk jug raft race, pancake breakfast, children's activities, and concerts in the nearby park. Visitors can enjoy riding on an old-time ferry, called the *Princess Laura*, down the river. Nearby, individuals can rent canoes and paddle the rivers themselves if they wish. Also located near the Tridge is the Midland Farmers' Market.

Bay County

The shoreline of Saginaw Bay was the final destination for much of the lumber from the valley, with 32 sawmills clustered on the waterfront of Bay City. The city flourished on timber and shipbuilding, and a drive down Center Avenue shows where much of it went. The lumber barons seemed infatuated with building the most elaborate homes they could afford, and the restored mansions in this historic district overwhelm visitors. In the middle of this Victorian-era street at 321 Washington Ave. is the ***Historical Museum of Bay County*** (989-893-5733; bchsmuseum.org), which spins the story of Bay City's golden era through 3-dimensional exhibits. The newest exhibit is "Bay City: Seaport to the World" in the Kantzler Maritime Gallery, where kids can climb behind the wheel to steer the tug *Witch*. The museum is open 10 a.m. to 5 p.m. Mon through Fri and noon to 4 p.m. Sat. There is no admission charge, but donations are welcomed.

More impressive than the grand homes, however, is the ***Bay City City Hall***. Built in 1894, the Romanesque-style stone building dominates the city skyline with its 125-foot clock tower at the southeast corner. It was listed on the National Register of Historic Places, and in 1976 the building underwent major renovation that preserved the original woodwork and distinctive metal pillars in the huge lobby. Visitors are welcome to stroll throughout the massive structure and view the 31-foot Chmielewska Tapestry that hangs in the council chambers. Woven with hand-dyed yarns of 500 colors by a young artist from Poland, the tapestry depicts the historic buildings of the community. A climb of 68 steps up the clock tower brings you to a most impressive view of Bay City, the Saginaw River, and the surrounding countryside.

The city hall (989-894-8200; baycitymi.org) is located downtown at 301 Washington Ave. and open from 8 a.m. to 5 p.m. Mon through Fri. Inquire at the personnel office in room 308 for a trip up to the clock tower. There is no admission fee. Guided tours also are offered by the Historical Museum of Bay

County. The hour-long tours are given the second Fri of each month. Cost is $1 per person and limited to the first 20 people. Call the museum for more information at (989) 893-5733.

Another attraction in Bay City is the **Delta College Planetarium and Learning Center.** Opened in 1997 with funding from NASA, the center is a striking red-domed building that looks like a spaceship in the middle of Bay City. The planetarium uses state-of-the-art equipment to take visitors on simulated outer-space journeys, while the exhibit hall features displays on astronomy and space travel. Outside there is a sundial.

The center is at 100 Center Ave. and Water Street and stages 2 to 3 shows daily. Contact the planetarium (989-667-2260; delta.edu/planet) for the times. Admission for most shows is $10 for adults and $5 for children ages 3 to 18.

michigantrivia

Bay and Saginaw Counties are the heart of Michigan's sugar beet industry and the home of Pioneer Sugar. The state's first sugar beet factory opened in Bay City in 1889 after Dr. Robert Kedzie of Michigan Agricultural College (now Michigan State University) encouraged local farmers to grow the crop the year before. Within a few short years, Saginaw Valley became the sugar bowl of Michigan.

The best way to escape from Bay City is aboard an **Appledore Schooner.** Departing from a dock in downtown Bay City, the pair of tall sailing ships begin in the Saginaw River but soon are unfurling their massive sails in Saginaw Bay for a variety of cruises. The 3-hour "Legends of the Saginaw Sails" day cruises include lunch onboard and a local historian immersing passengers in stories of Bay City's golden era of lumber and shipping. In the evening the Appledores offer dinner cruises and unusual "Stargazer Sails" that are hosted in conjunction with Delta College Planetarium.

Day cruises are at 11 a.m. on most Saturdays and Sundays in the summer and $45 for adults and $35 for children. Sunset tours last about 3 hours and cost $50 for adults and $40 for children. Many other cruise options, including a fall color sail, are offered during the year. For a schedule of trips or to make a reservation, contact **BaySail–Appledore Tall Ships** (989-895-5193; baysail-baycity.org).

Arenac County

Out in the middle of Saginaw Bay, 10 miles from Au Gres, is **Big Charity Island,** a 300-acre sanctuary of forests, beaches, rare plants such as Pitcher's thistle, bald eagles, and a lighthouse that was built in 1857. Until recently the island, with its miles of sandy shoreline and nature trails, was inaccessible to everybody but boaters experienced in navigating the choppy and often stormy Saginaw Bay.

Now even landlubbers can visit the island through *Charity Island Transport, Inc.* (989-254-7710; charityisland.net). For day trip cruises, passengers bring their own picnic lunches and dine at the lighthouse. The boat arrives about noon and passengers have 3 hours on the island before boarding the boat to return to the mainland. The day cruise costs $98 per person. Check the website for other cruises. In 2012, Charity Island Transport became licensed to sell adult beverages on its boats and at the lighthouse. Try some fine Michigan wines while you enjoy the scenery.

Iosco County

Perhaps the most famous river of the logging era was the *Au Sable,* which begins west of Grayling and ends at Lake Huron between the towns of Oscoda and Au Sable. In the 1890s it was assumed that forests were meant to be cut, and "driving the Au Sable" was a group of men known as "river rats" and "bank beavers," who floated logs down the to sawmills on Lake Huron. A century later it's "downstaters," "flatlanders," and "fudgies" driving the river. Now, however, they're following the *Lumberman's Monument Auto Tour,* an especially popular fall trip in Iosco County when tourists come to admire the color of the leaves rather than the size of the trunks.

Many motorists begin the 68-mile loop at the Tawas Area Chamber of Commerce (989-362-8643; tawas.com) at 228 Newman St. where they pick up a free copy of the Lumberman's Monument Auto Tour brochure. From Tawas City you head west on M 55 for a mile, then turn north (right) onto Wilber Road to reach Monument Road, which ends at River Road. A half mile to the east (right) is the entrance to the *Lumberman's Monument.*

The impressive bronze statue of three loggers was erected in 1931 and is now surrounded by trees very much like those they made a living cutting down. Even more impressive to many is the nearby interpretive area and museum, which give a good account of the logging era with displays and hands-on exhibits. They put the logger into perspective, a man viewed by many today as a colorful, Paul Bunyan–like character who ate apple pie and fry cakes for breakfast. In reality he provided cheap labor. In the middle of the winter, he made $2 for a 12-hour day spent pulling a saw while cold water sloshed in his boots. Little wonder that by the time most loggers turned 35 years old, they were too worn out or sick to continue their trade. The museum and interpretive area, which include overlooks, outdoor displays, and a cook's

Cruising in Iosco County

The best way to enjoy the fall colors in Iosco County is aboard the **River Queen,** a full-size paddlewheel riverboat that began operating on the Au Sable River in 1966. The *River Queen* departs from a dock on the Au Sable River 6 miles west of Oscoda and offers its 2-hour tours daily at noon and 3 p.m. from late June through late Aug and then at noon through late Sept. No tours are offered on Wed.

The tours most in demand are the weekend color tours from late Sept through mid-Oct at 10:30 a.m., 1 p.m., and 4 p.m. These are relaxing cruises along the Au Sable in which passengers enjoy the spectacular fall colors, beautiful scenery, and possibly even a few wildlife sightings such as bald eagles. Most trips are $20 per adult and $10 per child. Reservations are a must in the fall and can be made by contacting the *River Queen* office (989-739-7351).

raft on the Au Sable River known as a wanigan, are open from 10 a.m. to 5 p.m. daily from May to mid-Oct.

The auto tour continues west along River Road and in 1.5 miles comes to *Canoer's Memorial Monument.* The stone monument, topped off by a pair of paddles, was originally built as a memorial to Jerry Curley, a 17-year-old who died in 1953 practicing for the annual Au Sable River Canoe Marathon. Today it stands in honor of all racers who attempt the annual 150-mile event from Grayling to Oscoda, often cited as the toughest canoe race in the country (ausablecanoemarathon.org). From the monument site there is another fine overview of the Au Sable River Valley, and for those who keep one eye on the sky, bald eagles can often be seen in this area.

michigantrivia

One of the few remaining one-room log schools left in Michigan is the **Old Bailey School** along County Road F30 (Mikado-Glennie Road) near the hamlet of Mikado. Built in 1894, the school remained in use until 1941 and today is used by area residents for a strawberry shortcake social on the Fourth of July.

Still heading west on River Road, you reach *Iargo Springs* in another mile. *Iargo* is the Chippewa Indian word for "many waters," and this was a favorite spot for members of the tribe traveling along the Saginaw-Mackinac Trail. It's almost 300 steps and 8 rest stops down to the springs but well worth the exertion of the climb back up. The area below is pleasant and tranquil as the springs gurgle out of the moss-laden bluffs into the Au Sable River under a canopy of towering pine trees.

Alcona County

At Harrisville, US 23 swings away from Lake Huron and remains inland well into Alpena County. Taking its place along the water in northern Alcona County is Lakeshore Drive, the route to two interesting attractions. The first is *Cedar Brook Trout Farm,* reached 2.5 miles north of Harrisville immediately after turning off US 23 to 1543 N. Lake Shore Dr. Because of the almost perfect conditions for raising rainbow and brook trout, Cedar Brook was established in the early 1950s as the first licensed trout farm in Michigan. The key to the farm's success is the cold-water springs that flow from the nearby sandy bluffs. The water is funneled into the 13 ponds and rearing tanks, and its year-round constant temperature (47 degrees) and high level of oxygen are ideal for trout. The constant flow allows owner Jerry Kahn to manage without pumps. He begins with eggs and raises the trout from frylings to rainbows that will measure well over 16 inches.

The bulk of Kahn's business is shipping thousands of trout in a tank truck to individuals and sportsmen's organizations for stocking their own lakes and rivers. He also lets travelers stop by and catch their own in two ponds, one stocked with rainbows, the other with brook trout. The water in the ponds is cold and clear, and below the surface you can easily see hundreds of fish swimming around. Throw some feed in the ponds (available from a coin-operated dispenser), and dozens of large fish rise to the surface in a feeding frenzy. Anglers are provided with cane poles, tackle, bait, and a warning that catching the trout is not as easy as it looks. No fishing license is needed.

Cedar Brook (989-724-5241; cedarbrooktroutfarms.weebly.com), one of the few farms in the state that raises brook trout, is open for anglers daily from noon until 6 p.m. from May to Oct. After Labor Day, it is open weekends noon to 5 p.m. through Oct 15. The cost depends on the size (60 cents per inch) of the trout caught, but for $5 or $6 and with a little fishing luck, you can depart with a hefty rainbow.

michigantrivia

Alcona County is the site of the only gold mine to operate in the Lower Peninsula. Prospectors went to the vicinity of Harrisville looking for silver or copper after hearing reports of Indians finding large quantities of the minerals in the area. What the miners found in 1912 wasn't copper or silver but gold nuggets. To avoid a gold rush, they kept the discovery secret for several months until a stock company was formed and a mine shaft sunk. Tons of Alcona black dirt was processed for gold, but the venture ended in disaster when the steam-operated equipment blew up.

From the trout farm Lakeshore Drive continues north and in less than a half mile passes the marked side road to *Sturgeon Point Lifesaving Station* (989-335-4183; alconahistoricalsociety.com) and the preserved lighthouse, built in 1869. The last lightkeeper left in 1941, but the US Coast Guard continues to maintain the light. In 1982 the Alcona County Historical Society began renovating the attached lightkeeper's house and soon opened it to the public. The structure is a classic Michigan lighthouse, but the unique feature is that you can climb to the top of the tower (85 steps) and not only be greeted by a panorama of Lake Huron but still view a working prism as well. Amazingly, all that is needed to throw a light miles out on the Great Lake is this huge work of cut glass and an electric light no larger than your smallest finger.

The lightkeeper's house is now a museum, with the 5 rooms downstairs furnished as a turn-of-the-20th-century residence for those who maintained the attached tower. The 4 rooms upstairs are also open, and each showcases

Negwegon State Park

The only development *Negwegon State Park* has ever experienced since the state picked up the tract in 1962 is the construction of a parking area and a 10-mile trail system. What has never been improved is Sand Hill Road. This sandy, deeply rutted county road provides the only access to Negwegon and, in effect, has made it the remotest state park in the Lower Peninsula. Four-wheel-drive vehicles are recommended, and during extended dry spells, spinning tires in shifting mounds of sugary sand is not an uncommon occurrence.

After an agonizing 2.5-mile drive along the Alcona County road, most first-time visitors are stunned to arrive at a huge park sign and a wide, graveled entrance drive in the middle of nowhere. From the parking area at the end, they head into the woods and suddenly emerge at a crescent-moon bay framed by towering red pines on one side and the turquoise waters of Lake Huron on the other. In between is a sweeping shoreline of golden sand unmarred by beach blankets and beer coolers.

In short, paradise.

This is as far as most people get in the 1,775-acre park. If you can tear yourself away from the beach, Negwegon's trail system offers some interesting hikes. Departing south from the parking lot is the Potawatomi Trail, a 3.3-mile loop that hugs Lake Huron for more than a mile. To the north is the Algonquin Trail, which in 2 miles reaches the spectacular views at the tip of South Point.

To reach the park from US 23, head east on Black River Road and north on Sand Hill Road. Follow the two-track for 2.5 miles to the park entrance. It is best to stop first at *Harrisville State Park* (989-724-5126) on US 23 for a map and current road conditions before trying to reach Negwegon.

a different aspect of the county's history: shipwrecks, fishermen, the original lightkeepers, and, perhaps the most interesting, the ice-collecting industry that boomed in the area during the winter so iceboxes could be kept cold in the summer.

The lighthouse museum is open from noon to 3 p.m. Mon through Thurs and 11 a.m. to 4 p.m. Sat and Sun from Memorial Day through Sept. The best time to drop in is Fri, Sat, and Sun between noon and 3 p.m. when the lighthouse tower is open to visitors. There is no admission fee, but donations are accepted to maintain the lighthouse.

Alpena County

Lumbering turned *Alpena* from a handful of hardy settlers in 1850 into a booming town of 9,000 in 1884, and when the white pine ran out, the community sustained itself by becoming Cement City, utilizing its huge supply of limestone. From the cement factories emerged Besser Manufacturing Company, the world leader in concrete block-making equipment. Today Alpena is a manufacturing center that can boast the largest population (9,963) and the only enclosed shopping mall in northeast Michigan. The residents of this modern community also value their past and have begun restoring the historic downtown area as *Old Town Alpena.*

The original shopping area is clustered around N. Second Street and features small and specialized shops that could have been found here as early as the 1920s. An Old Town favorite is the *John A. Lau Saloon.* The restaurant dates to the 1880s when it was a rough-and-tumble waterhole for lumberjacks with a reputation that reached far into the woods. Part of the reason is that Lau always had three bartenders on staff, one who could speak German, one French, and the other Polish, so any logger, no matter where he came from, could order a beer-and-whiskey.

The restaurant still maintains that lumberman's decor with its thick plank floors, tin ceiling, crosscut saws on the walls, and historic photos of the original saloon. Dinners range from $15 to $36. The John A. Lau Saloon (989-354-6898; johnalausaloon.com) is at 414 N. Second Ave. Stories have long circulated that a ghost from the past haunts the John A. Lau Saloon. Fleeting images of a woman dressed in period clothing, strange knocking noises, odd unexplainable odors, and glasses that appear to move of their own accord all are the stuff of ghost tales surrounding the restaurant. Some say that the ghost is Agnes Lau, wife of the original saloon owner. Stop by and find out for yourself.

Alpena's *Besser Museum for Northeast Michigan* is the only accredited museum in northern Michigan and boasts one of the finest collections of Great Lakes Indian artifacts in the country.

The museum also features a sky theater planetarium and outside a small historic village that is home to the **Katherine V,** a historic fish tug. Hours are 10 a.m. to 3:30 p.m. Mon through Sat, noon to 4 p.m. Sun. The museum (989-356-2202; bessermuseum.org) is a block east of US 23 at 491 Johnson St. Admission is $5 for adults and $3 for children. Admission is free every Wed from 3 to 5 p.m. Planetarium admission is $5 for adults and $3 for children.

Alpena's newest museum is devoted to its largest park, only this one is underwater. Offshore from the city, the *Thunder Bay National Marine Sanctuary* (989-356-8805; thunderbay.noaa.gov) extends over 448 square miles under Lake Huron and includes nearly 200 historic shipwrecks. The wrecks lie in water that ranges in depth from a few inches to 200 feet, making the sanctuary a popular destination for divers, snorkelers, and even kayakers who can look down and see pieces of wrecks in the clear freshwater of Lake Huron.

Don't dive? Then the best—and driest—way to explore the shipwrecks is to visit the *Great Lakes Maritime Heritage Center,* the sanctuary's riverfront headquarters. The center's exhibits are a combination of a traditional maritime museum and a hands-on discovery center design for children. Inside the large hall is a life-size recreation of a historic Great Lakes schooner, historic displays and artifacts on shipwrecks, and interactive learning stations where kids can climb aboard a boat or follow "Discovery Tubes" to explore a wreck as if they're diving. And if you do want to see a real shipwreck, the staff will tell you where to get your toes wet.

The Great Lakes Maritime Heritage Center (989-356-8805; thunderbay.noaa .gov) is at 500 W. Fletcher St. and is open May through Labor Day 9 a.m. to 5 p.m. daily, and until 7 p.m. in July and Aug. Winter hours are 10 a.m. to 5 p.m. Mon through Sat, noon to 5 p.m. on Sun. There is no admission fee.

Presque Isle County

Jesse Besser, founder of the massive concrete block corporation, was also a humanitarian, and in Alpena the Besser Museum for Northeast Michigan is named after him. But Besser also was responsible for leaving something in Presque Isle County—a small tract of land on Lake Huron whose towering white pines somehow escaped the swinging axes of lumbermen.

The industrial genius, realizing the rarity of the uncut pines and the beauty of the undeveloped Lake Huron shoreline, gave the area to the people of Michigan in 1966. Today it is the *Besser Natural Area,* managed by the

Limestone Capital of the World

The world's largest open-pit limestone quarry is Rogers City's **Port of Calcite** and located on the grounds is **Harbor View,** an observation area where visitors can watch huge freighters being loaded for ports throughout the Great Lakes. More than 500 US and Canadian freighters are loaded annually with each vessel carrying 12,000 to 30,000 tons of stone to be used in the production of steel, cement, chemicals, and construction materials. To reach Harbor View, turn east on Quarry Road from Business US 23 and then right on Calcite Road and follow the signs. During the shipping season the port maintains a recorded message (989-734-2117) of what freighters are being loaded and when.

Department of Natural Resources. The remote preserve, reached from US 23 by taking County Road 405 to the south end of Grand Lake, offers a small niche of beauty and a little history in a quiet setting. Looping through the Besser Natural Area is a sandy 1-mile foot trail, which takes you past a small lagoon that once was part of Lake Huron. Look carefully at the bottom of the lagoon (you need polarizing sunglasses on sunny days) and you'll spot the hull of an old ship. The vessel served the community of Bell, which was located here in the 1880s and consisted of 100 residents, several homes, a sawmill, a saloon, a store, and a school.

The most noticeable remains of Bell are the rock pier along Lake Huron, a towering stone chimney, and the collapsed walls of a building whose steel safe and icebox counter indicate it might have been the saloon. Toward the end of the walk, you pass through some of the oldest and largest white pines remaining in a state once covered with the trees. There is no fee to enter the preserve, nor is there a visitor center or any other facility. Descriptive brochures that coincide with the footpath are available from a small box near the trailhead.

Visitors who exit US 23 for the east side of Grand Lake, which is the state's 19th-largest lake with more than 5,000 acres of water, usually want to view lighthouses. They take in the beautifully renovated **Old Presque Isle Lighthouse** (989-595-9917) near the end of County Road 405 (Grand Lake Road) at 4500 E. Grand Lake Rd. Built in 1840, this squat, stone lighthouse is open to the public and features an interesting museum crammed with artifacts and exhibits. The lighthouse is open daily from 9 a.m. to 6 p.m. from mid-May through Oct 15. There is a small admission charge.

Just a mile north of it at 4500 E. Grand Lake Rd. is **New Presque Isle Lighthouse Park** (989-595-9917) with nature trails, a picnic area, and a small museum of its own. Built in 1870, the New Presque Isle Lighthouse is one of

Take a Drive

The 56-mile stretch of US 23 between Mackinaw City and Rogers City is one of the most scenic drives in the Lower Peninsula, featuring a dozen parks and scenic turnouts overlooking Lake Huron.

Many of them are clustered around Rogers City. Five miles north of the town is **Forty Mile Point Lighthouse Park.** The small but delightful park is crowned by the towering lighthouse and includes a picnic area and beach. On the north side of Rogers City is **Seagull Point Park,** a mix of Lake Huron shoreline, low dunes, and woods that are best enjoyed in the fall by walking a 2-mile interpretive trail.

the tallest on the Great Lakes, standing 109 feet tall. An unattached keeper's residence, constructed in 1905, is now a museum while in the original keeper's quarters in the lighthouse is a gift shop where for a small fee you can climb the 130 steps to the top of the tower. Needless to say the view is incredible. The lighthouse is open daily mid-May through mid-Oct from 10 a.m. until 6 p.m. The 1905 House Museum is open from Memorial Day through Labor Day from 10 a.m. to 4 p.m. Fri through Mon.

The **Fireside Inn** is yet another reason to come to this part of the country, especially for anyone whose idea of a vacation in northern Michigan is renting a quaint log cabin on the edge of a lake. The Fireside Inn began its long history as a resort when the original lodge was built in 1908, and the first few authentic log cabins soon began to appear around it. Little has changed about the lodge or the dining room inside with its rustic wooden beams, plank floor, and large windows looking over Grand Lake. They still ring a dinner bell to signal suppertime and serve only one entree family-style; afterward guests still wander out to the rambling porch, an immense sitting area 215 feet long, to claim a favorite wicker chair or rocker.

michigantrivia

Posen, a village of 222 residents, is the agricultural heart of Presque Isle County with its farmers ranking third in the state as producers of packed and graded table potatoes. The best time to visit the community is during the **Posen Potato Festival** (989-766-8128; posenpotatofestival.com), held the first weekend after Labor Day.

You can rent one of the cabins with a wood interior and stone fireplace or just a room (shared bath) in the lodge itself. Rooms with private baths are $70 per person per day, upstairs rooms with shared bath are $45, and cabins are $510 per week per person, and includes all meals. Or you can stop in just for dinner, a delightful experience in itself. Dinner prices range from $12 to $20, depending on what is being served that night, and you should call ahead if possible. The Fireside Inn (989-595-6369; firesideinngrandlake.com) is located off County Road 405 at the end of the spur at 18730 Fireside Hwy.

Presque Isle County is home to another unique inn, **Nettie Bay Lodge.** Located 14 miles west of Rogers City, the lodge is on the shores of Lake Nettie and surrounded by 2,000 private acres. Originally developed as a hunting and fishing camp, Nettie Bay Lodge has since become known as a wildlife-viewing destination, offering not only accommodations but also the use of photography and observation blinds that overlook marshes and other prime spots to sight wildlife.

Because of the area's diverse habitat, it is not unusual to sight 100 different birds in a single weekend. Loons nest on a small island right in front of the lodge; bald eagles and ospreys often feed in the shallow waters of the lake; flocks of wild turkeys can be spotted in the woods. Several times in May the Nettie Bay School of Birding is held at the lodge and includes 2 nights' lodging, some meals, and bird identification workshops and field trips with professional ornithologists.

Nettie Bay Lodge (989-734-4688; nettiebay.com) is west of Hawks at 9011 W. 638 Hwy. and offers 8 cottages, 4 duplexes, and 2 A-frames. The birding school is $750 per person and includes lodging, meals, and instruction. Crafts schools include rod-making, stonemasonry, photography, and more. The Cobblestone Restaurant at Nettie Bay Lodge also offers a sumptuous dinner followed by a musical performance. The weekend specials are by reservation only.

Montmorency County

One of the most popular attractions in Montmorency County isn't a museum or a scenic overlook but a 700-pound elk. Almost 1,500 elk thrive on state forest land between Gaylord and Hillman, making it the largest herd east of the Mississippi River. A unique way to view the animals is an **Elk Viewing Sleigh Ride Dinner** arranged through the Best Western Thunder Bay Resort in Hillman. The popular wildlife-viewing adventure began in 1993 when Jack and Jan Matthias started offering sleigh rides to their 1940-vintage hunting cabin. But the high point for most guests was not the gourmet dinner at the cabin but seeing an elk along the way, including bulls whose antlers often exceeded a span of 4 feet.

The Matthiases eventually built a larger cabin to accommodate more people but still cook the 5-course meal—crown roast of pork, pear and apple crepes, and homemade soup, among other dishes—over a 1915 wood-burning

Dinosaur Gardens

Though it sounds like a tacky roadside attraction, **Dinosaur Gardens** is actually an interesting, even eerie, place to visit. The 40-acre park was the creation of the late Paul Domke, a self-taught artist and sculptor. In the 1930s Domke built 27 life-size dinosaurs from concrete, wire, and deer hair within the tangled branches of a cedar swamp forest. A winding path leads through the dark woods where a dino lies waiting for you around every bend.

Eeek!

Dinosaur Gardens (877-823-2408; dinosaurgardensllc.com) is right on US 23, 10 miles south of Alpena. It's open daily from 10 a.m. to 5 p.m. from Memorial Day through Labor Day. Admission is $10 for adults and $8 for children 3 to 15.

stove. The dinner includes 6 wine tastings. If you anticipate joining a sleigh ride, bundle up and grab one of the blankets that are provided. The ride through the snowy woods is a 45-minute trip each way.

The sleigh ride is offered year-round. A 2-night weekend package including accommodations at the Thunder Bay Resort, breakfasts, and the sleigh ride is $276 per person, while the 1-night is $192. When there is available space, you can also book just the dinner and sleigh at $112.68 per person.

michigantrivia

Located 11 miles inland from Rogers City along M 68 is *Ocqueoc Falls,* one of only two waterfalls in the Lower Peninsula. This cascade is a series of ledges that drops 6 feet in the Ocqueoc River. Ocqueoc is not the thundering waterfall that you experience throughout the Upper Peninsula, but it's still a beautiful spot, especially in the fall. The day-use area includes picnic tables and foot trails that follow the east bank of the river, while on the south side of M 68 is a rustic state forest campground.

Children must be at least 9 years old to participate in elk viewing and dinner. For more information or reservations, contact the *Best Western Thunder Bay Resort* (800-729-9375; thunderbayresort.com).

Garland Resort near Lewiston has another cure for cabin fever. Garland offers 4 championship golf courses. The best way to spend a winter afternoon at this sprawling resort of cozy cabins and romantic log lodges is by Nordic skiing and eating. Cross-country skiing, snowmobiling, and ice-skating are among popular winter activities at Garland Resort (989-342-1384; garlandusa.com). The resort is located at 4700 Red Oak Rd.

Oscoda County

The state bird of Michigan is the robin, but many argue that it should be the Kirtland's warbler. This small bird, the size of a sparrow, with a distinctive yellow breast, is an endangered species that breeds only in the jack pines of Michigan. It spends its winters in obscurity in the Bahamas and then migrates to areas between Mio and Grayling, arriving in mid-May and departing by early July. Only in these preserved nesting areas do birders and wildlife watchers have the opportunity to observe this rare bird, with fewer than 800 breeding pairs remaining.

The nesting areas are closed to the public, but you can join a **Kirtland's Warbler Tour,** which is sponsored by the US Forest Service. The tour, which lasts from 2.5 to 3 hours, includes a movie and a discussion by a Forest Service naturalist and then a short trip to the nesting area. The guided group hikes through the jack pines, usually covering 1 to 2 miles, until the warblers are spotted. Seeing a Kirtland's warbler is not guaranteed, but most tours do, especially in mid-May through June.

This tour is famous among birders, who come from all over the country for their only glimpse of the warbler, but it is also an interesting spot for anybody intrigued by Michigan's wildlife. The Forest Service office (989-826-3252), north of Mio on M 33, and the Michigan Audubon Society (michiganaudubon.org) jointly conduct guided tours from May 15 through July 4. Tours depart from the Michigan Forest Visitor Center with Hartwick Pines State Park, just north of Grayling at 4216 Ranger Rd. Visit the front desk upon your arrival for the meeting location. The tours are offered on weekdays at 7 a.m. and on weekends and holidays at 7 and 11 a.m. Tours are free of charge, but you must have a Recreation Pass to enter the state park. For Michigan residents, a Recreation Pass for a year costs $12. For nonresidents, a Recreation Pass costs $34 for the year or $9 for one day.

Places to Stay in the Lake Huron Region

ALPENA

Big Bear Lodge
2052 US Hwy 23 S
(989) 354-8573

Days Inn
1496 M 32
(989) 356-6118
wyndhamhotels.com

AU GRES

Rooster Inn Bed and Breakfast
198 N. Tonkey Rd.
(989) 876-6630
roosterinnaugres.com

BAY CITY

Americinn by Wyndham
3915 Three Mile Rd.
(989) 414-6796
wyndhamhotels.com

Doubletree by Hilton
1 Wenonah Park Pl.
(989) 891-6000
hilton.com

Historic Webster House
900 Fifth St.
(989) 316-2552
historicwebsterhouse.com

FLINT

Knob Hill Bed & Breakfast
1105 South Dr.
(810) 424-3888
knobhillbedandbreakfast
.com

Wingate by Wyndham
1359 Grand Pointe Ct.
(810) 694-9900
wyndhamhotels.com

FRANKENMUTH

Bavarian Inn Lodge
1 Covered Bridge Ln.
(989) 652-7200
bavarianinn.com

Frankenmuth Country Bed & Breakfast
2160 S. Gera Rd.
(989) 574-7000

Frankenmuth Motel
1218 Weiss St.
(989) 652-6171
frankenmuthmotel.com

Zehnder's Splash Village Hotel
1365 S. Main St.
(844) 207-7309
zehnders.com

HARRISVILLE

Alcona Beach Resort
700 N. Lake Huron Shore Dr.
(989) 724-5471

Springport Inn Bed and Breakfast
629 US 23
(704) 989-7513
springportinn.com

HAWKS

Nettie Bay Lodge
9011 W. County Hwy. 638
(989) 734-4688
nettiebay.com

HILLMAN

Thunder Bay Resort
27800 M 32
(800) 729-9375
thunderbayresort.com

LEWISTON

Garland Resort
4700 N. Red Oak Rd.
(877) 442-7526
garlandusa.com

Gorton House
4066 Wolf Lake Dr.
(989) 786-2764

Lewiston Lodge
1525 Fleming Rd.
(989) 786-5261
thelewistonlodge.com

MIDLAND

Best Western Valley Plaza Resort
5221 Bay City Rd.
(989) 496-2700
bestwestern.com

Sleep Inn
2100 W. Wackerly St.
(989) 837-1010
choicehotels.com

OSCODA

Camp Inn Lodge
3111 US 23
(989) 739-2021
campinnlodge.com

Huron House Bed & Breakfast
3124 N. Huron Rd.
(989) 739-9255
huronhouse.com

SELECTED CHAMBERS OF COMMERCE & TOURISM BUREAUS

Alpena Area Convention and Visitors Bureau
420 N. Second Ave.
Alpena 49707
(989) 340-2288
visitalpena.com

Flint Genesee Convention and Visitors Bureau
519 S. Saginaw St.
Flint 48502
(810) 600-1404
flintandgenesee.org

Frankenmuth Convention and Visitors Bureau
635 S. Main St.
Frankenmuth 48734
(989) 652-6106
frankenmuth.org

Great Lakes Bay Regional Convention & Visitors Bureau
515 N. Washington Ave.
Sagniaw 48607
(800) 444-9979
gogreat.com

Rogers City Area Chamber of Commerce
292 S. Bradley Hwy.
Rogers City 49779
(989) 734-2535
rogerscityareachamber.com

Shiawassee County Convention and Visitors Bureau
215 N. Water St.
Owosso 48867
(989) 723-1199
shiawassee.org

Tawas City Tourist Bureau
402 E. Lake St.
Tawas City 48764
(877) 868-2927
tawasbay.com

OSSINEKE

Oakapiney Beach Cottages
9611 US 23
(989) 471-2489
oakapiney.com

ROGERS CITY

Driftwood Motel
540 N. Third St.
(989) 734-4777
driftwoodmotelrc.com

Manitou Shores Resort
7995 US 23
(989) 734-7233
manitoushores.com

Purple Martin Lakeside Inn & Nature Center
194 E. Freidrich Depot
(989) 272-8111
purplemartininn.com

SAGINAW

Fairfield Inn
5200 Cardinal Square Blvd.
(989) 797-6100
marriott.com

Hampton Inn
2222 Tittabawassee Rd.
(989) 797-2200
hilton.com

Montague Inn
1581 S. Washington Ave.
(989) 752-3939
montagueinn.com

OTHER ATTRACTIONS

Chippewa Nature Center
400 S. Badour Rd.
Midland
(989) 631-0830
chippewanaturecenter.org

Crossroads Village and Huckleberry Railroad
6140 Bray Rd.
Flint
(810) 736-7100
geneseecountyparks.org

40 Mile Point Lighthouse
7323 US 23 N
Rogers City
(989) 734-4587

Great Lakes Lore Maritime Museum
367 N. Third St
Rogers City
(989) 734-0706
gllmm.com

Junction Valley Railroad
7065 Dixie Hwy.
Bridgeport
(789) 777-3480

Marshall M. Fredericks Sculpture Museum
7400 Bay Rd.
Bay City
(989) 964-7125
marshallfredericks.org

Saginaw Children's Zoo
1730 S. Washington Ave.
Saginaw
(989) 759-1408
saginawzoo.com

TAWAS CITY

Always a Holiday Bed and Breakfast
423 Newman St.
(989) 984-5300
alwaysaholidaybed
andbreakfast.com

East Tawas Junction Bed and Breakfast Inn
514 W. Bay St.
(989) 362-8006
east-tawas.com

Paradise Beach Resort
1029 Lake St.
(989) 362-3234
paradisebeachtawas.com

Tawas Bay Beach Resort
300 E. Bay St.
(989) 362-8600
tawasbaybeachresort.com

Places to Eat in the Lake Huron Region

ALPENA

Austin Brothers Beer Company
821 W. Miller St.
(989) 340-2300
austinbrosbeerco.com
Pub

Churchill Pointe Inn
5700 Bennett Rd.
Hubbard Lake
(989) 727-2020
churchillpointeinn.com
Fine Dining

Court Yard Ristorante
2024 US 23
(989) 356-9511
courtyardristorante.com
Italian American

Fresh Palate
109 N. Second Ave.
(989) 358-1400
freshpalategourmet.com
Fine Dining

John A. Lau Saloon & Restaurant
414 N. Second Ave.
(989) 354-6898
johnalausaloon.com
American

The Nest
628 W. Chisholm St.
(989) 340-1082
Casual

BAY CITY

Duece's Char House
432 N. Tuscola Rd.
(989) 893-5881
American

Gatsby's Seafood & Steakhouse
203 Center Ave.
(989) 922-5556
gatsbyssteakhouse.com
Steakhouse, Seafood

Krzysiak's House
1605 Michigan Ave.
(989) 894-5531
krzysiaks.com
Polish

Nino's Family Restaurant
1705 Columbus Ave.
(989) 893-0691
ninosfamrest.business.site
Italian

Old City Hall
814 Saginaw St.
(989) 892-4140
oldcityhallrestaurant.com
Fine Dining

BIRCH RUN

Oscar & Joey's Roadhouse
12027 Dixie Hwy.
(989) 624-9349
oscarandjoeys.weebly.com
American and Wild Game

Tony's I-75 Restaurant
8781 Main St.
(989) 624-5860
tonysi75restaurant.com
American

EAST TAWAS

Hsing's Garden Restaurant
600 E. Bay St.
(989) 362-5341
hsingsgarden.com
Chinese

Northwoods Steak House
1222 S. US 23
(989) 362-5321
thenorthwoodssteakhouse
.com
Steakhouse

Route 23 BBQ
1626 E. US 23
(989) 984-5123
route23bbq.com
Barbecue

FLINT

Bill Thomas' Halo Burger
800 S. Saginaw St.
(810) 238-4607
haloburger.com
Burgers

Cork on Saginaw
635 Saginaw St.
(810) 422-9625
corkonsaginaw.com
American, European

Luigi's Restaurant
2132 Davison Rd.
(810) 234-9545
luigissince1955.com
Italian

FRANKENMUTH

Bavarian Inn
713 S. Main St.
(989) 652-9985
bavarianinn.com
German

Harvest Coffeehouse & Beanery
626 S. Main St.
(989) 652-2203
harvestcoffeehouse.com
Cafe & Bakery

Honey B's Eatery
525 S. Main St.
(989) 262-8545
honeybseatery.com
Breakfast & Brunch

Wang's Bistro
207 N. Main St.
(989) 652-6888
frankenmuthwangsbistro
.com
Japanese

Zehnder's
730 S. Main St.
(800) 863-7999
zehnders.com
German

MIDLAND

Gratzi Midland
120 E. Main St.
(989) 486-9044
gratzimidland.com
Italian American

Maru Sushi & Grill
715 E. Main St.
(989) 633-0101
marusushi.com
Sushi

ONe Eighteen
111 W. Main St.
(989) 633-6099
oneeighteenmidland.com
Tavern

Pi's Chinese Restaurant
1815 S. Saginaw Rd.
(989) 832-5848
pichineserestaurant.com
Chinese

OSCODA

Bavarian Bakery & Restaurant
5222 N. US 23
(989) 739-8077
German

Tait's Bill of Fare
111 E. Dwight Ave.
(989) 739-1518
taits-bill-of-fare.business
.site
American

Wiltse's Brew & Family Restaurant
5606 F-41
(989) 739-2231
wiltsesbrewpub.com
Brewpub

SAGINAW

Artisan Urban Bistro
417 Hancock St.
(989) 401-6019
artisanurbanbistro.com
American

Fralia's
422 Hancock St.
(989) 799-0111
fralias.com
Sandwich

Jake's Old City Grill
100 S. Hamilton St.
(989) 797-8325
jakesforsteaks.com
Steakhouse

Pasong's Café
114 N. Michigan Ave.
(989) 791-5008
pasongs.com
Asian

Lake Michigan Region

The Lake Michigan shoreline may be the Lower Peninsula's western edge, but many will argue that its heart lies in Chicago. The shoreline is now connected to the city by an interstate, but that has only cemented what was already a long and enduring relationship between the Windy City and this watery edge of Michigan.

It began with the Great Chicago Fire of 1871, which left the city smoldering in ashes. Chicago was rebuilt with Michigan white pine, and the mill towns along the Great Lake, communities like Muskegon and Saugatuck, worked around the clock to supply the lumber. Maybe it was during these excursions to the sawmills that Chicagoans discovered that this region of Michigan possessed more than towering trees and two-by-fours.

They discovered the sand, the surf, and the incredibly beautiful sunsets of the Lake Michigan shoreline. By the 1880s, the tourist boom was on, and it was being fed by vacationers from cities outside Michigan, places like St. Louis and South Bend, Indiana, but most of all from Chicago. They arrived by steamships, trains, and eventually automobiles. They caused luxurious resorts and lakeside cottages to mushroom, beginning in New Buffalo on the edge of the Indiana-Michigan

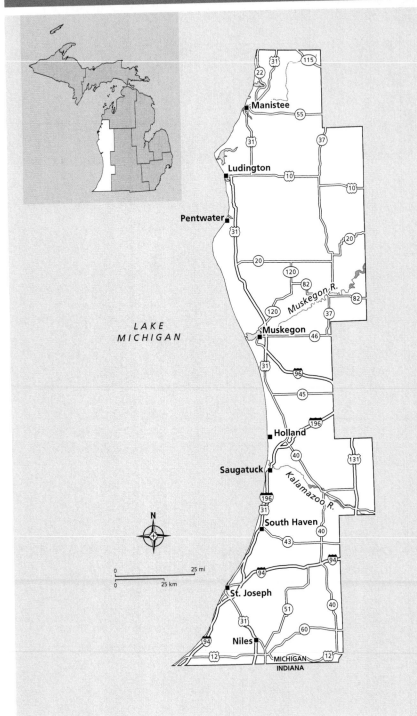

LAKE
MICHIGAN

Muskegon R.

Kalamazoo R.

N

0   25 mi
0   25 km

Manistee

Ludington

Pentwater

Muskegon

Holland

Saugatuck

South Haven

St. Joseph

Niles

MICHIGAN
INDIANA

AUTHOR'S TOP TEN PICKS

Gillette Sand Dune Visitor Center
6585 Lake Harbor Rd.
Hoffmaster State Park
(231) 798-3573

Great Lakes Naval Memorial and Museum
1346 Bluff St.
Muskegon
(231) 755-1230
silversidesmuseum.org

Historic White Pine Village
1687 S. Lakeshore Dr.
Ludington
(231) 843-4808
historicwhitepinevillage.org

Lakeshore Museum Center
430 W. Clay Ave.
Muskegon
(231) 722-0278
lakeshoremuseumcenter.org

Loda Lake Wildflower Sanctuary
4794 N. Felch Ave.
White Cloud
(231) 745-4631
fs.usda.gov

Ludington State Park
8800 M-116
Ludington
(231) 843-2423
visitludington.com

Saugatuck Chain Ferry and **Mount Baldhead Park**
528 Water St.
Saugatuck
(269) 857-2603
saugatuckcity.com

Shrine of the Pines
8962 M-37
Baldwin
(231) 745-7892
theshrineofthepines.com

Silver Lake State Park
9679 W. State Park Rd.
Mears
(231) 873-3083
visitbaldwin.com

Windmill Island
1 Lincoln Ave.
Holland
(616) 355-1036
cityofholland.com

border and continuing right up the coast: St. Joseph, South Haven, Saugatuck, Grand Haven, and Muskegon.

They call it the Michigan Riviera, and even Richard J. Daley, Chicago's famed political boss and mayor, had a summer home on the strip. With the completion of I-94, the two regions were linked by a four-lane belt of concrete. Many Chicagoans, eager to escape the city heat, were less than two hours from the cool breezes of their favorite resort.

The Lake Michigan shoreline is still the heart of Michigan tourism. This incredibly beautiful region is characterized by great dunes and watery sunsets, but it's also known for its bustling resorts, streets full of quaint shops, and attractive beachfront hotels. The region lies on the western edge of Michigan, but Chicago's influence is unmistakably clear.

Just go to the beach and look at the license plates of the cars, listen to the baseball games the radios are tuned to, or see what city's newspaper someone is snoozing under. You're in Chicago's playland.

Berrien County

You barely cross the state border from Indiana before the first lakeshore communities appear on the horizon with their hotels and motels clustered near the water. Many are new, each with features little different from the one next door. But if you search a little, you can find an old inn from another era unique in its appearance and half-hidden in a quiet neighborhood near the lake. If you search harder, you might even find the *Inn at Union Pier.*

Union Pier is a cluster of well-shaded streets and 19th-century summer homes about 10 miles north of the border. Locate Berrien Street and you'll pass the inn at 9708 Berrien St., 3 nautical buildings painted light blue with white railings. The inn began in 1918 as a single structure called the Karonsky Resort, but business was so good that by 1929 2 more had been added. An easy journey from Chicago (today it is only 90 minutes by car), the inn thrived in the golden age of the Lake Michigan resorts but by the 1960s had been abandoned and closed up. In 1983, Bill and Madeleine Reinke purchased the place, gutted it, and after two years of renovation, opened for business. The inn is now owned by Bill Jann.

From the outside the inn's most striking feature is the wraparound porch on one of the smaller lodges and the matching balcony above it, the ideal place to unwind after a day on the beach. Walkway decks connect the buildings; one has a large hot tub, and tables for breakfast outdoors are on another. Most of the rooms are furnished in light pine and include a Swedish ceramic woodstove. The heart of the main lodge is a spacious common area with a grand piano, overstuffed chairs and sofas, and lots to read. Guests begin each day with a full breakfast of local fruit and fresh baked goods on the deck and then head across the street to the beach, check out one of the inn's bicycles, or take to nearby roads for a winery tour or antiques excursion.

michigantrivia

Former Chicago mayor Richard M. Daley followed his father's footsteps by not only entering politics but also maintaining a second home in Michigan's Harbor Country, the communities along Lake Michigan from Indiana to Bridgman. Other celebrities with homes in the area include media personality Oprah Winfrey, actor George Wendt of TV show *Cheers* fame, and the late film critic Roger Ebert.

TOP ANNUAL EVENTS

MAY

Spring Sip and Savor
Traverse City
(231) 642-5550
traversecity.com

Tulip Time Festival
Holland
(800) 822-2770
tuliptime.com

JUNE

National Asparagus Festival
Shelby and Hart
(231) 861-8110
nationalasparagusfestival.org

JULY

Harbor Days/Venetian Nights
Saugatuck
(269) 857-1701
saugatuck.com

Manistee National Forest Festival
Manistee
(231) 723-2575
manisteeforestfestival.com

AUGUST

National Blueberry Festival
South Haven
(269) 637-5171
blueberryfestival.com

SEPTEMBER

Apple Cider Century
Three Oaks
(888) 877-2068
applecidercentury.com

OCTOBER

Goose Festival
Fennville
(616) 836-9979
fennvillegoosefestival.com

The Inn at Union Pier (269-469-4700; innatunionpier.com) has 15 rooms priced for double occupancy from $155 to $280 per night, including breakfast.

Three Oaks, in the southwest corner of Berrien County, is home to the *Three Oaks Spokes Bicycle Club.* Founded in 1974, the club is best known for the *Apple Cider Century* (888-877-2068; applecidercentury.com), when every September more than 7,000 cyclists depart from the tiny town on 1-day rides of 25, 50, 62, 75, or 100 miles.

The *Lake Michigan dunes,* the most spectacular natural feature of the region, begin in Indiana and hug the shoreline almost to the Straits of Mackinac. The largest preserve of dunes in Berrien County is at *Warren Dunes State Park,* on the lake 12 miles north of the state border. The park has more than 2 miles of fine sandy beaches and dunes that rise 240 feet above Lake Michigan. The dunes are a popular place in the summer for sunbathers and swimmers during the day and campers at night. What many people don't realize is that Warren Dunes is the only state park that permits hang gliding, and it is considered by most gliders to be one of the best places in the Midwest, if not the country, for soaring.

Gliders are drawn to the park because of **Tower Hill,** which looms over the beach parking lot. They trudge up the hill carrying their gliders and then soar into the winds from the top, flying over the sandy park or even above Lake Michigan. When the sport enjoyed its heyday in the mid-1970s, there would be almost 100 gliders on Tower Hill on a windy weekend, with as many as 20 in the air at one time. The park rangers were so burdened with accidents caused by unqualified fliers that they instituted a certification system and stricter regulations for gliders.

What makes the park so attractive for these soaring adventurers, especially those just learning the sport, are the smooth winds that come off the lake and the soft and relatively forgiving sand below. Although not nearly the rage it was in the 1970s, arrive on a weekend in the fall or spring with a wind out of the north-northwest and it's still possible to watch a glider or two take off from the top of Tower Hill. Occasionally glider instructors still set up school in the park, taking students through a 1-day lesson or a tandem glide. To find such an instructor, call Warren Dunes State Park (269-426-4013) or check the state-by-state list of schools on the website of the United States Hang Gliding Association (ushpa.aero).

Lake Michigan does more than provide water for the beaches or a view from the top of sand dunes. It also tempers the winter storms that roll in from the Great Plains and moderates the sweltering summer heat felt elsewhere in the Midwest. These effects, combined with the light soil of the region, have turned the lakeshore strip into a cornucopia of orchards, berry farms, and especially vineyards. Michigan is the third leading wine-producing state in the country after California and New York. Paw Paw in Van Buren County is the unofficial center for the state's winemakers, with the largest vineyards, St. Julian Wine Company and Warner Vineyards, located right off I-94.

Smaller wineries are also found throughout the region, including a frequent winner in national competition, **Tabor Hill Winery & Restaurant,** in the center of Berrien County. The winery began when two Chicago salesmen who sold steel but loved wine brought a selection of hybrid grapevines back from France in 1968. They chose their vineyard site in the rolling hills of the county, hoping the conditions there were similar enough to those in France to bring success. They were. The transplanted vines thrived, and the winery produced its first bottle in 1970. Seven years later a bottle of its 1974 Baco won a gold medal in the American Wine Competition, and since then both the vineyard and Leonard Olson, steel-salesman-turned-winemaker, have won numerous awards. The winery remains small, producing 40,000 gallons (or about 15,000 cases) of wine annually in almost two dozen types of whites, reds, and blends.

The best way to view Tabor Hill is on a walking tour that begins where workers bottle the wine and then heads out into the rows of trellised vines for a history of the grapes. You also descend into the wine cellar for a look at the huge vats and hand-carved oak casks that age the wine and then finish the tour in the tasting room for some tips on how to "judge" wine. The 25-minute tour ends with everybody age 21 or older sampling six of Tabor Hill's finest wines, including a souvenir glass (kids can sample grape juice).

The winery also includes an excellent restaurant with tables that overlook the rolling vineyard and a huge deck outside. A favorite activity of many, especially during fall, is to pack a picnic lunch and enjoy it on the open deck with a bottle of Tabor Hill wine.

Tabor Hill (800-283-3363; taborhill.com) is at 185 Mount Tabor Rd. and can be reached from I-94 by taking exit 16 and heading north on Red Arrow Highway to Bridgman. From Bridgman head east along Shawnee Road and keep an eye out for the signs. This vineyard is definitely off by itself. The $20 tours are offered every half hour from noon to 4:30 p.m. daily May through Nov. Video tours also are available upon request.

In between the sand dunes, the orchards, and the wineries of Berrien County is a lot of history. Niles, the community of four flags, was the first settlement in the Lower Peninsula and claimed one of the first museums in the country when a private one opened here in 1842. Eventually it became the ***Fort St. Joseph Museum,*** and today it houses more than 10,000 historical items on 2 floors. Much of the museum's collection relates to its namesake fort, for which the French built the stockade in 1691. The British took it over in 1761, and the Spanish captured it 20 years later. In 1783, the Americans arrived and raised the fourth and final flag over Fort St. Joseph.

Bear Cave

Bear Cave near Buchanan is one of the few caverns in Michigan. Formed in rare "tura rock," the cave is 15 feet deep, 6 feet wide, and 15 feet high and estimated to be 25,000 years old. The cave was part of the Underground Railroad for slaves in the mid-1800, and then in 1875 bank robbers used it to hide their loot. The heist inspired the 1903 movie, *The Great Train Robbery,* in which the cave served as a movie location.

Bear Cave (269-695-3050) is 6 miles north of Buchanan on Red Bud Trail at 4085 Bear Cave Rd. Tours of the cave are available during the summer and include following a winding stairway through the cavern.

The museum's most noted displays, however, are devoted to the Sioux Indians of the Great Plains, not to the residents of Fort St. Joseph. Many of the Indian artifacts were obtained by Captain Horace Baxter Quimby, whose daughter moved to Niles. While the US Army captain was based in the Dakota Territory in 1881 and 1882, he became friendly with Sitting Bull, the most famous Sioux chief. Among the gifts Quimby received from Sitting Bull were 13 pictographs of the chief's greatest battles. The set of pictures is one of only three known collections of the Sioux chief.

The museum (269-683-4702; nilesmi.org) is right behind the Niles City Hall (ci.niles.mi.us) at 508 E. Main St. Niles can be reached from US 12, 23 miles east of I-94 or 33 miles west of US 131. Hours are 10 a.m. to 4 p.m. Wed to Fri and 10 a.m. to 3 p.m. Sat. There is no admission fee.

More history can be seen at Berrien Springs' **The History Center at Courthouse Square.** The courthouse itself was built in 1839 and at various times was a militia drill hall, a college, and even a church. In 1967, the courthouse was repurchased by the county and restored as the 19th-century courtroom where law was interpreted and justice dispensed in Michigan's early years of statehood. The classic Greek Revival–style structure is the centerpiece of the Berrien County Courthouse Square, a complex of 5 buildings that is listed on the National Register of Historic Places. It gives visitors a glimpse of the machinery of old-fashioned government.

You can climb the wooden stairs to the second-floor courtroom where former Michigan Supreme Court Justice Epaphroditus Ransom presided over the first session in April 1839. Little in the building has changed since then. The wooden floors still creak as you approach the bench, and floor-to-ceiling windows still illuminate the courtroom furnishings of pewlike benches, wood-burning stoves, and the curved railing that separated the participants from the gallery.

The historic complex (269-471-1202; berrienhistory.org) is located in Berrien Springs at 313 N. Cass St. Berrien Springs is 11 miles southeast of exit 27 off I-94. Hours for the buildings are 10 a.m. to 5 p.m. Wed through Sun. Admission is free.

Van Buren County

South Haven has a long and colorful history spiced with Great Lakes vessels and shipbuilding, and much of it is explained at the **Michigan Maritime Museum,** which is dedicated to the boats that were built and used on the Great Lakes. Founded in 1976, the museum includes a 600-foot outdoor boardwalk around a historical fish tug and a vessel used in the US Life-Saving Service.

Inside the museum hall the exhibits range from collections of small vessel motors and tools used by local shipbuilders to personal belongings of mariners and exhibits on the role of the Great Lakes in the War of 1812.

Michigan Maritime Museum (269-637-8078; michiganmaritimemuseum.org) is at 260 Dyckman Ave. where it crosses the Black River and is reached from I-196 by taking exit 20 and heading west on Phoenix Street. Turn north on Broadway Street and then west on Dyckman Street. Open Wed through Sun 10 a.m. to 5 p.m. Admission is $8 for adults and $5 for children.

For excitement on the high seas, take a cruise starting at $35 on **Friends Good Will,** a tall ship sailing out of the Michigan Maritime Museum. The square topsail sloop is a replica of a ship of that name that fought for both the US and Great Britain during the War of 1812. The ship takes regularly scheduled sails on Lake Michigan from mid-May through mid-Sept, with crew dressed in full 1812-era regalia. During the summer months special "Pirate Chaser Adventure Sails" are scheduled for the younger set Wed though Sat. *Lindy Lou* is an electric river launch that cruises up and down the Black River, starting at and returning to the Michigan Maritime Museum in South Haven. The launch is a recreation vessel designed to be a replica of river launches found in South Haven in the early 1900s. Thirty-minute cruises also are available on the Coast Guard Motor Lifeboat 36460. Built in 1941, the lifeboat seats 6 passengers and starred in the Disney film *The Finest Hours*. The 1929 Chris Craft Cadet *Merry Time* takes cruisers back to the Roaring Twenties. Check the website for cruises and prices.

The good life on the lakes can also be enjoyed at dinnertime aboard the **Idler Riverboat,** a restaurant floating in the Black River downtown in Old Harbor Village. The *Idler* was built in Clinton, Iowa, in 1897 for Lafayette Lamb, a lumber baron who used the 120-foot houseboat for his own personal enjoyment on the Mississippi. He never installed an engine in the *Idler* because he didn't want to be disturbed by the vibrations, so the vessel was always pushed up and down the river by a small tug.

The *Idler* appeared at the 1904 World's Fair in St. Louis, but in 1910 it burned to the waterline. It was immediately rebuilt and eventually captured the fancy of actor Vincent Price's father. He owned it for 58 years, and in a letter now framed and hanging in the restaurant, Price said that what his father liked most about the riverboat was playing the piano on board. Eventually the boat was purchased, and it was brought to South Haven in 1979. Today it has been beautifully restored, and topside is the Creole Tavern, an open-air bar with sweeping views of the town and the Black River from every table. In the restaurant, located below, you can dine popular Cajun and Creole dishes. Also popular is the Fried Tomato BLT Burger—a prime steak burger, grilled to order and topped with fried green tomato, hickory smoked bacon, Swiss cheese, and roasted garlic parmesan mayo served on a Kaiser bun with kettle chips.

Idler Riverboat at 515 Williams St. (269-637-8435; idlersouthhaven.com) is open in season from 11 a.m. to 2 a.m. Mon through Fri and 9 a.m. to 2 a.m. on Sat and Sun. Dress is casual on the riverboat. Call to confirm riverboat hours.

Sportfishing fans throughout Michigan head for the streams, inland lakes, and Great Lakes to fill their creels with a variety of catch. If they are passing through Van Buren County on M 43, they should also head for the **Wolf Lake State Fish Hatchery,** one of the main reasons fishing is so good in Michigan. The hatchery dates to 1928 and by 1935 was the largest in the world. Construction of the present facility began in 1980, and three years and $7.2 million later, the technological upgrading had made Wolf Lake the finest complex in the country for producing both warm-water and cold-water species. No other hatchery in Michigan raises as many species as Wolf Lake, which hatches steelhead, brown trout, chinook salmon, and grayling along with the warm-water species of tiger muskie, northern pike, walleye, bass, and bluegill.

Hatchery tours should begin at the interpretive center, which will fascinate anybody who dabbles in sportfishing. Hanging on the wall in the lobby is the state record sturgeon—one very big fish—plus displays of trout fishing on the state's renowned Au Sable River. Off to one side is the "Michigan Room," a walk-through exhibit area that begins with an interesting series of habitat

Caruso's Candy Kitchen

Since the Roaring Twenties, vacationing families have been stepping up to the Italian marble soda fountain bar at *Caruso's Candy Kitchen* in Dowagiac to sip a creamy soda or indulge in an ice cream concoction served in a tall glass sundae dish. They're still doing it today because little has changed at this venerable ice cream parlor.

Founded in 1822 by Antonio Caruso, who had just sailed to the United States from Italy with his wife, Caruso's still features pedestal stools, a wavy mirror behind the counter, lime green Hamilton Beach malt mixers, and high wooden booths. This is where you come for a real milkshake, made with hand-dipped ice cream in a metal malt glass. The specialty of the shop is the Green River: lime phosphate syrup on the bottom of a sundae dish, two scoops of vanilla ice cream, and topped off with crushed cherries, pineapple, mixed nuts, and real whipped cream. It is based on the green, white, and red flag of Italy and was Antonio Caruso's way of saluting his native country.

Caruso's (269-782-6001) is in downtown Dowagiac at 130 S. Front St. and open from 8:30 a.m. to 5 p.m. Mon through Fri, and 9 a.m. to 3 p.m. Sat.

dioramas, cross sections of every type of water you might drop a line into, from trout streams to the Great Lakes. Each diorama shows the species that will be found, the habitat they like, and the lure of a frustrated angler trying to land the lunkers that lie below. There are also exhibits on fish anatomy, slide presentations of Michigan's commercial fisheries, and an area devoted to sportfishing gear, including a delightful display of more than 100 historic lures, plugs, and other tackle.

After viewing the exhibits and a short slide presentation in the auditorium, visitors are encouraged to wander through the hatchery itself to view millions of fish in the ponds. If you want to see something bigger, ask for some fish feed at the interpretive center and walk out on the small pier at the show pond. The small lake was developed so that people, especially children, could actually see some large fish. Among the species in it is a pair of sturgeons, each one more than 6 feet long and weighing more than 60 pounds. Imagine that at the end of your line!

The center (269-668-2876; michigan.gov) is open Mon through Sat 10 a.m. to 6 p.m., and Sun from noon to 6 p.m. during the summer with guided half-hour tours at 10 and 11 a.m. and at 1, 2, and 3 p.m. The center has shorter hours in Mar, Apr, May, Sept, and Oct. There is no admission fee to visit Wolf Lake, which is reached from I-94 by heading north on US 131 for 4 miles and then west on M 43 for 6 miles to 34270 County Road 652. Check the website for hours.

Michigan has no short supply of vineyards and wine-tasting rooms to visit, but few have the old-world character of **Warner Vineyards** in Paw Paw. The building itself is a Michigan Historical Site, constructed in 1898 as the town's first waterworks station. The vineyard purchased it in 1967 and proceeded to renovate the structure using lumber from old wine casks to transform it into a wine haus and bistro.

Today the brick and stone building is reached by crossing a footbridge over the east branch of the Paw Paw River, which gurgles its way through the shaded grounds and around an outdoor deck. The whole setting is one of idyllic enjoyment. A self-guided tour of Warner's champagne caves will answer the question of how they get the bubbles into the bottle, or skip the tour and simply stop for a little wine tasting.

Warner Vineyards (800-756-5357; warnerwines.com) is reached from I-94 by taking exit 60 and heading north on M 40 into Paw Paw. The winery is at 706 S. Kalamazoo St. and open from noon to 5 p.m. Sun through Fri, 10 a.m. to 5 p.m. on Sat. The winery also has tasting rooms in Holland, South Haven, and Marshall.

Just down the road in Paw Paw at 716 S. Kalamazoo St. is the **St. Julian Winery,** the state's oldest and largest vineyard. Founded in 1921, St. Julian (800-732-6002; stjulian.com) produces 40 types of wines and also offers tours and tastings as well. Open Mon to Thurs from 10 a.m. to 6 p.m., Fri and Sat from 10 a.m. to 7 p.m., Sun from 11 a.m. to 6 p.m. St. Julian Winery also has locations in Dundee, Union Pier, Metro Detroit, Rockford, and Frankenmuth.

Allegan County

On the map **Saugatuck** looks like just the next beachfront community along the lake, but in reality it is a trendy resort whose streets are lined with fine restaurants, quaint shops, and lots of tourists. Perhaps the most striking sight in Saugatuck is at the docks along the Kalamazoo River, where moored at the edge of the shopping district is an armada of cabin cruisers and sailboats 30, 40, or 50 feet in length or even longer. You can pick up the boardwalk that winds past the boats anywhere along Water Street, and if you follow it north, eventually you'll come to the most unusual vessel afloat, the **Saugatuck Chain Ferry** (269-857-1701) at 528 Water St. It's the only chain-powered ferry in the state and has been carrying passengers across the Kalamazoo River since 1838. An operator hand-cranks a 380-foot chain attached at each shore, pulling the small white ferry through the water. Dogs, bikes, and strollers ride free, but motorized vehicles are not permitted on the ferry. The ferry operates, give or a take a day or two, from Memorial Day to Labor Day from 9 a.m. to 9 p.m. In May, it runs weekends from 9 a.m. to 9 p.m.

It's only $2 for the 5-minute ride, and it is your escape from the bustling downtown shopping district to one of the most beautiful beaches on the lake. Once on the other side, you walk north for a few hundred yards until you reach **Mount Baldhead Park,** with tables, shelter, and a dock on the river. There is also a stairway that takes you (after a little huffing and puffing) to the top of the 200-foot dune, where you are greeted with a glorious panorama of Saugatuck, Kalamazoo Lake to the southeast, and Lake Michigan to the west. On the other side you have a choice. You can descend to **Oval Beach** along the Northwoods Trail, an easy walk that includes a view of the lake and beach along the way. Or you can dash madly down the steep and sandy Beach Trail, right off the towering dune, across the beach, and into the lake for a cool dip.

Saugatuck's most entertaining tour by far is **Harbor Duck Adventures.** It's almost impossible to miss this big, blue half-boat and half-truck wheeling through town. What was an amphibious vessel in World War II has been turned into a 20-passenger wet taxi that offers a forty-five-minute narrated tour of Saugatuck and Douglas and even crosses the Kalamazoo River between them.

Even better, you are free to leave the vessel to shop trendy Saugatuck and then board a later tour.

Harbor Duck Adventures (269-857-3825; harborducks.com) departs Coughlin Park at Colver Street in Saugatuck every hour from 10 a.m. to 7 p.m. May through Sept. Fare for adults is $19 and $10 for children ages 6 to 12, $6 for children ages 3 to 5. Harbor Duck accepts cash only.

Moving inland, another interesting attraction is the old *Allegan County Jail* in Allegan. Seriously. The imposing redbrick building was built in 1906 and features Greek Revival architecture with a peaked roof and columns along the porch. It has bars on the windows, a hexagonal turret in the corner, and a three-story grandeur that is lacking in its newer counterpart across the street.

But most unusual is the small red sign on Walnut Street that says *Allegan County Old Jail Museum.* Go to jail and get a history lesson in penitentiary punishment. Within the museum are a variety of exhibits, including a country store loaded with 19th-century merchandise, a display devoted to Allegan's General Benjamin Pritchard, whose men captured Confederate president Jefferson Davis during the Civil War, and a historical laundry room.

But coat hangers and wringers are not what draw more than 1,000 visitors to the museum every year. It's a macabre fascination with slammers and pokeys. To that end, a guide leads you through the sheriff's living quarters and the large kitchen, where his wife would prepare meals for up to 30 prisoners a night and then pass plates through a small door in the wall. On the second floor are rows of 6-by-8-foot cells, complete with the graffiti that disheartened convicts scratched on the walls in the 1930s. You can even walk through the maximum-security cells, now filled with a historical toy collection, view the old padded cell, and examine the holding pen for "ladies."

michigantrivia

Beneath the sand near the mouth of the Kalamazoo River on Lake Michigan lies the site of *Singapore,* one of Michigan's most famous ghost towns. The town was founded in the 1830s by New York land speculators who hoped it would rival Chicago or Milwaukee as a lake port. Singapore bustled as a lumbering town for almost forty years, but once the trees were gone by the 1870s, the residents fled.

The Old Jail Museum (269-673-8292; alleganoldjail.com) is open 10 a.m. to 4 p.m. Fri and Sat May through Aug and Sat 10 a.m. to 4 p.m. Sept through Apr. There is no admission fee. To reach the museum, take M 222 (exit 55) off US 131 and head west into Allegan. The old jail is at 113 Walnut St., between Hubbard and Trowbridge.

Ottawa County

Every spring Holland bursts into a rainbow of colors thanks to the millions of tulips that residents plant seemingly everywhere. The event climaxes during the **Tulip Time Festival** (800-822-2770; tuliptime.com) in mid-May, when the flowers are in full bloom and the Dutch-founded city hosts more than a half-million visitors, who book hotel rooms months in advance.

But historical Holland can be an interesting trip the rest of the year as well. Founded in 1847 by Dutch religious dissenters, Holland celebrated its sesquicentennial in 1997 and today is the undisputed center of Dutch culture in Michigan. For a dose of old Holland, visit Nelis's **Dutch Village.** This 15-acre theme park is a re-created 19th-century Dutch village complete with canals, tulip gardens, and historical displays along with some kitschy attractions like a wooden-shoe slide to keep the kids happy. Among the many buildings are a wooden-shoe factory and Queen's Inn, Holland's only restaurant serving Dutch food.

At the wooden-shoe factory, shoes are carved by hand and with antique automated machines. Try on a pair of klompen (wooden shoes), feed the farm animals, ride the restored antique carousel, and take a big swing on the Zweefmolen (Dutch Swing Ride). There is no extra charge for rides. Adults can step onto the Heksenwaag (a 200-year-old witch's scale) to find out who is guilty of witchcraft, hand crank an Amsterdam street organ, and sample Dutch specialty foods. Educational movies, enjoyed by both adults and children, are shown throughout the day. A Klederdracht (costume) Museum features authentic costumes in typical settings and a doll exhibit showcases 150 provincial costumes. Attractions include pedal-pumper cars, Dutch cheese making, Dutch delftware making, Dutch dancing lessons, and walking the goat. Dutch Village (800-285-7177; dutchvillage.com) is along US 31, 2 miles northeast of downtown Holland at 12350 James St. Hours vary throughout the year so call for correct times. Admission is $14 for adults and $12 for children ages 3 to 15.

Windmill Island is a city park that features **De Zwaan,** the only working Dutch windmill allowed to be shipped out of the Netherlands. The 5-story-high windmill is still operating as it grinds whole wheat flour that is sold in shops nearby. Also at Windmill Island are the Posthouse Museum, Little Netherlands Museum, an 1895 carousel, and 36 acres of manicured gardens, dikes, canals, and picnic areas. The park (616-355-1036 or 888-535-5792; cityofholland.com) is just northeast of downtown Holland at Seventh and Lincoln Streets at 1 Lincoln Ave. and open mid-Apr through mid-Oct 9:30 a.m. to 5 p.m. daily. Admission is $10 for adults and $5 for children ages 5 to 15.

Holland also has two wooden-shoe factories where you can buy the oaken loafers or simply see a demonstration of how they are made. The best is the **Deklomp Wooden Shoe & Delft Factory,** which also includes a display on the many kinds of wooden shoes worn in Europe. The Wooden Shoe Factory (616-399-1900; veldheer.com) is off US 31 just south of Sixteenth Street at 12755 Quincy St. Hours are 9 a.m. to 5 p.m. Mon through Fri and 10 a.m. to 4 p.m. Sat from Apr through Oct. At this double Dutch delight, you can talk with the artists as they mold, hand-paint, and glaze the only authentic blue and white delftware made in the US, or watch the wooden-shoe carving on machines that were imported from the Netherlands. All handmade items, and other Dutch delicacies, are available for purchase.

Grand Haven has developed its waterfront along the Grand River and includes a riverwalk that extends several miles from downtown to the pictur-esque **Grand Haven Lighthouse** (grandhaven.org), out in Lake Michigan. But by far the most noted aspect of the river is the city's **Musical Fountain** (616-842-4499; ghfountain.com) at 101 N. Harbor Dr. , the world's largest, which performs nightly during the summer with electronically controlled and synchro-nized music. Performances begin around dusk, and most people enjoy the free concerts by assembling in the Waterfront Stadium. Nightly performances begin Memorial Day weekend and run until Labor Day. From Labor Day through Sept, performances are only on Fri and Sat.

Muskegon County

In the late 1800s this county was the heart of lumbering on Michigan's western side, and the city of **Muskegon** grew during the prosperous era to be known as the Lumber Queen of the World. A drive down W. Webster Avenue shows how much money was made and where much of it went: The Victorian man-sions are fabulous. The most elaborate houses were built by the two men who prospered most of all from Michigan white pine, Charles H. Hackley and his partner Thomas Hume. They built their homes next to each other, and it reportedly took 200 artisans and craftsmen two years to complete them. Behind the homes the men shared the same carriage house. The **Hackley House** and **Hume House** are listed on the National Register of Historic Places and have been called two of the nation's most outstanding examples of Victorian architecture.

The Hackley House is especially impressive, a virtual museum of carved woodwork that strikes you from the moment you walk into the home and are greeted by unusual figures along the walls. Almost every aspect of the house is overwhelming, from its original furnishings and stained-glass windows to

michigantrivia

The world's largest weather vane is located in Montague. Erected in 1884 by the Whiteall Metal Studios across the street, the vane is 48 feet tall and weighs 3,500 pounds. It has a 26-foot-long arrow and directional letters that are 3 feet, 6 inches tall, and is topped off by a 14-foot-long schooner. The vane is right off Business US 31 in a park overlooking the town harbor.

the hand-stenciled walls and the 11 fireplaces, each made unique with imported ceramic tiles. If you see only one restored home in Michigan, it should be the Hackley House, where it's hard to imagine living in such style.

The **Hackley and Hume Historic Site** (231-722-7578; lakeshoremuseum .org) is at 484 W. Webster Ave. Tours are offered. Check the website for hours. Admission is $15 for adults and $5 for children ages 3 to 12. Another interesting museum in Muskegon is partly underwater. The USS *Silversides* is a US Navy submarine that was commissioned just eight days after the Japanese attacked Pearl Harbor on December 7, 1941. It went on to serve in the Pacific Fleet during World War II and ranked third among all US submarines for enemy ships sunk. Today *Silversides* is docked at the Muskegon Channel Wall in Père Marquette Park at 1346 Bluff St. and is the main attraction of the **Great Lakes Naval Memorial and Museum.**

The museum itself, at 1346 Bluff St., opened its doors in 2009 and features military exhibits, a theater, and a gift shop. From there guides lead tours on the USCGC *McLane*, a Prohibition-era "buck-and-a-quarter boat" (125 feet long) that earned the honor of sinking an enemy vessel during WWII, and then USS *Silversides*. The 312-foot-long submarine is often the first one most visitors have

Cruising to Milwaukee

Bored with Michigan or just hungry for a good bratwurst? An interesting side trip from Muskegon is Milwaukee. Wisconsin's beer-and-brat capital is only a 2.5-hour ride away thanks to *Lake Express LLC* (866-914-1010; lake-express.com). The company's high-speed catamaran connects the two cities with 3 round-trips across Lake Michigan daily from July through Aug, and 2 trips daily in May, June, Sept, and Oct. During the summer you can arrive at Milwaukee before noon and not leave until 7 p.m. That's a lot of brats and fried cheese curds.

The basic round-trip fare for passengers is $165 for adults, $70 for children, and $202 if you choose to take your vehicle. The Premier Cabin offers free Wi-Fi, steward service, complimentary headsets for movies, and complimentary nonalcoholic drinks. Premier Cabin is limited to children 12 years and older with $211 round-trip fare for adults and $183 for seniors age 65 and older.

Michigan's Best: Dune Climbs

The first time my children saw the Dune Climb in Sleeping Bear Dunes National Lakeshore, it might as well have been Mt. Everest. And in a way it was. Climbing it was a knee-bender. Reaching the top was exhilarating. Bounding and leaping down the steep sandy slope is as close as they have ever come to rappelling.

In Michigan, a towering sand dune is the first mountain every kid (and their parents) needs to conquer. There is certainly no shortage of sand on the west side of the state, but here are our top five dune climbs in no particular order:

Pikes Peak: In the 1970s Warren Dunes State Park (269-426-4013) was one of the most popular places to hang glide in Michigan. That's how steep and high its dunes are. Today thousands climb Pikes Peak in the day use area to enjoy the views of Berrien County and the wide sandy beaches that greet them at the end of their romp.

Mount Baldhead: From downtown Saugatuck, you can hop on the city's Chain Ferry for a quick ride across the Kalamazoo River and then tackle the 282 steps to the top of this 220-foot-high dune. Three routes lead down the other side; Northwoods Trail and South Ridge Trail are gentle descents through the woods. Skip them for Beach Trail, a wild run down through the sand that will have you at Saugatuck's beautiful Oval Beach (269-857-1701) in minutes.

Tunnel Park: This 22-acre Ottawa County park is home to a 140-foot dune with a tunnel through the middle of it so visitors can easily reach the beach on the west side. The east side of the sandy mountain is roped off as a dune climb and features a long staircase to make the climb even easier. From US 131 depart at the Lakewood Boulevard exit and head west to Lakeshore Drive where Tunnel Park (616-738-4810) is just a quarter mile to the south.

Silver Lake State Park: Lying between Silver Lake and Lake Michigan is a strip of some of the largest and purest dunes in the state, giant mountains of windblown sand, lacking trees, scrub, even dune grass. From the Dune Pedestrian Parking Area, it's a 10-minute hike to the dunes that tower right above the beaches on Silver Lake's west side. Run and dive! From US 31, depart at Shelby Road and head west for 6 miles to County Road B15 and follow the signs to Silver Lake State Park (231-873-3083).

Dune Climb: This is the original, a steep sandy slope that rises 130 feet above a picnic area in Sleeping Bear Dunes National Lakeshore (231-326-5134) near Empire. It's a major effort for little legs, but the view of Glen Lake from the top is stunning and the run back down wild.

ever boarded, and they find the cramped torpedo rooms, crew quarters, and the galley fascinating.

Great Lakes Naval Memorial and Museum (231-755-1230; silversides-museum.org) and the USS *Silversides* are open daily June through Aug from 10 a.m. to 5:30 p.m. From Sept through May hours are Sun through Thurs from

10 a.m. to 4 p.m., Fri and Sat from 10 a.m. to 5:30 p.m. Admission is $15 for adults and $10.50 for children ages 5 to 18.

The towering dunes along the eastern side of Lake Michigan are the world's largest accumulation of dunes bordering a body of freshwater and are renowned throughout the country. One of the best places for learning about dunes is the *Gillette Sand Dune Visitor Center* within P. J. Hoffmaster State Park. This beautiful facility was built in 1976 as a bicentennial project and then totally renovated in 2002. It's located at the base of Mount Baldy, a towering sand dune, and its west wall is a 2-story viewing window where visitors can stare up at the migrating mountain of sand. As Michigan's official sand dune interpretive center, Gillette is a natural history museum filled with state-of-the-art displays devoted to the state's unique sand dunes.

Its main exhibit hall is entitled "Michigan Coastal Sand Dunes . . . Like Nowhere Else on Earth" and features dioramas that depict dune habitats in all seasons, an animation station where visitors can see how sand dunes are formed, and an interactive computer station that outlines the great sand dune areas in the state. There is also an 82-seat auditorium where multimedia presentations on the dunes are shown, a gift shop, and classrooms that host a wide range of nature programs throughout the year.

Most visitors view the exhibits and then tackle *Dune Climb Stairway* that begins near the center. This 193-step structure climbs 190 feet to the top of one of the park's largest parabolic dunes where an observation deck gives way to a sweeping view of Lake Michigan and the surrounding sand dunes. There is a vehicle permit fee to enter the state park (231-798-3573; michigan.gov), which is reached by heading south of Muskegon on US 31, exiting at Pontaluna Road, and heading west. The Gillette Visitor Center at 6585 Lake Harbor Dr. is open daily during summer from 10 a.m. to 5 p.m.; the rest of the year, hours are Tues through Fri noon to 4 p.m. and Sat 10 a.m. to 4 p.m. The center is closed mid-Nov through mid-Jan for annual maintenance. A $12 Recreation Passport is required to visit all 98 state parks and recreation areas. Or visitors can pay a $9 daily entrance fee.

Newaygo County

The most distinctive structure in the southern Newaygo County town of *Grant* is its wooden water tower. Built in 1891, it's the classic *Petticoat Junction* water tower, the last one standing in the state. Driving down Main Street, you half expect to see Uncle Joe and the rest of the cast from that zany old sitcom.

Drive through the town to see the water tower, but stop because of its train depot. Former owner Chuck Zobel transformed the once bustling passenger station into the **Grant Depot Restaurant,** one of the county's best eateries—unless you're a railroad enthusiast, then it's a fascinating train museum that serves a very good lemon meringue pie.

After purchasing the empty depot in 1979, Zobel spent a year renovating it, and in the process of tearing down walls and replacing floors, he turned up a variety of artifacts from the era of the iron horse: tickets and train orders from 1903, bottles, telegrams, signs, even the remains of a copper sulfate battery that powered the telegraph before the age of electricity. Today you can sit at a table in what a century ago was the passenger waiting room, or in a bay window overlooking the tracks, where a station agent once worked a telegraph. What was the baggage room is now the kitchen, and the dining room walls are covered with memorabilia—from lanterns and oilcans to warning lights, and tickets.

The Grant Depot Restaurant (231-834-7361; thegrantdepot.weebly.com) is open from 6 a.m. to 9 p.m. Mon through Sat and 7 a.m. to 3 p.m. Sun. From I-96 in Grand Rapids, head north on M 37 (exit 30). Grant is reached in 24 miles, and the depot is right off M 37 at 22 W. Water St.

Wildflower lovers ought to stay on M 37 in Newaygo County to reach the **Loda Lake Wildflower Sanctuary.** In 1938, Forest Service rangers invited the Federated Garden Clubs of Michigan to help them create a sanctuary for native plants, including endangered and protected species, to ensure their survival. Although part of the Manistee National Forest, the preserve is still managed by

michigantrivia

One of the most unusual festivals in Michigan is the **Blessing of the Bikes**, which is held the third weekend in May in Baldwin. Hundreds of motorcyclists, many of them riding classic Harley-Davidsons, arrive in town for the weekend and gather on Sunday at the local airstrip to have their bikes blessed by a priest.

the Federated Garden Clubs, and over the years it has evolved into a unique haven for botanists, wildflower enthusiasts, and families who just want to know the difference between Michigan holly and Holly, Michigan.

The self-guiding trail is a mile loop of easy hiking where you encounter the first numbered post in less than 20 feet, and before you return to the picnic area, you'll pass 38 others. The interpretive posts mark the locations of trillium, blueberries, swamp rose, insect-eating sundew plants, and fragrant water lily, among other plants, and they correspond to a trail guide available near the parking area.

From White Cloud head north on M 37 and then left on Five Mile Road, where the directional sign to Loda Lake is posted on the corner. Head a mile west and turn right on Felch Road. The entrance to the sanctuary is a mile to the north. For a trail guide, call or stop at the **US Forest Service Ranger Station** (231-745-4631) at 650 N. Michigan Ave. in Baldwin.

Lake County

When you look at a stump, what do you see? A stump? Is a tree root just a tree root? Not to Ray Overholzer. This hunting guide-turned-craftsman would stroll along the Père Marquette River, find a stump left over from Michigan's logging era, and see a table or maybe a piece of a rocking chair. Then he would spend months fashioning it by hand until his unique vision became reality. This is woodworking as an art, and it's preserved today at the **Shrine of the Pines,** a small but—to those of us who struggled in shop class just to build that birdhouse—intriguing museum.

Overholzer constructed a rocking chair from roots that is so perfectly balanced it rocks 55 times with a single push. His gun rack holds 12 hunting rifles and rotates on hand-carved wooden balls like ball bearings—not a screw or a hinge in the elaborate cabinet. A stump became a bootlegger's table with a hidden compartment for the whiskey bottle and another for the shot glasses. Perhaps most amazing is the dining room table that began as a 700-pound stump of a giant white pine. By the time Overholzer was done working with the piece of discarded wood, it was a 300-pound table with roots carved into legs and storage bins hollowed out of the sides. In 1940 and 1941 Overholzer built a huge lodge on the banks of the Père Marquette at 8962 M 37 and originally intended to operate it as a hunting lodge. But his furniture was too dear to him by then and, fearing it would get scratched, he changed his mind. The intended lodge became a museum of more than 200 pieces, the world's only collection of handcrafted white pine furniture.

The Shrine of the Pines (231-745-7892; theshrineofthepines.com) is open from 10 a.m. to 5 p.m. Mon, Tues, Fri, and Sat and 1 to 5 p.m. on Sun. Admission is $7 per person. Call ahead of time to be sure Shrine of the Pines is open. Hours sometimes change.

Oceana County

County Road B15 turns off from US 31 north of Whitehall and swings west toward Lake Michigan before returning to the highway at Pentwater, the bustling resort community at the northwest corner of Oceana County. Along the way the county road passes **Silver Lake,** an impressive sight that slows most cars bearing sightseers to a crawl. The lake is bordered to the west by a huge dune that towers over it, and from the car window you see beach and sunbathers, crystal clear lake and sailboats, the mountain of sand and dune climbers. Much of what you see, including the strip of dunes between the inland lake and Lake Michigan, is part of *Silver Lake State Park.*

Silver Lake is different from other state parks along Lake Michigan because the dunes have been divided into three areas for three types of users. The section in the middle is the pedestrian area, where people scramble up the huge dunes and hike across them to Lake Michigan.

The region to the south is one of only two places in the state where dune rides are offered in large open-air jeeps that hold up to 12 passengers. *Mac Wood's Dune Rides* date back to the 1930s, and today thousands enjoy the popular rides every year from early May through early October. The scenic 40-minute ride takes passengers through the heart of the Silver Lake dune country from the top of the tallest dunes to the edge of Lake Michigan. It's a wild ride down sandy hills and through the surf of Lake Michigan, but never too scary for small children to handle. The tour is even more spectacular near sunset on a clear summer evening.

Mac Wood's Dune Rides (231-873-2817; macwoodsdunerides.com) is located at 629 N. 18th Ave. in Mears. Hours are 9:30 a.m. to sunset daily from Memorial Day through Labor Day. The cost is $20 for ages 12 and up, $12 for children ages 3 to 11.

Tiny *Hart,* population 2,091, is known for two things: asparagus and rail trails. Hart hosts the *National Asparagus Festival* (231-259-0170; nationalasparagusfestival.org) in the second weekend of June because Oceana County grows more of the green stuff per capita than anywhere else in the world. The 4-day event includes parades, farm tours, fun runs, and the opportunity to feast on the asparagus that has been prepared every which way, from dip to cakes.

Not into vegetables? Then arrive with your bicycle. Hart is the northern end of the *Hart-Montague Trail.* The 22.5-mile paved path became one of the first rail trails in Michigan when an abandoned track of the Chesapeake and Ohio Railroad was converted into recreational use in 1987. A trailhead with maps and parking is located in Hart's John Gurney Park. The northern 8 miles of the trail, from Hart to Shelby, is by far the most scenic section.

Mason County

Continue on S. Lakeshore Drive, pass the huge Ludington Power Plant, and then after a few miles keep an eye on the east side of the road for *Bortell's Fisheries.* From the outside the fish market is not glamorous, but it has been in business since 1937 and gradually has evolved into western Michigan's finest shop for fish and seafood. It carries a variety of frozen seafood, makes delicious marinated herring in cream and wine, and smokes one of the best selections of fish in the state, including trout, chub, salmon, sturgeon, blind robin, and menominee. Want something fresher? When in season, its cases are filled with fresh perch, pike, walleye, trout, and even smelt in the spring, all half buried in ice.

Still not fresh enough? Then you can wander around back with a pole and catch a rainbow trout out of one of its stocked ponds. Bortell's will cook any fresh fish right there in the market and serve it with french fries and homemade potato salad or coleslaw. You can enjoy your meal outside at one of a half dozen picnic tables next to the market, or better yet, cross the street to Summit Park, where you have a view of Lake Michigan from your table. The freshest fish, good food, and beautiful scenery at a little out-of-the-way county park—it doesn't get much better than that.

Bortell's Fisheries (231-843-3337) is 7 miles south of Ludington at 5510 S. Lakeshore Drive between Meisenhiemer and Deren Roads. From May through Labor Day, the store is open Tues through Sat from 11 a.m. to 8 p.m. and Sun from 11 a.m. until the store sells out of fish. On Labor Day weekend, the store closes for the season when it sells out of fish. Cash and check only.

The first frame house in Mason County was built by Aaron Burr Caswell in 1849. Six years later the 2-story home was still the only frame building in an area that was trying to organize itself into Michigan's newest county. So

Lake Michigan Car Ferry

In 1897 the *Père Marquette* departed Ludington, offering the first ferry transportation across Lake Michigan between Michigan and Wisconsin. A century later you can still hop on a ferry for a trip to Manitowoc, Wisconsin, thanks to the SS *Badger*, the only steam-powered auto passenger ship on the Great Lakes.

Launched in 1952, the 410-foot ferry was extensively refurbished in 1991 and now includes staterooms, a maritime museum, food and beverage service, theater and bingo hall, an outdoor deck, and live entertainment. The 60-mile crossing takes 4 hours but saves you the 450-mile drive around the lake between the two cities. The cruise, a throwback to when luxurious steamers sailed the Great Lakes in the 1920s, is so popular that the company offers a single-day ticket. The round-trip fare for an adult without a vehicle is $131 and $44 per child.

In the summer the ferry departs Ludington at 8:30 a.m. and 8:30 p.m. and Manitowoc at 1:30 p.m. and 1 a.m. In spring and fall, the ferry departs Ludington at 8:30 a.m. and Manitowoc at 1:30 p.m. For tickets or reservations call the SS *Badger* at (800) 841-4243 or go online at ssbadger.com.

Death of Father Jacques Marquette

Located on Lakeshore Drive just north of White Pine Village is a memorial to **Father Jacques Marquette,** a 45-foot-tall metal cross set in stone. The 17th-century missionary explorer is famous for founding St. Ignace and Sault Ste. Marie and for joining Louis Jolliet on a 3,000-mile paddle in discovering the Mississippi River. Realizing he was losing his health, Marquette tried to return to his beloved St. Ignace mission in 1675 but never made it. Instead he died on the banks of Lake Michigan in Buttersville at the site of the cross. He was buried here, but his remains were later exhumed and taken to St. Ignace for final burial.

that year Caswell offered the front half of his home as the first courthouse and county seat of Mason. Today the preserved building is a state historic site and the centerpiece of **Historic White Pine Village,** a museum complex operated by the Mason County Historical Society.

The village at 1687 S. Lakeshore Dr. is composed of some 20 preserved buildings or replicas, all from the surrounding county and set up along streets on a bluff overlooking Lake Michigan. Each of the buildings, which range from an 1840s trapper's log cabin to a hardware store of the early 1900s, is completely renovated inside and can be viewed on a leisurely self-guided walk. Throughout the village people in traditional dress ply their trades, everything from a blacksmith to a turn-of-the-20th-century housewife cooking on a woodstove to a violin maker.

What makes White Pine Village an enjoyable experience is the active visitor participation in the exhibits. A documented trial that was held in the Caswell home in the 1860s is reenacted today with visitors filling in as the jury, and 9 out of 10 times handing down the same verdict as the first time. A log chapel on the rise overlooking the area still holds a Sunday service, and afterward people are encouraged to help the village cooks and enjoy their fresh-baked treats.

White Pine Village (231-843-4808; historicwhitepinevillage.org) has changing hours so check the website. The museum complex is located off US 31, 3 miles south of Ludington, and is reached by exiting west onto Iris Road and then turning north at S. Lakeshore Drive for a quarter of a mile to 1687 S. Lakeshore Dr. Admission is $12 for adults and $9 for children.

From Ludington the famous dunes of Lake Michigan continue to the north, and the area immediately adjacent to the city has been preserved as **Ludington State Park** at 8800 M 116. It's a popular place where visitors enjoy miles of beach and rolling dunes, as well modern camping, or a hike to historic Point Sable Lighthouse. Along with a 300-site campground, the state park

Skyline Trail

Anyone who loves boardwalk paths with benches will savor the **Skyline Trail,** a short but spectacularly scenic hike in Ludington State Park. The path follows the crest of a wooded dune, and erosion of the original trail prompted the park staff to replace it with a boardwalk path in 1981. The two-year project included use of Air National Guard helicopters to airlift much of the lumber to the top of the dune.

The sweeping views of Lake Michigan and the park's open dune country are so good that numerous benches were built into the boardwalk. Sure, the trail is only a half mile long, but if you sat on every bench and admired the scene, it would take you most of the afternoon to hike it. The view from the bench at Post Number 11 is especially scenic as you gaze south at the miles of open dunes stretched out to the Lake Michigan shoreline, the Ludington Harbor Lighthouse, and, on a clear day, even the Silver Lake dunes 25 miles away.

Beside the benches are 13 numbered posts along the boardwalk that correspond to information in a brochure available from map boxes at the foot of each staircase. They identify the three common evergreens in Michigan, explain dune country succession, and point out stumps and other remnants of the loggers who arrived in 1851 to cut down the white pine.

(231-843-2423; michigan.gov) also features the Great Lakes Interpretive Center, an unusual nature trail in Hamlin Lake for canoers, and a lighthouse that can only be reached on foot.

At the tip of the Big Sable Point is **Big Sable Point Lighthouse,** whose black-and-white tower is Ludington State Park's distinctive trademark. The classic structure was authorized by President James Buchanan in 1858 after the barge *Neptune* sank off the point and 37 people drowned. Actual construction began in 1866, and a year later its light was illuminated by Burr Caswell, Mason County's first resident and the first caretaker of the lighthouse.

The light was placed on the National Register of Historic Places in 1983 and today is an interesting maritime museum that is reached on foot by following the lighthouse service road or the beach, either one a 1.5-mile walk. The attached lightkeeper's residence contains furnished rooms, historic displays, and a gift shop. You can then climb a circular, iron stairway of 130 steps to the top of the tower and step outside. The view is worth every step as the park's sandy shoreline lies to the east and the blue horizon of Lake Michigan to the west.

Big Sable Point Lighthouse (231-845-7343; spika.com) at 5611 N. Lighthouse is open from 10 a.m. to 5 p.m. daily from May through Oct. Admission is $5 for adults and $2 for children. Outside there are picnic tables while nearby is the marked Lighthouse Trail that heads east to the heart of the park and the rest of the trail system.

Where Ludington State Park ends, the **Nordhouse Dunes** begin, a 1,900-acre preserve in Manistee National Forest that is not as well known or as frequently visited as the state park but is equally beautiful.

A Michigan governor called the Nordhouse Dunes "one of the most outstanding scenic resources" in the state, and in 1987 they were given a federal wilderness designation. What makes these dunes unique is that the area is entirely undeveloped. Travel through the dunes is only on foot either along 10 miles of easy-to-follow trails or by simply making your way across the open hills of sand. The area is the only place in Michigan where you can hike in and camp among the dunes. Because of its inaccessibility to motorized traffic, the dunes area also offers those willing to hike in the opportunity of having a beach to themselves along its 4 miles of sandy lakeshore.

Access into Nordhouse Dunes is through the Lake Michigan Recreation Area, a semiprimitive campground on the northern end of the preserve that is maintained by the national forest's **Manistee Ranger District** (231-723-2211; fs.usda.gov). Trails into the dunes begin from the recreation area, which also contains 100 camping sites, a beach, and observation towers overlooking the lake. To reach the recreational area, take US 31 to Lake Michigan Road (also known as Forest Road 5629) located 10 miles south of Manistee. Follow Lake Michigan Road 8 miles west to the area. There is a $5 vehicle permit fee for exploring the dunes or for day use of the recreational area. There is no nightly fee for camping.

Manistee County

Manistee is another lakeshore town that boomed during the lumbering era; at one time in the late 1800s, it boasted 32 sawmills and 17 millionaire lumber barons among its residents. Almost the entire town was destroyed in the Great Fire of 1871 on the same day Chicago experienced its famous blaze. One of the first buildings erected after the fiery mishap was the **Lyman Building,** which was a place of business throughout its existence until the Manistee County Historical Society turned it into the only "storefront museum" in the state.

The Lyman Building Museum is not just another county museum displaying local artifacts. The many fixtures, walk-in vault, and wraparound balcony have been preserved, and part of the first floor has been restored as an early drugstore with brass apothecary scales, pill makers, an impressive selection of antique medicines and balms, and fading posters on the walls selling Pe-Ru-Na, which "cures catarrh." The other half of the first floor is set up as a general store, while in the back is an old newspaper office with original Linotype machines. Upstairs are 10 more rooms, including a dentist's office, a bank, and the living room of an early 1900s home. The hallway between the rooms is filled with Victor talking machines and Victrolas. The Lyman Building Museum (231-723-5531; manisteemuseum.org), at 425 River St. in downtown Manistee, is open from 10 a.m. to 4 p.m. Mon through Sat from June through Sept, 10 a.m. to 4 p.m. Thurs through Sat Jan through Mar, and 10 a.m. to 4 p.m. Tues through Sat Apr through May and Oct through Dec. Admission is $3 for adults and $1 for students and $8 for families.

michigantrivia

A historical marker in Orchard Beach State Park 2 miles north of Manistee commemorates the Great Fire of 1871. On October 8, the day the famous Chicago fire began, fires also broke out in Michigan after an exceptionally long, hot summer. Most of Holland and Manistee was ruined within hours, with the flames sweeping east across the state and eventually reaching Port Huron.

Manistee is a city full of museums, and one of them isn't even on dry land. Permanently moored on Manistee Lake at the Moonlite Motel and Marina is the **SS** *City of Milwaukee,* the last traditional Great Lakes railroad car ferry still afloat. The 360-foot-long steamship was built in 1931 for the Grand Trunk Western Railroad and could hold an entire freight train of 32 boxcars on its freight deck and 300 passengers on the cabin deck above. Its triple expansion engines were monsters at 1,400 horsepower each, and their combined power could propel the ship at 14 mph or break through 3 feet of solid ice. The ship served as "Rails Across the Water" until 1981 when the state of Michigan shut down its cross-lake ferry system.

Destined to be scrapped, the SS *City of Milwaukee* was saved by residents of her home port of Frankfort, and in 2000 was declared a National Historic Landmark and towed to a new home in Manistee. Today this floating maritime museum offers guided tours that take you from the freight deck to the engine room to the wheelhouse to the Pullman staterooms and everywhere in between. In October the railroad ferry becomes a "Ghost Ship" haunted house to the delight of wide-eyed children. Visitors are invited to experience lodging aboard a 1920s Great Lakes steamship. Passenger, crew, and other cabins are available for overnight stays. Walk the decks and enjoy the stars from a deck chair or watch a movie in the observation room.

The SS *City of Milwaukee* (231-723-3587; carferry.com) at 99 Arthur St. is open for tours from 11 a.m. to 5 p.m. Thurs through Mon from June through Aug; Fri, Sat, and Sun mid-Apr through mid-Sept. Admission is $10 for adults, $8 for children. Overnights on Fri and Sat nights from June through early Sept are $45 per single person bunk bed with $15 for another person, 4-bed room for $85, and a double bed for $85.

Places to Stay in the Lake Michigan Region

DOUGLAS

Douglas House Inn
41 N. Spring St.
(269) 857-1119
douglashouseinn.com

Sherwood Forest Bed & Breakfast
938 W. Center St.
(269) 857-1246
sherwoodforestbandb.com

GRAND HAVEN

Boyden House Bed & Breakfast
301 S. Fifth St.
(616) 846-3538
boydenhouse.com

Harbor House Inn
114 S. Harbor Dr.
(616) 846-0610
harborhousegh.com

Looking Glass Beachfront Inn
1100 S. Harbor Dr.
(616) 842-7150
lookingglassmi.com

LUDINGTON

Candlelite Inn Bed & Breakfast
709 E. Ludington Ave.
(231) 845-8074
candleliteinnludington.com

Lamplighter Bed & Breakfast
602 E. Ludington Ave.
(231) 843-9792
ludington-michigan.com

Ludington Pier House
805 W. Ludington Ave.
(231) 845-7346
ludingtonpierhouse.com

Viking Arms Inn
930 E. Ludington Ave.
(231) 843-3441 or
(800) 748-0173
vikingarmsinn.com

MANISTEE

Dempsey Manor Bed & Breakfast Inn
506 Maple St.
(616) 802-4588
dempseymanorbandb.com

Lakeshore Motel
101 S. Lakeshore Dr.
(231) 723-2667
lakeshoremotelmanistee.com

Ramsdell Inn
399 River St.
(231) 398-7901
ramsdellinn.net

Riverside Motel & Marina
520 Water St.
(231) 723-3554
riversidemotelmarina.com

NEW BUFFALO

Harbor Grand Hotel
111 W. Water St.
(888) 605-6800
harborgrand.com

New Buffalo Inn & Spa
231 E. Buffalo St.
(844) 340-5240
newbuffaloinn.com

Victorian Inn
123 E. Mechanic St.
(312) 985-6535
victorian-inn-new-buffalo-michigan.com

ONEKAMA

Portage Point Resort
8567 Portage Point Dr.
(231) 889-7500
portagepointresort.com

PENTWATER

Hexagon House Bed & Breakfast
760 Sixth St.
(231) 869-4102
hexagonhouse.com

SAUGATUCK

Bayside Inn
618 Water St.
(269) 857-4321
baysideinn.net

Belvedere Inn
3656 63rd St.
(269) 857-5777
thebelvedereinn.com

Hotel Saugatuck
900 Lake St.
(269) 416-0731
thehotelsaugatuck.com

Judson Heath Colonial Inn
607 Butler St.
(269) 416-0871
judsonheath.com

Maplewood Hotel
428 Butler St.
(269) 857-1771
maplewoodhotel.com

Rosemont Inn Resort B&B
83 Lakeshore Dr.
(269) 857-2637
rosemontinn.com

Wickwood Inn
510 Butler St.
(269) 857-1465
wickwoodinn.com

SOUTH HAVEN

Inn at the Park
233 Dyckman Ave.
(269) 639-1776
innpark.com

Old Harbor Inn
515 Williams St.
(269) 637-8480
oldharborinn.com

Sunset Inn
72 N. Shore Dr.
(269) 637-7777
sunsetinn.us

ST. JOSEPH

Boulevard Hotel
521 Lake Blvd.
(269) 983-6600
theboulevardinn.com

Duncan House Bed and Breakfast
1117 State St.
(269) 930-9698
duncanhousesjmi.com

Painted Turtle Inn
3205 Lakeshore Dr.
(269) 982-9463
paintedturtleinn.com

South Cliff Inn
1900 Lakeshore Dr.
(269) 983-4881
southcliffinnsj.com

UNION PIER

Goldberry Woods
9902 Community Hall Rd.
(269) 469-9800
goldberrywoods.com

OTHER ATTRACTIONS

Curious Kids Museum
415 Lake Blvd.
St. Joseph
(269) 983-2543
curiouskidsmuseum.org

Fernwood Botanic Gardens
13988 Range Line Rd.
Niles
(269) 695-6491
fernwoodbotanical.org

Manistee Fire Hall
281 First St.
Manistee
(231) 723-1549
manisteemi.gov

Ramsdell Regional Center for the Arts
101 Maple St.
Manistee
(231) 398-9770
ramsdelltheatre.org

Southwestern Michigan College Museum
58900 Cherry Grove Rd.
Dowagiac
(269) 782-1374
swmich.edu

Trillium Ravine
Niles

Inn at Union Pier
9708 Berrien St.
(269) 469-4700
innatunionpier.com

Lakeside Inn
15251 Lakeshore Rd.
(269) 469-0600
lakesideinns.com

WHITE CLOUD

The Shack
2263 W. Fourteenth St.
(231) 924-6683
shackcountryinn.com

Places to Eat in the Lake Michigan Region

BUCHANAN

Tabor Hill Winery & Restaurant
185 Mount Tabor Hill Rd.
(269) 422-1161
taborhill.com
Fine Dining

Wheatberry Tavern & Restaurant
15212 Red Bud Trail N.
(269) 697-0043
wheatberrytavern.com
Southwestern

GRANT

Grant Depot Restaurant
22 W. Main St.
(231) 834-7361
thegrantdepot.weebly.com
American

Old Iron Bar & Grill
189 S. Maple St.
(231) 834-5388
oldironbargrill.com
American

HOLLAND

Alpenrose Restaurant
4 E. Eighth St.
(616) 393-2111
alpenroserestaurant.com
Austrian

Boatwerks Waterfront Restaurant
216 Van Raalte Ave.
(616) 396-0600
boatwerksrestaurant.com
American

Crazy Horse Steak House–Saloon
2027 N. Park Dr.
(616) 395-8393
crazyhorsesteakhouse.com
Steakhouse

Hops at 84 East
84 E. Eighth St.
(616) 396-8484
hops84east.com
Gastropub

Mizu Sushi
99 E. Eighth St.
(616) 395-0085
mymizusushi.com
Japanese

Windmill Restaurant
28 W. Eighth St.
(616) 392-2726
windmill-restaurant
.business.site
American

LUDINGTON

Jamesport Brewing Company
410 S. James St.
(231) 845-2522
jamesportbrewingcompany
.com
Brewpub

Old Hamlin Restaurant
122 W. Ludington Ave.
(231) 843-4251
oldhamlin.com
American

P. M. Steamers
502 W. Loomis
(231) 843-9555
pmsteamers.com
American

The Q Smoke House
225 S. James St.
(231) 425-3933
ludingtonbbq.com
Barbecue

Table 14
130 W. Ludington Ave.
(231) 843-6555
table14restaurant.org
Southern

MONTAGUE

Big Cat Daddy Walleye Bar & Grill
8875 Water St.
(231) 893-6605
bcbwbarandgrill.com
American

Dog 'n Suds
4454 Dowling St.
(231) 894-4991
dog-n-suds.com
American

NEW BUFFALO

Beer Church Brewing Co.
24 S. Whitaker St.
(269) 586-3864
beerchurchbrewing.com
Brewpub

Bentwood Tavern
600 W. Water St.
(269) 469-1699
bentwoodtavern.com
American

Brewster's Italian Café
11 W. Merchant St.
(269) 469-3005
brewstersitaliancafe.com
Italian

Casey's New Buffalo
136 N. Whittaker
(269) 469-6400
caseysnewbuffalo.com
American

ONEKAMA

The Glenwood
4604 Main St.
(231) 889-3734
glenwoodrestaurant.com
American

PENTWATER

Boathouse Bar & Grille
5164 Monroe Rd.
(231) 869-4588
boathousebarandgrille.com
American

SELECTED CHAMBERS OF COMMERCE & TOURISM BUREAUS

Grand Haven Area Convention and Visitors Bureau
225 Franklin Ave.
Grand Haven 49417
(616) 842-4499
visitgrandhaven.com

Holland Area Visitors Bureau
76 E. Eighth St.
Holland 49423
(800) 506-1299
holland.org

Ludington Convention and Visitors Bureau
5300 W. US 10
Ludington 49431
(800) 542-4600
pureludington.com

Manistee Convention and Visitors Bureau
310 First St.
Manistee 49660
(877) 626-4783
visitmanisteecounty.com

Muskegon Convention and Visitors Bureau
610 Western Ave.
Muskegon 49440
(800) 250-9283
visitmuskegon.org

Saugatuck/Douglas Visitors Bureau
2902 Blue Star Hwy.
Douglas 49406
(269) 857-1701
saugatuck.com

South Haven Van Buren County Convention and Visitors Bureau
546 Phoenix St.
South Haven 49090
(800) 764-2836
southhaven.org

Southwestern Michigan Tourist Council
2300 Pipestone Rd.
Benton Harbor 49022
(269) 925-6301
swmichigan.org

Gull Landing
438 S. Hancock St.
(231) 869-3160
gulllanding.com
American

SAUGATUCK & DOUGLAS

Bowdies Chophouse
230 Culver St.
(269) 455-5481
bowdieschophouse.com
Steakhouse

The Butler
40 Butler St.
(269) 857-3501
butlerrestaurant.com
American

Everyday People Cafe
11 Center St.
(269) 857-4240
everydaypeoplecafe.com
Fine Dining

Marro's Italian Restaurant
147 Water St.
(269) 857-4248
marrosrestaurant.com
Italian

Mermaid Bar & Grill
340 Water St.
(269) 455-5949
mermaidofsaugatuck.com
Seafood

Saugatuck Brewing Company
2948 Blue Star Hwy.
(269) 857-7222
saugatuckbrewing.com
Brewpub

The Southerner
880 Holland St.
(269) 857-3555
thesouthernermi.com
Southern

SOUTH HAVEN

Captain Lou's
278 Dyckman Ave.
(269) 637-3965
captainloussouthhaven.com
Seafood

Idler Riverboat
515 Williams St.
(269) 637-8435
idlersouthhaven.com
Cajun

Tello Italian Bistro
524 Phoenix St.
(269) 639-9898
tellorc.com
Italian

STEVENSVILLE

Grand Mere Inn
5800 Red Arrow Hwy.
(269) 429-3591
grandmereinn.com
American

Tosi's
4337 Ridge Rd.
(269) 429-3689
tosis.com
Italian

ST. JOSEPH

Bistro on the Boulevard
521 Lake Blvd.
(269) 983-6600
theboulevardinn.com
Fine Dining

Clementine's Too
1235 Broad St.
(269) 983-0990
ohmydarling.com
American

Plank's Tavern on the Water
800 Whitwam Dr.
(269) 408-9108
American

221 Main — Restaurant & Cocktail House
221 Main St.
(269) 982-4000
221stjoe.com
Steakhouse

THREE OAKS

Froehlich's
26 N. Elm St.
(269) 756-6002
shopfroehlichs.com
Bakery & Cafe

Journeyman Distillery
109 Generations Dr.
(269) 820-2050
journeymandistillery.com
American

UNION PIER

Red Arrow Roadhouse
15710 Red Arrow Hwy.
(269) 469-3939
redarrowroadhouse.com
American

Timothy's Restaurant
16409 Red Arrow Hwy.
(269) 469-0900
timothysrestaurant.com
American

Northwest Michigan

In many ways Northwest Michigan is a continuation of the region stretching along Lake Michigan. It's accented by vast tracts of dunes, miles of beaches, and a handful of well-developed resort towns whose specialty shops bustle in the summer and winter. But it is also distinctly different.

This is "the land of many little bays," with scenic Grand Traverse Bay dominating the center of the region, Little Traverse Bay farther up the shoreline, and remote Sturgeon Bay at its northern tip. For many tourists this is Mackinaw City, a tour of Fort Michilimackinac, and a ferry ride to Mackinac Island, the summer resort island known throughout the country for its horse-and-carriage transportation and the Grand Hotel.

Most of all, this is Michigan's Cherry Country. Moderate weather from the Great Lakes and light soils help this region produce 80 to 85 percent of the state's total cherry crop. Drive along US 31 from Traverse City to Charlevoix in spring, and you'll pass rolling hills of trees in full bloom and air scented by cherry blossoms.

Arrive in July and you can enjoy the bountiful harvest these fruit farms produce. Along this 50-mile stretch of road, you'll pass dozens of farms and will undoubtedly see

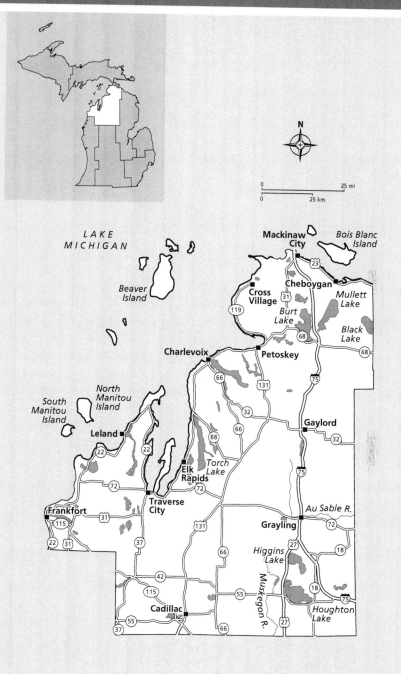

LAKE
MICHIGAN

Mackinaw
City

Bois Blanc
Island

Cheboygan

Cross
Village

Mullett
Lake

Beaver
Island

Burt
Lake

Black
Lake

Charlevoix

Petoskey

North
Manitou
Island

South
Manitou
Island

Leland

Gaylord

Torch
Lake

Elk
Rapids

Traverse
City

Frankfort

Au Sable R.

Grayling

Higgins
Lake

Muskegon R.

Cadillac

Houghton
Lake

harvesting crews "shaking" one tree after another, with the cherries ending up in a large metal tank of water.

You'll also see numerous roadside fruit stands that will be hard to pass up, and you shouldn't even try. The most common sweet cherries sold are Bing and Schmidt; tourists often call them black cherries, though if they are, the fruit is overripe. Look for cherries that are firm and dark maroon, and be prepared when you bite into your first one. The juice will explode from the cherry, dribble down your chin, and send your taste buds into a state of ecstasy. There are few things as wonderful in this state as a northern Michigan cherry in July.

Benzie County

One of the smallest counties in the state, Benzie is also one of the most scenic. It features rolling forested hills, spring-fed trout streams, towering sandy bluffs, and endless beaches along Lake Michigan and Crystal Lake, a body of water whose clarity lives up to its name. In the natural beauty of this north woods setting, Gwen Frostic emerged as one of Michigan's most noted poets and publishers from her background as an artist and a conservationist. Her love of nature had always been with her, but she began writing and carving blocks for prints in the mid-1940s in the blue-collar community of Wyandotte, south of Detroit. In the early 1960s she moved to a wooded spot 2 miles west of Benzonia and set up *Gwen Frostic Prints* on a personal wildlife sanctuary of 285 acres.

Her large gallery is housed in a building of native stone, glass, and old wood, which seeks to "bring the outdoors in" while blending into the natural surroundings. She accomplished that surprisingly well. Inside you'll walk below rough-cut beams past huge stone fireplaces and view the tumbling water of natural fountains. You'll be surrounded by Frostic's woodblock prints, tables covered with books of her poetry, and bird carvings by some of the country's leading wildlife carvers. There is a small library overlooking a pond where waterfowl usually are feeding, and another room displays all the honors she has received, including a Michigan governor's proclamation of an official "Gwen Frostic Day." Frostic passed away April 25, 2001, but her company and gallery live on.

Most impressive, perhaps, is the publishing aspect of the gallery. From a balcony above, visitors can view 12 original Heidelberg presses clanking away as workers print a wide selection of cards, notepaper, wall prints, and books, all using block designs carved by Frostic, featuring natural subjects and sold in the gallery.

Gwen Frostic Prints (231-882-5505; gwenfrostic.com) is at 5140 River Rd., 2 miles west of US 31 and 6 miles east of M 22 in Frankfort. The gallery is open

AUTHOR'S TOP TEN PICKS

Avalanche Bay Indoor Waterpark
1 Boyne Mountain Rd.
Boyne City
(866) 976-6972
avalanchebay.com

Beaver Island
Charlevoix
(231) 448-2505
beaverisland.org

Dennos Museum Center
1701 E. Front St.
Traverse City
(231) 995-1055
dennosmuseum.org

Grass River Natural Area
6500 Alden Hwy.
Bellaire
(231) 533-8576
grassriver.org

Gwen Frostic Prints
5140 River Rd.
Frankfort
(231) 882-5505
gwenfrostic.com

Historic Mill Creek Discovery Park
9001 US 23
Mackinaw City
(231) 436-4100
mackinacparks.com

Michigan Forest Visitor Center
Hartwick Pines State Park
4216 Ranger Rd.
Grayling
(989) 348-2537
michigan.gov/dnr

Pierce Stocking Scenic Drive
Empire
(231) 326-5134

South Manitou Island
Leland
(231) 256-9061
nps.gov

Tunnel of Trees Shore Drive and Legs Inn
6425 N. Lake Shore Dr.
Cross Village
(231) 526-2281
legsinn.com

Mon through Sat from 10 a.m. to 5 p.m. The presses are in operation only Mon through Fri.

More art in an unusual outdoor setting can be seen at the ***Michigan Legacy Art Park*** (231-378-4963; michlegacyartpark.org). This "gallery," a 30-acre forest at Crystal Mountain Resort on M 115 near Thompsonville at 12500 Crystal Mountain Dr., can be viewed any time of the year, even on cross-country skis in the winter, but is a perfect fall destination.

Scattered along a wooded ridge and reached by short footpaths are 35 major works of art, ranging from wind machines and poetry rocks to a winding piece that incorporates 3,500 cubic feet of oak logs. The park is open year-round from dawn to dusk, and in early October the outdoor sculptures are framed by colorful foliage that is almost as appealing as the art itself. Admission is $5 per person and free for children.

Hit the Trail in Michigan

When somebody in Michigan tells you to "hit the trail" they mean it . . . literally. That's because the state is blessed with thousands of trails and footpaths. The Michigan State Park system and four national forests are laced with nature walks, footpaths, and mountain bike areas, while crisscrossing the state are more than 2,000 miles of rail trails. Isle Royale National Park has 160 miles of hiking trails; Michigan State Forests have 65 pathways that total 750 miles. The North Country Trail crosses the Upper Peninsula and then the Lower Peninsula for a hike of 1,150 miles!

Where to find a path? Here are a few websites that will lead you to the trail of your choice:

michigantrails.org: Go to the Michigan Trails & Greenways Alliance and click on "Trail Finder" to locate a rail trail.

mmba.org: The Michigan Mountain Biking Association has information on more than 100 mountain bike trails across the state.

northcountrytrail.org: On the North Country Trail Association website you'll find maps and descriptions for much of the NCT in Michigan and other states.

michigantrailmaps.com: Maps, photos, and descriptions for hiking and backpacking trails around the state with the ability to locate them by county.

traversetrails.org: Traverse City is home to Michigan's premier trail network, all managed by TART Trails and used by cyclists, in-line skaters, Nordic skiers, hikers, and mountain bikers.

Of all the dunes along Lake Michigan, the best known are those in **Sleeping Bear Dunes National Lakeshore,** administered by the National Park Service. Thousands of people visit the area every year, and many head straight to the **Dune Climb,** a 150-foot-steep hill of sand located right off M 109 in Leelanau County. This is the park's most famous feature, a knee-bending climb up the towering dune and a wild run down through the soft sand. In addition, there are other aspects of the park, many having nothing to do with dunes and often overlooked by visitors who rush through the area in an afternoon.

The national lakeshore begins in Benzie County and includes one of the most scenic beaches on Lake Michigan. **Platte River Point** is a long, sandy spit divided from the mainland by the crystal

michigantrivia

In 1873 a canal was built to Lake Michigan that drained the water out of inland Crystal Lake. The level of Crystal Lake dropped 25 feet, creating the beautiful beaches that make it such a popular resort area today. The canal, on the other hand, eventually became a swamp.

clear Platte River. It's pure sand, this narrow strip, with endless Lake Michigan on one side, the knee-deep salmon and trout river on the other, and panoramas of towering dunes off in the distance. To reach it, sunbathers turn west from M 22 onto the marked Lake Michigan Road and follow it to the end. Then it's a quick wade through the rippling waters of the Platte River with dad holding a young one or the picnic lunch high on his shoulder. There is no bridge.

People at Platte River Point swim, build sandcastles, and beachcomb as on any other beach, but the favorite activity here is floating. They bring out an old inner tube or an air mattress, hike a few hundred yards up the point, and then let the Platte River give them a free ride right out to Lake Michigan if they wish. It's debatable who enjoys it more, the kids or the parents. If you don't have an inner tube, you can rent one from **Riverside Canoe Trips** (231-325-5622; canoemichigan.com) located on M 22 right before you turn off for the beach. Tubes for 1 to 4 people can be rented, and there are drop-off and pickup services for those who want to spend an afternoon "tubing" the Platte River from the Platte Lake to the Great Lake. Rental rates depend on the length of your float and the size of your tube.

You can relive the 1950s and catch a flick in Benzie County at the **Cherry Bowl Drive-In,** northern Michigan's last drive-in movie theater. The drive-in has been showing movies since 1953 and still honors that swinging era by

Best Cherry Pie in Northern Michigan

A sure way to start an argument in northern Michigan is to ask who bakes the best cherry pie in this land of cherries. You're bound to get a wide range of opinions, and one of them will surely be the Cherry Hut.

Located in Beulah, right on US 31, the *Cherry Hut* has been around since 1922 and has been run by the Case family since 1959. Locals call the smiling cherry on the restaurant sign "Cherry Jerry" and know it marks a good place to go for turkey dinners or giant cinnamon rolls.

But it's a thick slice of cherry pie, made with locally grown tart cherries and wrapped in a golden flaky crust, that is the Cherry Hut's claim to fame and why it has received recognition from such national media powerhouses as the *New York Times, People* magazine, *Bon Appétit* magazine, and National Public Radio. The fruit in the pies is so fresh that on the menu is this warning: "Cherries may contain an occasional pit."

The Cherry Hut (231-882-4431; cherryhut.com) is open Mon through Wed from 11 a.m. to 4 p.m. and Thurs through Sun 11 a.m. to 8 p.m. serving lunch and dinner. A slice of cherry pie is $3.95, and a whole pie is $9.75.

Might as well buy a whole pie—they're that good.

TOP ANNUAL EVENTS

MAY

National Morel Mushroom Hunting Festival
Boyne City
(231) 582-6222
bcmorelfestival.com

JULY

Alpenfest
Gaylord
(989) 732-6333
gaylordalpenfest.com

Au Sable River Canoe Marathon and River Festival
Grayling
(989) 348-4425
ausablecanoemarathon.org

Beaver Island Music Festival
Beaver Island
(231) 830-2883
bimf.net

National Cherry Festival
Traverse City
(231) 947-4230
cherryfestival.org

Traverse City Film Festival
(231) 392-1134
traversecityfilmfest.org

AUGUST

Buckley Old Engine Show
Buckley
(231) 269-3669
buckleyoldengineshow.org

Harbor Days
Elk Rapids
(231) 342-1058
elkrapidsharbordays.org

Suttons Bay Art Fair
Suttons Bay
(231) 590-9944
suttonsbayartfestival.org

Waterfront Art Fair
Charlevoix
(231) 547-2675
charlevoixwaterfrontartfair.org

SEPTEMBER

Harbor Springs Cycling Classic
Harbor Springs
(231) 526-2151
birchwoodinn.com

OCTOBER

Apple Festival
Charlevoix
(234) 547-2101
Visitcharlevoix.com

serving malts and chili fries in its diner while workers dress as if they were in the cast of *Happy Days*. Admission includes 2 movies, and kids 12 years old and younger get in free. Families haven't paid so little to see a movie since, well, the 1950s.

Cherry Bowl Drive-In (231-325-3413; cherrybowldrivein.com) is on US 31 just a mile west of Honor at 9812 Honor Hwy. Admission for adults is $10. Children age 12 and under admitted free with a paid adult. The drive-in promises that it will never show any movie stronger than PG-13 or any movie that glorifies teen drinking or drug use.

Leelanau County

For a view of spectacular dune terrain, take a ride along the ***Pierce Stocking Scenic Drive*** at Sleeping Bear Dunes National Lakeshore. Often called "the slowest, shortest, but most scenic stretch of pavement in the state," the drive is only a 7.4-mile loop but passes three stunning overlooks of the national lakeshore's perched dunes. Pierce Stocking, the self-taught naturalist who built the road in the early 1960s and operated it until his death in 1976, charged each car $2. The next year the National Park Service took over the road and changed its name to honor the man who'd built it.

The speed limit is only 15 miles per hour, but even that seems fast at times. Along with the scenic viewing points of the dunes and the sweeping shoreline, there are also 12 interpretive stops that correspond with information in a brochure provided at the fee station. From the Dune Overlook you can also walk the Cottonwood Trail, a short nature trail that leads you to within view of the Dune Climb. Feel energetic? There is also a bicycle lane along the road, but keep in mind that it's a very hilly bike ride. Above all, pack a lunch and plan to picnic at the Lake Michigan Overlook.

The entrance to Pierce Stocking Scenic Drive is on M 109, 3 miles north of the ***Sleeping Bear Dunes National Lakeshore Visitor Center*** (231-326-4700; nps.gov/slbe) in Empire. A weekly or annual vehicle pass is required to enter the drive.

The dunes are one of the main attractions of the area today. At the turn of the 20th century, however, the noted feature was the ***Manitou Passage,*** between the Manitou Islands and the mainland. During the heyday of Great Lakes shipping from the 1860s to 1920, when a hundred vessels might pass through on a single day, this was a shoal-lined shortcut they all took. The narrow Manitou Passage's shallow, reeflike shoals, and often violent weather, produced more than their share of shipwrecks, and eventually several lighthouses and lifesaving stations were built on the mainland and the islands.

One of them has been preserved by the National Park Service as ***Sleeping Bear Point Coast Guard Station Maritime Museum.*** The facility began its service in 1901 as a US Life-Saving Station and was actually situated on Sleeping Bear Point. When a migrating sand dune threatened to bury it in 1930, the US Coast Guard (having replaced the US Life-Saving Service) moved the buildings 1.5 miles toward Glen Haven. The station ended its duty in 1942 and now is a well-restored museum that tells the story of the US Life-Saving Service, which monitored the coastline all around the country.

Anywhere from 6 to 10 men would live at the remote station, and their former living quarters, a huge 2-story building, is now the main exhibit area.

It allows visitors a glimpse of the regimented work they performed and the isolated life they lived. Nearby the boathouse contains the lifesaving boats, complete with tracks down to the beach for a quick launch, and other equipment, including the beach cart. When ships ran aground within 400 yards of shore, the lifesavers would pull out the beach cart and use the small cannon on it to shoot a guideline to the distressed vessel. That rope was used to string more lines across the water, and a breeches buoy was sent to the ship on a pulley. Then, one by one, sailors would step into the breeches buoy and ride the line to the shore and safety. The museum is open daily from 11 a.m. to 5 p.m. from Memorial Day through Labor Day and noon to 5 p.m. Sat and Sun Sept through mid-Oct. A vehicle permit is required to enter. Check with the park headquarters (231-326-4726, nps.gov/slbe) for other information. During summer at 3 p.m. each day, there is a reenactment of a breeches buoy rescue drill using Raggedy Ann and Andy as shipwreck victims. Children are encouraged to participate in the drill.

From the Dune Climb, M 109 climbs to a panoramic view of Lake Michigan and the Manitou Islands then sharply descends to Grand Haven on the shores of Lake Michigan.

What used to be lumber baron D. H. Day's company town in the mid-1800s is now the ***Glen Haven Historic District*** with several of the buildings restored as museums.

Michigan's Famous Dune Climb

The Dune Climb in Sleeping Bear Dunes National Lakeshore is the most popular dune to climb in Michigan and possibly the country. Park officials estimate that more than 300,000 people climb it annually . . . or try to. This is no easy climb.

It's 130 feet to the top of the first hill at the Dune Climb and another 130 feet to the top of the second hill, or a total ascent of 260 feet. Jockey's Ridge on the Outer Banks of North Carolina, the largest dune on the Atlantic coast, is just a little over 100 feet. Then there is the fact that you're trudging through soft sand that gives way under each step. You may be taking a 12-inch step up the dune but the sand gives way underneath and your foot slides down 8 inches. Thus the net gain is only 4 inches, so in reality you will climb the dune three times before reaching the top.

The Dune Climb is a little easier to climb in the spring when the sand just below the surface is still damp, but it gets harder as thousands of visitors churn up the sand to dry in the summer sun. The easiest time to climb is a cool, cloudy day just after a rainfall. No matter when you climb or how hard it is, the effort is well spent as the view of Glen Lake to the east is stunning, one of the best in Sleeping Bear Dunes National Lakeshore.

You can view a collection of historic wooden boats and motors at the ***Cannery Boathouse,*** watch a blacksmith turn iron into horseshoes at the ***Blacksmith Shop,*** and step inside the ***Glen Haven General Store*** as it appeared in the 1920s.

A vehicle permit is required to visit Glen Haven. The General Store (231-334-3710) is open noon to 5 p.m. daily from July to Labor Day and the same hours on Fri, Sat, and Sun in May and June. The Blacksmith Shop and the Cannery Boathouse have slightly shorter hours, depending on volunteers.

Just east of Glen Haven is ***Glen Arbor,*** a small village on M 22 that bustles in the summer with shops, restaurants, and galleries. One of the most unusual stores is ***Cherry Republic,*** the self-proclaimed world's largest cherry retailer whose goal is "to put a cherry in every home."

Needless to say, everything here is cherry. In the Cherry Republic cafe you can choose from 12 different flavors of cherry ice cream, sip a glass of cherry lemonade, or feast on a cherry hot dog, cherry hamburger, or cherry chili. Next door in its Winery, people taste sparkling cherry wine or cherry ginger ale while its Great Hall of the Republic is a store stocked with everything from dried cherries and jars of cherry salsa to salad bowls carved out of cherry wood.

Cherry Republic (231-226-3016; cherryrepublic.com) is at 6026 S. Lake St. and open from 9 a.m. to 9 p.m. daily during the summer with shorter hours in the winter.

The village of Leland's trademark is a row of weathered dockside shacks along the Leland River that at one time housed commercial fishermen and today is a historic district known as ***Fishtown.*** All the commercial fishermen except Carlson's Fishery have disappeared from the strip, but their buildings have been preserved and now house specialty shops and stores. With its unique setting and atmosphere, Fishtown is the proper place to begin a nautical adventure to ***South Manitou Island,*** a portion of the Sleeping Bear Dunes National Lakeshore located 17 miles from Leland in Lake Michigan.

Island visitors board a ferry at the end of Fishtown and begin with a 90-minute cruise to South Manitou that passes a lighthouse and the scenic shoreline of Sleeping Bear Dunes. The island, with its hardwood forests and natural harbor, attracted settlers, a lighthouse, and a lifesaving station as early as 1840, and it has an interesting history. The ferry has a 4-hour layover at the national park dock, more than enough time to view the small museum at the visitor center, climb the 116 steps to the top of the lighthouse, and enjoy a lunch on a nearby beach.

For the more energetic, there are trails and old farm roads across the island, and it's possible to hike the 6-mile round-trip to the **Francisco Morazan** and return to the mainland the same day. The *Morazan* was a Liberian freighter

A Fall Driving Tour

If you visit Leelanau in the fall, use it as your springboard for a driving tour of Northwest Michigan. This popular color tour is a 190-mile drive that focuses on two delightful peninsulas: Leelanau and Mission. Both are crowned by a lighthouse in a park (Leelanau State Park and Old Mission Point) and feature more than two dozen vineyards where you can stop, taste, and purchase some of Michigan's finest wines. The other highlight of the tour is Sleeping Bear Dunes National Lakeshore. Fall colors peak between late September and mid-October. For a wine trail map check the **Leelanau Peninsula Vintners Association** website at lpwines.com.

that ran aground in November 1960 at the southwest corner of the island, and a large portion of the battered vessel is still visible above the waterline today. For the best adventure on South Manitou, camp for a night or two at Weather Station Campground, a national park facility that is free. The campground is a 1.5-mile hike in from the dock, and you can explore the tract of sand dunes on the west side of the island. The dunes, perched on bluffs high above Lake Michigan, are probably the remotest and least visited ones in the state.

All visitors must bring their own food to South Manitou, and campers have to be self-sufficient with tent, sleeping bags, and other equipment. Contact Manitou Island Transit (231-256-9061; manitoutransit.com) about the ferry that sails to the island daily from mid-May through Sept. The round-trip fare is $42 for adults and $21 for children 12 and under. Children 2 and under free.

The growing conditions in southwest Michigan that made Paw Paw the wine-producing center of the state are also found in **Leelanau** and **Old Missionary,** two peninsulas filled with fruit farms and a half dozen vineyards of surprising quality. All the vineyards have a tasting room, and an interesting day can be had visiting each of them.

At the tip of the Leelanau Peninsula is the 1,350-acre **Leelanau State Park.** From this park you can enjoy spectacular views along miles of lakeshore, from platforms on top of dunes and even from the tower of a lighthouse. In addition to a campground, picnic area, and hiking trails, the park also includes the historic Grand Traverse Lighthouse.

Built in 1916, the **Grand Traverse Lighthouse** is the most recent light in a series of lighthouses that have guided ships around the peninsula since 1852. Today it is an interesting maritime museum where visitors can tour the first floor, which has been restored as a lightkeeper's home of the 1920s, and then climb the tower for a grand view of Lake Michigan. The foghorn building next door has also been restored and is now a gift shop with a maritime theme.

Traverse City Film Festival

It's not the Sundance Film Festival, not yet, but it's getting there. When Academy Award–winning filmmaker Michael Moore, whose antiwar film *Fahrenheit 9/11* is the highest-grossing documentary of all time, founded the *Traverse City Film Festival* in 2005, many questioned his intentions. As it turns out, all he wanted to do was show great films near his home in northern Michigan.

The Traverse City Film Festival was a huge hit from the start. It has become one of the biggest film festivals in the Midwest, registering 80,000 admissions to nearly 100 screenings and pumping millions of dollars into the Traverse City tourism economy. Staged in the last week of July, the festival presents the best of independent, foreign, and documentary cinema in several indoor movie houses, including the city's State Theatre, the City Opera House, and the Old Town Playhouse. Even more popular are the classic movies shown free of charge on a giant, inflatable outdoor screen overlooking Grand Traverse Bay at dusk.

For more information on the Traverse City Film Festival or to book tickets, call (231) 392-1134 or go online at traversecityfilmfestival.org.

Leelanau State Park is 8 miles north of Northport on County Road 629. The Grand Traverse Lighthouse (231-386-7195; grandtraverselighthouse.com) is open 10 a.m. to 5 p.m. daily from June through Aug; noon to 4 p.m. daily May, Sept, Oct; noon to 4 p.m. on Sat and Sun in Nov. A state park vehicle permit is required to enter the park, and admission to the lighthouse is $4 for adults and $2 for children ages 5 to 12 years old.

Grand Traverse County

The most noted feature of the county is *Grand Traverse Bay,* a beautiful body of water with Traverse City at the south end and old Mission Peninsula splitting it up the middle. Its protected waters have become a haven for sailboats, catamarans, and sailboarders, but by far the most impressive vessel afloat during the summer is the **Manitou,** a replica of a two-masted, gaff-rigged, topsail 1800s coasting cargo ship. The 114-foot, 100-ton ship was built in 1983 to look and sail like a traditional schooner, and it's that love for old wooden boats that draws most of its passengers on deck. From May through Sept the *Manitou* offers 3 sailings daily, with 2-hour cruises at noon and 3 p.m. and a 2.5-hour evening sail with picnic meal—the most popular trip, of course—at 6:30 p.m. Passengers who dream about a life on the high seas go a step further and book a cabin on the *Manitou,* which at night becomes Michigan's only floating bed-and-breakfast. The quarters are tiny, with bunks built into the curves and angles of the hull. The head (bathroom) is shared, and the showers are back on land. In the evening guests wander topside to take in Traverse City lights shimmering on the bay or snuggle up in their bunks to be put to sleep by the gentle swells and the creaking of the wooden hull.

The *Manitou* is operated by the **Traverse Tall Ship Company** (231-941-2000; tallshipsailing.com). Its office and dock are at 13258 SW Bay Shore Dr. Daily cruises range from $44 to $60 for adults. Ranging from $775 to $845 per person, Windjammer cruises offer 3- and 4-day getaways featuring Stories of the Stars, Historic & Haunted Lighthouses, and more.

You can also enjoy the water from above through **Traverse City Balloon Tours,** which offers hot-air balloon rides across Grand Traverse Bay, often beginning at the Château Grand Traverse vineyards on Old Mission Peninsula. This may well be the most spectacular view from any hot-air balloon in Michigan, as below you lies the narrow peninsula, the rippling waters of the bay, Traverse City, and the endless rows of the cherry orchards to the northeast. Tethered rides and private charters are also available. Flight prices range from $249 for shared rides to $2,799 for a private flight for 6 to 8 passengers. Reservations are recommended for Traverse City Balloon Tours (231-818-8331; tcballoontours.com), last-minute urges to float above the bay can often be fulfilled.

For another unusual view of the bay, head to the highest ridge on the Mission Peninsula just before sunset. At this high point, Robert Begin built a beautiful vineyard, **Château Chantal Winery and Inn,** and included a brick terrace that overlooks both the West Arm and East Arm of Grand Traverse Bay. With vineyards and cherry orchards at your feet, you settle back with a glass of Chardonnay or a semidry Riesling and some sharp cheeses or freshly cut fruit and watch the sky melt into a collage of oranges and reds over the bays of northern Michigan.

Begin has built the unique winery on a former ridgetop cherry farm and named it after his daughter. You can stop by for a tour or a sip in the vineyard's wine-tasting and sales area, a great room that features hardwood floors, a polished granite bar top, and a grand piano in front of a 20-foot-wide bay window overlooking Grand Traverse Bay. Or you can simply stop for the night and unwind. That's because this winery is also a bed-and-breakfast, featuring 12 rooms and suites with sitting areas and private baths.

Château Chantal (800-969-4009; chateauchantal.com) is just off M 37 on Mission Peninsula, 12 miles north of Traverse City at 15900 Rue Devin. Tours are offered daily during summer at 1, 2, and 3 p.m. The tasting room is open year-round Sun through Wed from 11 a.m. to 5 p.m., Thurs through Sat from 11 a.m. to 8 p.m. Rooms range from $165 to $315 per night. An Executive

A Singer Named Jewel

In the mid-1990s, regulars at Ray's Coffeehouse in Traverse City remember they would hear a young singer with a distinctly sweet and high voice. By 1997 they knew her well, though she had been gone for years. Her name—the only name she goes by—was Jewel. Jewel was a student at the *Interlochen Fine Arts Camp* that summer and playing for tips in local coffeehouses. In time she would become one of the hottest singers on the pop music scene.

You can catch other possible future stars at the internationally acclaimed music camp that overlooks Green Lake near the town of Interlochen. The camp hosts more than 750 performances each year by faculty members, students, and big-name entertainers, with many of them taking place in its open-air pavilion overlooking Green Lake. For ticket information call (800) 681-5920 or visit interlochen.org.

Apartment with 2 bedrooms and 1 bath, full kitchen, fireplace, and 2 private decks is also available for about $600 per night.

One of Michigan's newest art museums is no stuffy gallery with ancient masterpieces in gilded frames. Located on the campus of Northwestern Michigan College, the **Dennos Museum Center** at 1410 College Dr. opened in 1991 after more than a decade in the planning.

The jewel of the museum is its permanent Inuit Art Gallery, a collection that began in 1960 and was housed in the college library. Today there are 550 pieces of sculptured soapstone and colorful prints depicting the harsh life and fascinating culture of these Arctic people. Carvings and prints depict hunters pulling a walrus out of the ice with a rope, kayaking through the open seas, bedding down in an igloo, and waiting patiently at a breathing hole in the frozen Arctic Ocean for a seal to surface.

But families and kids usually head for the Discovery Gallery, which combines art, science, and technology into an intriguing set of hands-on displays. One of the exhibits is the Recollections Piece. With the use of video cameras and computer-generated images, visitors can watch themselves "come alive in color" as they move in front of a room-size screen. The museum staff calls it "painting with your body."

From downtown Traverse City head north on US 31 to the Northwestern Michigan College campus. The Dennos Museum Center (231-995-1055; dennosmuseum.org) is on the small campus at 1701 E. Front St. The center is open Mon, Tues, Wed, Fri, and Sat from 10 a.m. to 5 p.m.; Thurs from 10 a.m. to 8 p.m.; and Sun from 1 to 5 p.m. Admission is $6 for adults and $4 for children.

More fun for kids can be found on the west side of Traverse City at the **Great Lakes Children's Museum,** whose hands-on and interactive exhibits are focused on water and the Great Lakes. At the museum's Lighthouse Keeper's Quarters, children can dress up and experience life in a lighthouse, while the Water Table lets them create standing waves and eddies and channel-flowing water a hundred different ways without getting too wet. Never been on a freighter before? There's one at the museum especially sized for kids to explore. When the sun is out, you want to be on the beach in Traverse City, but if it's raining, this is a great place to spend an afternoon with the family.

The Great Lakes Children's Museum (231-932-4526; greatlakeskids.org) is at 13240 SW Bayshore Dr. (M 22) and open 10 a.m. to 5 p.m. Tues through Sat, 1 to 5 p.m. on Sun. During the summer the museum is also open on Mon from 10 a.m. to 5 p.m. Admission is $7 per person.

If you're traveling just north of Traverse City on US 31 and pass a place called the **Music House,** turn off the car stereo. Strip the headphones and cellphones from your kids' ears. Then turn around and see how music used to be enjoyed. Housed in an old granary built in 1905, the Music House is a showcase for automatic musical instruments from the 1880s to the 1920s. Visitors are entertained rather than educated, as the hour-long tour is a musical journey with toe-tapping demonstrations ranging from small music boxes to one of the largest ballroom dance organs ever made.

Tours begin in the phonograph gallery, where a huge model of Nipper, the famous RCA Victor dog, greets you. There are rows of "talking machines" beginning from 1900 with their wax cylinders instead of records and colorful morning glory horns instead of speakers. In the main portion of the barn are larger musical machines set up in the environments in which they were enjoyed. The most impressive sight for many visitors is upstairs in the loft, which is home to the 30-foot facade of the Amaryllis dance organ. Built in 1922 for a palace ballroom in Belgium, the instrument plays a folded perforated cardboard book using hundreds of wooden and metal pipes along with percussion instruments.

The Music House (231-938-9300; musichouse.org) is located on a 180-acre cherry farm off US 31, 1.5 miles north of the highway's junction with M 72 or 8 miles north of Traverse City at 7377 US 31 North. It is open daily from "cherry blossoms through fall colors," or, to be more exact, May 1 through Oct 31, 10 a.m. to 4 p.m. Mon through Sat; noon to 4 p.m. Sun. From mid-Nov through Dec, it is open Sat and Sun 10 a.m. to 4 p.m. Admission is $16.50 for adults and $6 for children.

Antrim County

Speeding along US 131 in the middle of Antrim County, you pass one of the most spectacular inland viewing points in the Lower Peninsula, though you would never know it from this road. The side road to ***Deadman's Hill*** is 7 miles north of Mancelona, but there is little fanfare about the scenic overlook: Only a small brown sign points the way. Follow Deadman's Hill Road for 1.5 miles until it dead-ends at a pair of Department of Natural Resources pit toilets and a wood-chip path. Some 15 yards up the path is a spectacular panorama from a high point of more than 1,200 feet. You take in a 180-degree view of the Jordan River Valley stretching 15 miles to rugged hills that fill the horizon. During October the view from this spot is priceless, as the entire valley with the river winding through it is on fire with autumn reds and oranges.

Deadman's Hill earned its name from the logging era at the turn of the 20th century. The steep hills made the Jordan River Valley a treacherous place to log, and numerous accidents occurred. But people grieved the most in 1910 when "Big Sam" Graczyk, 21 years old and soon to be married, was killed while driving a team of horses and a big wheel of logs. The name for the ridge stuck. You can admire the view and have a picnic while sitting on the edge, and the more adventurous can hike the Jordan River Pathway, which begins at this point. Part of the trail is a 3-mile loop down to the river and back, or it can be turned into an 18-mile overnight walk to a hike-in campground for backpackers.

Where there is a boardwalk or similar planking along a trail, there is usually a swamp, marsh, or bog surrounding it. At the ***Grass River Natural Area,*** there are an awful lot of boardwalks. Some trails are nothing but boardwalks, because a good slice of this 1,165-acre Antrim County park is sedge meadow, marsh, and cedar swamp.

Grass River itself is only 2.5 miles long and just chest deep. It's a crystal clear waterway that connects Lake Bellaire to Clam Lake as part of Antrim County's "Chain of Lakes." But the extensive floating sedge mats and other wetlands that surround the river are so intriguing that they prompted a fundraising effort to buy the land and dedicate it as a natural area in 1976.

They've been building boardwalks ever since. Along with an interpretive center, which features several rooms of displays and a small bookstore, Grass River has a 5-mile trail system that is marked with interpretive posts and winds through a variety of habitats.

The Woodland/Wildfire Trail is the longest at 2.2 miles; the quarter-mile Tamarack Trail is designed to be accessible for people with disabilities. But to many the Sedge Meadow Trail is the most enjoyable. It's one long boardwalk—almost every step of it is on wood—that passes through a variety of wetlands where plants have been identified and numbered posts correspond with information in a trail guide. Eventually the trail emerges at the edge of Grass Lake where observation platforms and towers have been built on the boardwalk along with a series of benches.

From US 131 in Mancelona, head west on M 88 toward Bellaire and within 2 miles continue on Alden Highway (County Road 618). The entrance road to Grass River Natural Area (231-533-8314; grassriver.org) is off CR 618 before you reach Alden at 6500 Alden Hwy. Exciting news happened in October 2011 when the long-awaited (original plans were developed 42 years ago) Grass River Center was opened. The building sits exactly where it was planned, in a fern field off the cabin trail. The building offers teaching facilities, restrooms, and covered areas for water quality studies, eating, meeting or just plain resting.

The trails are open from dawn to dusk. The interpretive center is open Tues through Fri from 10 a.m. to 4 p.m. June through Aug. Winter hours are 11 a.m. to 4 p.m. Sat and Sun.

Charlevoix County

South of Charlevoix off US 31 is yet another state park along Lake Michigan. *Fisherman's Island State Park* possesses many of the same features as the other parks: 3 miles of sandy shoreline, excellent swimming areas, scenic views of the Great Lake. But Fisherman's Island also has a couple of unique features. Not nearly as popular or crowded as some other locales, the park offers 10 rustic campsites right on Lake Michigan. Each one is tucked away in the trees with a table and a spot to pitch a tent only a few feet from the lapping waters of the lake. These are some of the most beautiful campsites in the Lower Peninsula, and naturally they are the first to be chosen in the campground. But you can reserve those particular sites, or any other in the park, up to 6 months in advance through the *Michigan Campground Central Reservation System* (800-447-2757; midnrreservations.com). The other noted feature of the state park is the *Petoskey stones.* The state stone is actually petrified coral, a leftover fragment of the many coral reefs that existed in the warm-water seas from Charlevoix to Alpena some 300 million years ago. Today the stones are collected by rock hounds, and many of them end up polished and used in jewelry, paperweights, and other decorative items. Dry stones are silvery with no apparent markings to the untrained eye, but when the rocks are wet, it's easy to see the ringlike pattern that covers them. Rock hounds searching for the stones are usually seen closely inspecting the waterline or washing off handfuls of rocks in the lake.

Splashing & Sliding at Avalanche Bay

In 2005 Michigan's largest ski resort, **Boyne Mountain Resort,** opened the state's largest indoor water park, **Avalanche Bay.** While some traditionalists in the ski industry wondered about combining waterslides with ski slopes, the indoor park was envisioned as a solution to Michigan's finicky winters and a way to attract more families in the summer to what is basically a golf resort.

Now while dad is out hitting the links, the kids are making a splash in 88,000 square feet of spraying gushers, falling water, splash pools, and wild rides. To the theme of a Swiss village hit by an avalanche, the park offers more than a dozen rides and attractions all surrounding Splasherhorn Mountain, a 3-story structure that at the sound of a horn dumps 800 gallons of water on the unsuspecting below. Kids can also float down a lazy river in an inner tube, ride the wild Vertigo tube slide, even surf a simulated rip curl. The indoor water park is always 84 degrees and open year-round.

Parents can join in the watery fun or soak away weary ski muscles in a pair of giant Jacuzzis known as Glacier Hot Springs.

Boyne Mountain is on US 131 just south of Boyne Falls at 1 Boyne Mountain Rd. For information on skiing, lodging, or golf vacation packages call the resort at (855) 688-7024 or go online at boynemountain.com.

The 2.5-mile park road begins at the ranger station and ends at the sandy beaches of the state park but along the way passes an extended rocky shoreline. Many gem enthusiasts say this is one of the best places in northern Michigan to find Petoskey stones. Stop at the ranger station for a park map and information on the famous stones. There is a vehicle fee to enter Fisherman's Island State Park (231-547-6641) and an additional charge to camp overnight.

The Great Lakes, which have blessed Michigan with miles of magnificent shoreline, also have given it many islands that have become unique destinations for visitors. The most popular is **Mackinac Island,** a nonmotorized resort (no cars or buses) that tourists flock to each summer, taking ferries out of Mackinaw City on the Lower Peninsula or St. Ignace across the Mackinac Bridge on the Upper Peninsula. There are also many islands without the crowds, commercialization, and fudge shops of Mackinac that make for an interesting side trip. One of the largest is **Beaver Island,** reached by a ferry from Charlevoix.

Known as Emerald Isle for its strong Irish heritage, Beaver Island lies 32 miles northwest of Charlevoix and is 55 square miles of forests, inland lakes, and farms. Its recorded history dates to 1832, when Bishop Frederic Baraga, the "Snowshoe Priest," brought Christianity to a small Indian settlement here. The island's most bizarre period began in 1847 after James Jesse Strang arrived. Strang and his band of Mormon followers had just broken away from the leadership of Brigham Young and established St. James, the island's only village. Eventually Strang would crown himself "king of Beaver Island" and rule the island and its religious sect with an iron fist before being shot in 1856 by a disgruntled subject. Irish immigrants followed in the 1870s to fish the waters of northern Lake Michigan, and today many of the 551 people who live year-round in or near St. James have roots back in Ireland.

Beaver Island has an assortment of lodge and hotel accommodations and restaurants for overnight visitors, but on Saturdays in July and August, it also makes an ideal day trip. You can depart from Charlevoix at 8:30 a.m. on the ferry and reach the island by 10:30 a.m. for a 6-hour visit before catching the last ferry back to the mainland at 5:30 p.m. In St. James there are several museums, including the **Old Mormon Print Shop** (231-448-2254), which was built by King Strang in 1850, and the Marine Museum, a 1906 net shed dedicated to the time when the area bustled with fishermen.

The museums are open from June through Aug. Hours are 11 a.m. to 5 p.m. Mon through Sat, noon to 3 p.m. Sun. There is a small admission charge.

Another interesting attraction in St. James is the **Toy Museum and Store** (231-448-2480). Once known as "the last nickel toy store in the US," the Toy Museum is still affordable to anybody on a weekly allowance: Chinese fans 3 for a dollar, a disappearing dagger for 75 cents, and green army men at a nickel apiece. Suspended from the high-peaked ceiling is the "museum," an interesting collection of antique toys that range from foot-pedal Roadsters and "rocket cars" from the 1930s to clay marbles and dolls that predate the 1900s. The shop at 37970 Michigan Ave. is open daily from 11 a.m. to 4 p.m. from Memorial Day weekend to Labor Day.

You can also rent a mountain bike or a jeep and tour the island, which has more than 100 miles of roads, most of them dirt and gravel. On a pleasant summer day, this is a most delightful adventure and a great way to see the old farmhouses, inland lakes, remote shoreline, and lighthouse located outside St. James. Pack a picnic lunch and plan on driving 3 to 4 hours to circle Beaver Island.

The **Beaver Island Boat Co.** (888-446-4095; bibco.com) operates the ferry and charges $55 for a round-trip adult ticket and $30 for children ages 5 to 12 during nonpeak times and $65 for adults and $40 for children ages 5 to 12 during peak times. You can rent a vehicle for $65 a day from **Burton Car Rental** (231-838-2883; stjamesboatshop.com) or a mountain bike from **Lakesports Rentals** (231-448-2166). For a complete list of businesses, lodging, and sites, contact the **Beaver Island Chamber of Commerce** (231-448-2505; beaverisland.org).

A number of writers have ties to Northwest Michigan but none as famous as Ernest Hemingway, who spent the summers of his youth at his family's cottage on Walloon Lake. Hemingway buffs often tour the area to see artifacts and places that made their way into his writing. Most begin in Petoskey's Little Traverse Historical Museum (see Emmet County) and then head down US 141 past Walloon Lake. Some go to **Hemingway Point** on the south shore of Lake Charlevoix, to which the young author once fled (it was owned by his uncle) when being pursued by a game warden.

Of course, almost all eventually stop at the **Horton Bay General Store,** located across the lake on Boyne City Road. Built in 1876 with a high false front, the store's most prominent feature is its large front porch with benches and stairs at either end. Hemingway idled away some youthful summers on that porch and fished nearby Horton Creek for rainbow and brook trout. He also celebrated his first marriage in Horton Bay's Congregational Church, and eventually the general store appeared in the opening of his short story "Up in Michigan." The Horton Bay General Store has had a string of owners, but remarkably little has changed about its appearance. It is still the classic general store; only the bright red benches outside receive a new coat of paint every now and then.

michigantrivia

By following Michigan's Chain of Lakes (Mullett, Burt, and Crooked Lakes), Native Americans and fur traders had only one short portage in traveling from Lake Huron to Little Traverse Bay on Lake Michigan. Thus they avoided a paddle through the Straits of Mackinac and facing its strong winds and wicked currents.

You enter through a flimsy screen door with a bell above it, and inside you find the worn wooden floors and shelves stacked with canned goods and other merchandise. There is an old wooden tub filled with ice and cold drinks, a small freezer that holds 4 or 5 flavors of ice cream, and the lunch counter where the morning coffee drinkers gather. Then as your eyes wander toward the ceiling, you realize this is more a preserved shrine to Hemingway than a store for the local residents. On one wall hang guns, old traps, mounted deer heads, and a panel of photographs of the author during his days in Northwest Michigan. The Horton Bay General Store (05115 Boyne City Rd.; 231-582-7827; hortonbaygeneralstore.com) has evolved to include a B&B upstairs and a tavern in the back with a garden patio that serves breakfast and lunch seven days a week. At press time, the whole shebang was up for sale so call to find out the latest.

From Horton Bay you can continue around Lake Charlevoix in a scenic drive that will take you past Young State Park, through the historic downtown area of Boyne City, and near Hemingway Point, where Ferry Road abruptly ends at the South Arm of the lake. If you want to continue, you'll have to take passage on the *Ironton Ferry,* one of Michigan's most delightful boat rides, even though it's only 5 minutes long.

Ferry service on the South Arm dates back to 1876, when the first barge was pulled back and forth by horses. It was apparently a moneymaker right from the start, as the 1884 rates are still listed on the side of the ferry office. The present ferry was installed in 1926 and is guided by cables 35 feet down on the lake bottom, making it, say officials, one of two cable-operated automobile ferries in the country.

That's only one of the Ironton Ferry's many little oddities, the reason it was once featured in *Ripley's Believe It or Not.* Consider its size (so small it holds only 4 cars), the length of its trip (a mere 575 feet of water), and the fact that it doesn't have a rudder. Perhaps most unusual is that the Ironton Ferry doesn't make regularly scheduled crossings. It's operated on demand because the South Arm is so narrow that passengers can be seen waiting on the other side.

The ferry operates from mid-Apr to Thanksgiving Eve, 6:30 a.m. to 10:50 p.m. daily. A trip across is $3 per vehicle, 50 cents per walker, $1 per person with bicycle.

On the shores where Hemingway's family had their cottage are a number of historic buildings, including the *Walloon Lake Inn.* The century-old inn has a number of rooms upstairs, a fine lakeside restaurant downstairs, where you can arrive by car or boat.

Walloon Lake Inn at 4178 West St. (231-535-2999; walloonlakeinn.com), in the heart of Walloon Lake Village, is 8 miles south of Petoskey and reached from US 31 by heading west a quarter of a mile on M 75.

For a wonderful respite, plan to spend some time in the resort community of Walloon Lake where the lovely *Hotel Walloon* (231-535-5000, hotelwalloon.com) makes a luxurious home base at 4127 N. M 75. Opened in May 2015, the three-story year-round waterfront Hotel Walloon offers 32 rooms with such pleasures as heated marble floors in guest bathrooms, a private beach, and lakeside spa tub.

michigantrivia

At one time Michigan was a favorite nesting ground for the passenger pigeon. Vast quantities of beechnuts attracted them, and each spring immense flocks arrived, literally darkening the skies for hours at a time as they flew over.

At Crooked Lake in Emmet County, a nesting in 1878 covered 90 square miles, drawing the attention of thousands of hunters who quickly converged on the area. Millions of birds were killed, packed in barrels, and shipped to Petoskey. Such wanton slaughter led to the extinction of the passenger pigeon by 1914.

Next to the hotel is the ***Barrel Back Restaurant*** (231-535-6000, barrel-back.com), a year-round upscale dining spot that opened in 2013 overlooking the lake. The restaurant is open daily at 8:30 a.m. for breakfast, lunch, and dinner. It closes at 9:30 p.m. The menu for the fresh American cuisine changes frequently so look for specials online. Barrel Back features almost two dozen beers on tap. Under the restaurant is a 60-slip marina operated out of Tommy's Michigan (231-535-6039; tommyswalloon.com), a water sports retailer.

Barrel Back Restaurant's namesake refers to the iconic, curved barrel backs of the classic wooden boats that cruised Walloon Lake in the 1930s, '40s, and '50s and still do today. Look for the 1942 Chris Craft boat that restaurant owner Matt Borisch often keeps at a private dock in front of the restaurant. The 26-foot runabout has a barrel back design.

Emmet County

Housed in Petoskey's Chicago and West Michigan railroad depot, which was built in 1892, the ***Little Traverse Historical Museum*** is the first logical stop on any Hemingway tour. The display case is small but contains photographs, other memorabilia, and some rare first-edition books that Hemingway autographed for his friend Edwin Pailthorp, whom he visited in Petoskey in 1947. There is also a display case devoted to another famous writer, Bruce Catton, who was born in the Emmet County town and grew up in nearby Benzonia. Later Catton would pen *A Stillness at Appomattox,* for which he won a Pulitzer Prize in 1953. The original manuscript of that book and other personal artifacts are in the museum.

The museum (231-347-2620; petoskeymuseum.org) is at 100 Depot Ct. on Petoskey's picturesque waterfront and open Memorial Day to Sept from 10 a.m. to 4 p.m. Mon through Fri and 1 to 4 p.m. Sat and Sun. Admission is $3 for adults, free for children under 10.

From the well-developed resort town of Harbor Springs, M 119 heads north and hugs the coastline for 31 miles until it ends at Cross Village. The drive is scenic, but not for the views of Lake Michigan you might expect when tracing it on a map. This is the ***Tunnel of Trees Shore Drive,*** a narrow road that climbs, drops, and curves its way through the thick forests along the rugged coast. At times the branches from trees at each side of the road merge overhead to form a complete tunnel, shading travelers even when the sun is beaming down at midday. You finally emerge from the thick forest at Cross Village, a small hamlet and home of ***Legs Inn.***

The inn is the creation of one man, Stanley Smolak, a Polish immigrant who fell in love with this part of Michigan and moved here from Chicago in 1921.

Smolak quickly made friends with the local Ottawa Indians, who inducted him into their tribe as Chief White Cloud. Then in 1930, with a Polish past, a love for northern Michigan, and his new Indian heritage, Smolak began building the inn. He combined the driftwood and stones he found along the shoreline to construct an unusual building on a bluff overlooking Lake Michigan. From the outside the architecture of the Legs Inn is bizarre at best, but the interior is even more fascinating, for Smolak loved to carve the driftwood. He would take a piece, see something in it, and then whittle away. The inn has several rooms, all filled with Smolak's driftwood sculpture.

Naturally, the menu reflects Smolak's homeland and includes entrees of pierogi, gotabki, and bigos, a hearty Polish stew. The restaurant even serves a beer imported from Poland. The Legs Inn (231-526-2281; legsinn.com) is located in the heart of Cross Village at 6425 N. Lake Shore Dr. (you'll know it when you see it) and is open mid-May to mid-Oct from noon to 8 p.m. and even later in July and Aug. Dinner entrees on the menu range from $20 to $30. Each freestanding cottage has two bedrooms, bathroom, living room, and equipped kitchen. It does not have air conditioning, television, telephones, or Wi-Fi. Rooms are priced from $98 to $228 depending on the night and the season.

Cheboygan County

The residents are certainly friendly in **Cheboygan.** Arrive in this Lake Huron town of 4,826 during the summer or early fall and the first place people want you to go is the jail. Stay as long as you like, they say. Plan to spend a few minutes in each cell, because that's where you'll find the pride and heritage that is Cheboygan—in the **Historical Cheboygan County Museum** housed in the old county jail. At this museum you not only get to view the history of the area in an interesting series of displays and exhibits, you also have the opportunity to wander through a 19th-century jail. It's debatable which is more fascinating.

Built in 1890, the facility served as the area jail until 1970, when the county board of commissioners gave the building to the historical society. You enter the attached brick home where the county sheriff and his family lived, and the first room you walk into is a huge kitchen, where his wife cooked not only for him and his family but for all the prisoners as well. From the home you pass through a metal door, entering the jail. Little has changed about the facility except that the historical society has filled each cell with a display, ranging from the town's first hardware stores to its maritime history to an exhibit on logging. Call it "history behind bars."

The museum is at Huron and Court Streets at 427 Court St. From US 23 within town, head south on M 27 and then west on Court Street for 3 blocks.

The jail museum (231-627-9597; cheboyganhistory.org) is open from early July through early Oct from 1 to 4 p.m. Tues through Sat. Adult admission is $5; children have free admission.

Built in 1995, Spies Heritage Hall houses primary exhibits which chronicle the history of Cheboygan County. Exhibits include the Native American presence in the Straits Area, the military service of local residents in wars from the Civil War to Iraq and Afghanistan, the maritime industry, and the lumber industry.

A Native American log cabin built in the mid-1800s was moved to the center. It was one of three remaining cabins when the Cheboygan County sheriff dispatched deputies in 1900 to foreclose on property because of unpaid taxes. The cabins were part of a Native American village on Burt Lake in the late 1800s. Most of the cabins were burned. The cabin had been used as an icehouse and then a storage shed. When it was moved to the history center, the cabin was taken apart log by log. Each log was numbered to permit exact reconstruction of the cabin. Notice the notched corner construction, which assured a close fit and stability. Originally, the chinking—the filler between the logs—was moss, clay, or mud. The roof is covered with wood shingles. The original floor was hard-packed dirt, which could be swept or even scrubbed if it was packed hard enough. The cabin had a loft for storage and sleeping. The ladder to the loft could be pulled up at night for security. The door is made of wood split lengthwise. It is locked by unknotting the rope pull and pulling it through to the inside at night. By removing the rope, the door could not be opened from the outside.

Another intriguing historical spot in Cheboygan County is just a few miles north at 9001 US 23. ***Historic Mill Creek Discovery Park*** is an excellent destination for families, especially for those with children who think history is "borrrring!" The Mackinac Historic State Park was opened in 1984 after the site was "rediscovered" in 1972 by a local archaeologist. It dates to the 1780s, when a Scottish trader named Robert Campbell obtained a 640-acre tract of land around the only stream in the area with enough power to operate a mill,

michigantrivia

You can only drive north on I-75 so many times before the billboard about a "man-eating clam" entices you off the highway at exit 326 and into the parking lot of Sea Shell City.

Inside the huge gift shop, between the rows of rubber tomahawks and other tacky souvenirs for tourists, is a 505-pound giant clam (*Tridacna gigas*) from the Philippines. This is reputed to be the largest mollusk in the world and "has the capacity to snuff out a man's life with one sharp snap of its shells." Reality is that the clam is a vegetarian that feasts on algae.

making the creek one of the oldest industrial centers in the Midwest. There was a great demand for lumber at the time, since the British were moving their military post from Fort Michilimackinac at the tip of the Lower Peninsula to Mackinac Island. The island's high limestone bluffs made it easier to defend against the Americans, who were thought to be on their way.

Today the 625-acre park is a combination of re-created history and high adventure. You learn the history of Mill Creek from exploring the interactive exhibits in its museum and watching interpreters cut logs at a reconstructed sawmill or by hand in a saw pit. Then you can hit the park's 3.5 miles of forest trail for a little adventure that includes the Forest Canopy Bridge, Nature Trail Climbing Wall, the 50-foot-high Treetop Discovery Tower, and Eagle's Flight Zip Line that sends you flying through the canopy over Mill Creek like an eagle. History has never been so fun.

The park is reached from I-75 by taking exit 338 and heading south on US 23 for 4 miles to 9001 W. US 23. Mill Creek (231-436-4226; mackinacparks.com) is open from May through mid-Oct from 9 a.m. to 5 p.m. daily, until 6 p.m. from mid-June through early Sept, and from 11 a.m. to 5 p.m. Mon through Fri and from 9 a.m. to 5 p.m. on Sat and Sun from Sept through early Oct. Admission is $9.50 per adult and $7 per child ages 5 to 12.

Otsego County

The eastern elk, once a common sight to Indians in the Lower Peninsula, disappeared from Michigan around 1877. After several unsuccessful attempts to reintroduce the animal in the early 1900s, seven Rocky Mountain elk were released in Cheboygan County in 1918, and today biologists believe Michigan's herd of 1,400 elk descended from those animals. The herd ranges over 600 square miles in Cheboygan, Montmorency, Otsego, and Presque Isle Counties, but its heaviest concentration is in the wilderness areas of the *Pigeon River Country State Forest.*

The 95,000-acre state forest features rustic campgrounds, miles of hiking trails, and fishing opportunities, but come fall most visitors have their hearts set on seeing the elk. As big as the adults are (ranging from 700 to 900 pounds), they're tough to spot during the summer, for they break up into small groups or are solitary and lie low in the thick forest. But in September the bulls begin the "bugling season," when they move into open areas and form harems of 15 to 20 cows by calling out to them with a high-pitched whistlelike sound. Watchers will see from 30 to 100 elk gathered in an open field and then hear the most amazing sound—the huge bull making his high-pitched mating call.

To witness one of Michigan's great wildlife scenes, head to the Pigeon River forestry field office (989-983-4101), 13 miles east of Vanderbilt, just off Sturgeon River Road at 996 Twin Lakes Rd. The office is open from 8 a.m. to 4:30 p.m. Mon through Fri, and workers can provide maps and suggest open areas to view the elk. The rule of thumb is that the 2 weeks on either side of Sept 20 are the best time to catch the bugling, or rutting, season. Plan to be at an open area just before dawn or dusk, and sit quietly to await the movement of the herd. One traditional spot to see elk is off Ossmun Road near Clark Bridge Road northeast of the forestry office. Here you will find a large open field, a small parking lot off the road, and a few elk viewers waiting patiently during September.

If you can't find elk in Pigeon River Country State Forest, head south to **Gaylord's City Elk Park.** The city herd began in 1995 when three elk needed a home after a local nature center closed. Today the herd numbers around 70 and lives on a 108-acre enclosure. A few of the bulls tip the scales at well over 800 pounds and stand 6 feet tall, donning massive horns during the fall and winter and dropping them in the spring.

The most popular viewing area of Elk View Park (800-345-8621) is adjacent to the Elk's Lodge (how appropriate!) and reached by departing I-75 at exit 279 and heading north on S. Otsego Avenue and then east on Grandview Boulevard to 116 Grandview Blvd.

Crawford County

The best-known attraction in this county is **Hartwick Pines State Park** and its **Michigan Forest Visitor Center,** the interpretive center dedicated to Michigan's lumber era at the turn of the 20th century. On the outside the building, decks, and wooden walkways blend naturally into a grove of pines. Inside there are sitting areas with glass walls looking out over the ancient trees, the reason the state park was created.

The hands-on displays, dedicated to Michigan's vast forests, are excellent. There is a mounted wolf that looks so real a sign was needed saying PLEASE DON'T PET THE WOLF. Instead you touch a piece of fur and immediately a pack of wolves begins to howl all around you. The Living Giant is a white pine that talks to you, explaining what heartwood is or how its needles produce food. But the most captivating display is "Reading the Rings." The computerized program displays a cross section of a white pine. Touch one of its rings and the screen flashes to what happened that year, including 1994 when the tree was blown down in a windstorm and cut up for firewood.

The Holy Waters

The most revered trout stream east of the Mississippi River is an 8-mile stretch of the Au Sable River east of Grayling that is known among fly-fishers as the Holy Waters. It was on the banks of the Holy Waters that Trout Unlimited was founded in the 1950s.

Ironically, trout are not native to the river but were introduced. The original fish of the Au Sable was grayling, the trout-like fish with the distinctively high dorsal fin. These were first classified by biologists in 1864, and within a decade, after railroads had penetrated northern Michigan, anglers from all over the country were arriving in Grayling to fish for grayling.

The fishing was so easy that anglers could often catch three or four grayling at a time by tying multiple hooks to their line. Such heavy fishing pressure and the deforestation caused by the lumber industry made the Michigan grayling rare by the turn of the 20th century and extinct by 1930.

For more on the history of fly-fishing or to see a grayling stop at the *Crawford County Historical Museum* (989-348-4461; crawfordcountyhistoricalsociety.com) at 97 Michigan Ave. in Grayling. The historical complex surrounds the Grayling Depot and in the depot itself is an intriguing first-floor exhibit of trout fishing in the Au Sable. Along with century-old bamboo rods and flies are displays on early Au Sable boatbuilders, guides, and a mounted grayling that measures 18 inches in length. The museum is open from Memorial Day to Labor Day Sun to Thurs from 10 a.m. to 6 p.m., Fri from 10 a.m. to 5 p.m., and Sat from 9 a.m. to 8 p.m.

From the interpretive center you can walk the *Virgin Pines Trail* that loops through a 49-acre stand of 300-year-old virgin white pine. Along the way you will pass through a reconstructed loggers' camp with various lumber machines on display, including "Big Wheels" that were used to haul giant logs out of the woods.

The state park (989-348-7068) is north of Grayling and can be reached by exiting I-75 at M 93 and following the park signs. The Michigan Forest Visitor Center is open from 10 a.m. to 6 p.m. daily from Memorial Day to Labor Day and 9 a.m. to 4 p.m. the rest of the year. A vehicle permit is required to enter the park.

In 1959, in a cabin called the Barbless Hook on the banks of the Au Sable River, 16 anglers met one evening and formed *Trout Unlimited.* Today TU is the most recognized organization dedicated to the protection of cold-water fisheries, and it's no surprise to anybody who tosses a fly in search of a trout in Michigan that it was founded in Crawford County.

The county is steeped in the history of trout fishing and nowhere is that better seen than tiny *Lovells,* a village split by the North Branch of the Au Sable and home of the ***Lovells Museum of Trout Fishing History*** (989-889-5580; lthsmuseums.org). Set up in 2002 by the Lovells Township Historical Society, the cabin is the only museum in the state dedicated to the history of trout fishing, particularly fly-fishing. Its display cases are filled with rods, reels, the fly collection of noted flytier Bob Smock, and a lot of historical photos and articles from Lovells' golden era of fly-fishing at the turn of the 20th century.

Whitefish on a Plank

The most valuable fish caught in the Great Lakes isn't walleye, lake trout, or even perch, it's whitefish (*Coregonus clupeaformis*). During the summer Michigan restaurants from the Thumb to the Upper Peninsula serve it every way imaginable: from baked in a pastry puff to grilled on a cedar plank. This is especially true in the northwest corner of the Lower Peninsula.

Whitefish is a deep-bodied fish characterized by a small head with a blunt snout overhanging the lower jaw. The average commercially caught whitefish is 17 to 22 inches in length and weighs 2 to 4 pounds, but in 1918 a 41-pounder was landed in Lake Superior, still the heaviest on record. The fish itself isn't actually white; rather, the skin is greenish-brown on the back, with silver sides and a silvery-white belly.

But its delicate flesh is white and possesses such an exceptional flavor that whitefish has been extolled ever since the first commercial nets were dropped into the Great Lakes. In 1918 the renowned *Fannie Farmer's Boston Cooking School Cookbook* called whitefish "the finest fish found in the Great Lakes."

There is still active commercial fishing for whitefish in northern Michigan, and it's possible to purchase fillets that were swimming just the day before. The best-known commercial shop is ***Carlson's*** (231-256-9801; carlsonsfish.com) at 205 River St. in Leland's Fishtown that sells both fresh and smoked whitefish throughout the summer.

Even better is to let somebody else prepare it for you. Whitefish grilled on cedar planks is the most popular way to serve it, but restaurants also encrust it in ground pecans or macadamia nuts, blacken it Cajun style, or sauté the fillets in a white wine, garlic, and caper sauce, to name but a few of the ways whitefish is served. A couple of the restaurants where you can find good fish would be ***The Cove*** (231-256-9834; thecoveleland.com), at 111 W. River St. in Leland, and ***Old Mission Tavern*** (231-223-7280; oldmissiontavern.com) at 17015 Center Rd. on Mission Peninsula. Even ***Legs Inn*** (231-526-2281; legsinn.com) at 6425 N. Lake Shore Dr. in Cross Village, renowned for its Polish entrees, serves whitefish 3 different ways.

Another northern Michigan treat is smoked whitefish spread where the fish is blended with cream cheese, herbs and spices, and sometimes even a touch of brandy and then enjoyed on a slice of crusty bread. Some of the best whitefish spread is made and sold at ***Burritt's Market*** (231-946-3300; burrittsmarket.com) at 509 W. Front St. in Traverse City.

Located at 8405 Twin Bridges Rd., the museum is open the last Sat in Apr to the last Sat in Sept. Hours are 1 to 4 p.m. on Wed and Fri, 11 a.m. to 4 p.m. on Sat, and 10 a.m. to 1 p.m. on Sun. But the best time to visit is the last Sat in Apr when Lovells stages its annual Trout Opener Festival with speakers, fly-tying demonstrations, and casting competitions.

More trout fishing history is only a short walk away. What began as the Douglas Hotel in 1916 is today the **North Branch Outing Club,** a lodge overlooking the North Branch of the Au Sable that is still dedicated to fly anglers. At its height, the North Branch Outing Club boasted such members as Henry and Edsel Ford, Harvey Firestone, and the Dodge brothers. In 1996 the Fuller family bought the historic but vacant lodge and opened it as a 12-room inn after two years of extensive renovation. The Fullers' North Branch Outing Club (989-348-7951; northbranchoutingclub.com) is at 6122 E. County Rd. 612 and is a classic angler's inn. The lodge overlooks 400 feet of the North Branch and features a complete fly shop on the first floor, a comfortable lounge and dining area, and a room to hang and dry out your waders. Outside there are often as many Au Sable River boats in the parking lot as cars.

Wexford County

Hunting and fishing have a long tradition in Michigan. How long? In 1994 the state celebrated the 100th year in which deer licenses had been issued. There is no better place to see the history of hunters and anglers in Michigan than at the **Carl T. Johnson Hunt and Fish Center,** a state interpretive site in Cadillac. Located adjacent to Mitchell State Park at 6087 M 115, the center features a variety of exhibits and hands-on displays, including a marsh diorama, a wall-size aquarium stocked with native fish, and a full-size stuffed elk, a species reintroduced to the state thanks to the efforts of sportsmen's groups. Push a button and you can hear the call of the elk along with the calls of many other Michigan species in the exhibit hall. From the center a trail leads north into the Heritage Nature Study Area, which includes observation platforms and marshes where you have a reasonably good chance of spotting many of Michigan's wild species. The Carl T. Johnson Hunt and Fish Center (231-779-1321) is open daily from 10 a.m. to 6 p.m. from Memorial Day through Dec 1 and the rest of the year from noon to 5 p.m. Fri and 10 a.m. to 5 p.m. Sat and Sun. A $12 recreation passport is required for vehicle entry into the park.

Back in the 1930s, a small group of Frankfort residents discovered the thrill of soaring in gliders. They would take off from the high bluffs overlooking Lake Michigan and fly through the air, sometimes for hours, before landing on the beach. What emerged was the ***Northwest Soaring Club of Frankfort,*** which at one time hosted a national soaring championship in this small town.

The art of soaring has changed over the years, but the club is still around, offering lessons and, for visitors passing through on vacation, introductory rides. In 2011, the club moved to Wexford County Airport in Cadillac and

Get a Thrill with Shemhadar Dog Sled Adventures

When 8-year-old Chris Dewey read about heroic sled dog Balto, the little girl knew what she wanted for her upcoming gift days.

A Siberian husky in Nome, Alaska, Balto was credited with saving children's lives when his Alaskan village was affected by diphtheria in 1925. Diphtheria vaccine was needed and the closest supply was 483 miles away. Led by Balto and a team of dogs and guides, the journey was made and the children were saved.

"Our daughter promptly told us that she wanted a sled and some dogs for her birthday and for Christmas," said Chris's mother, Gina Dewey. "We agreed and that's what started it all."

Before long, Gina and her husband Tim Dewey had opened a place called ***Shemhadar Dog Sled Adventures*** in Cadillac, Michigan.

"We started giving public tours in 2007/2008 and we have 23 dogs right now," Dewey said. "The name comes from the words *Shem* which means 'Place' and *Hadar* which means 'Fruit in all seasons' because we have something going on here in every season."

Depending on snowfall, dogsledding is offered from mid-December through February, plus a few weekends in March.

Shemhadar offers several types of tours including a special one for groups called "A Taste of Mushing." The tour includes a custom kennel visit and short rides for everyone.

"We like to keep the group sizes to 12 to 18 people," Dewey said. "We have one rider and one driver on the sled so it takes a while to give everyone a ride."

If the group is larger, it could be done in two sessions with one half of the group doing "A Taste of Mushing" while the other half visits attractions in Cadillac. Then the groups could switch places.

"We don't want to have people standing outside too long in the cold while they are waiting their turn to take a ride," Dewey said. "But it is exciting to watch the dogs take off and return."

For more information, contact Shemhader Dog Adventures at (231) 779-9976; vbs20.com/shemhadarkennels.

became the Northwest Soaring Club. Soaring conditions accessible from Cadillac were identified as the strongest in the state on many days. Passengers join a certified pilot in a 2-seat glider 25 to 35 feet long, with a wingspan of about 50 feet. The glider is towed to a height of 2,000 to 3,000 feet by a small plane and then released. What follows is a spectacular ride above the wonders of northern Michigan with extensive views of Lake Mitchell, Lake Cadillac, and the surrounding area. The length of the ride depends on the wind and thermal conditions, but it ranges from 30 minutes to sometimes several hours. Introductory rides are offered from May through Oct and cost $25 per person for a 3,000-foot tow, $45 for a 4,000-foot tow, and $85 for a 5,300-foot tow. The higher the tow, the longer the flight. Participants also must pay a daily membership fee of $50. Interested persons should contact the Northwest Soaring Club (231-352-9160; northwestsoaringclub.com). Club rides take off from Wexford County Airport, located at 8040 E. 34 Rd.

Places to Stay in Northwest Michigan

BAY VIEW

Stafford's Bay View Inn
2011 Woodland Ave.
(800) 258-1886
thebayviewinn.com

Terrace Inn
1549 Glendale Ave.
(231) 347-2410
theterraceinn.com

BEAVER ISLAND

Beaver Island Lodge
38210 Beaver Lodge Dr.
(231) 448-2396
beaverislandlodge.com

The Emerald Isle Hotel
37985 Kings Hwy.
(231) 448-2376
emeraldislehotel.com

Lazy K Farms Bed & Breakfast
27996 Barney's Lake Rd. N.
(231) 448-2150

BELLAIRE

Applesauce Inn Bed & Breakfast
7296 S. M 88
(231) 533-6448
applesauceinn.com

Bellaire Bed and Breakfast
212 Park St.
(231) 533-6077
bellairebandb.com

Grand Victorian Bed & Breakfast
402 N. Bridge St.
(877) 438-6111
grandvictorian.com

CHARLEVOIX

Horton Creek Inn B&B
5757 Boyne City Rd.
(231) 582-5373
hortoncreekinnbb.com

Inn at Grey Gables B&B
306 Belvedere Ave.
(231) 547-2251
innatgreygables.com

Pointes North Inn
101 Michigan Ave.
(866) 547-0055
pointesnorthcharlevoix.com

Weathervane Terrace Hotel
111 Pine River Ln.
231-547-9955
weathervane-chx.com

ELK RAPIDS

Cairn House Bed & Breakfast
8160 Cairn Hwy.
(231) 264-8994
cairnhouse.com

The Spring Lighthouse B&B
106 Oak St.
(231) 264-6282
springlighthouse.com

White Birch Lodge
571 Meguzee Point Rd.
(231) 264-8271
whitebirchlodge.org

ELLSWORTH

House on the Hill Bed & Breakfast
9661 Lake St.
(231) 588-6304
thehouseonthehill.com

FRANKFORT

Chimney Corners Resort
1602 Crystal Dr.
(231) 352-7522
chimneycornersresort.com

GAYLORD

Heart Lake Cottages
9603 N. Old 27
(989) 732-5081
heartlakecottages.com

Sojourn Lakeside Resort
2332 E. Dixon Lake Rd.
(989) 370-7873
sojournlakesideresort.com

GLEN ARBOR

Glen Arbor Bed & Breakfast and Cottages
6548 Western Ave.
(231) 334-6789
glenarborlodging.com

SELECTED CHAMBERS OF COMMERCE & TOURISM BUREAUS

Beaver Island Chamber of Commerce
26215 Main St.
Beaver Island 49782
(231) 448-2505
beaverisland.org

Benzie County Visitors Bureau
826 Michigan Ave.
Benzonia 49616
(800) 882-5801
benzie.org

Charlevoix Area Convention and Visitors Bureau
109 Mason St.
Charlevoix 49720
(800) 367-8557
visitcharlevoix.com

Gaylord Area Convention and Tourism Bureau
319 W. Main St.
Gaylord 49735
(800) 345-8621
gaylordmichigan.net

Mackinaw Area Tourist Bureau
10800 US 23
Mackinaw City 49701
(231) 436-5664
mackinawcity.com

Petoskey Area Visitors Bureau
401 E. Mitchell St.
Petoskey 49770
(800) 845-2828
petoskeyarea.com

Sleeping Bear Dunes Visitors Bureau
12 Wood Ridge Rd.
Glen Arbor 49636
(231) 334-2000
sleepingbeardunes.com

Traverse City Convention and Visitors Bureau
101 W. Grandview Pkwy.
Traverse City 49684
(800) 940-1120
traversecity.com

M-22 Inn Glen Arbor
5793 S. Ray St.
(231) 334-3773
m22inn.com

Sylvan Inn
6680 W. Western Ave.
(231) 334-4333
m22inn.com

HARBOR SPRINGS

Birchwood Inn
7291 S. Lake Shore Dr.
(231) 526-2151
birchwoodinn.com

Boyne Highlands Resort
600 Highland Dr.
(855) 688-7022
boynehighlands.com

Colonial Inn
210 Artesian Ave.
(231) 526-2111
harborsprings.com

LELAND

Falling Waters Lodge
200 A Ave.
(231) 256-9832
fallingwaterslodge.com

Whaleback Inn
1757 N. Manitou Trail
M 22
(231) 256-9090
whalebackinn.com

OMENA

Sunset Lodge Bed and Breakfast
12819 E. Tatch Rd.
(231) 631-2636
sunsetlodgeomena.com

PETOSKEY

Apple Tree Inn
915 Spring St.
(800) 348-2900
appletreeinn.com

Bay Harbor Resort
4000 Main St.
(888) 229-4272
bayharbor.com

Inn at Bay Harbor
3600 Village Harbor Dr.
(855) 351-4295
marriott.com

Quality Inn
1314 US 31 N.
(231) 347-3220
choicehotels.com

Stafford's Perry Hotel
100 Lewis St.
(800) 737-1899
staffords.com

TRAVERSE CITY

Beach Haus Resort
1489 US 31 North
(231) 947-3560
thebeachhausresort.com

Cherry Tree Inn
2345 US 31
(800) 439-3093
cherrytreeinn.com

Grand Beach Resort Hotel
1683 US 31 North
(800) 968-1992
tcbeaches.com

Grand Traverse Resort & Spa
100 Grand Traverse Village Blvd. (Acme)
(231) 534-6000
grandtraverseresort.com

Oviatt House Bed & Breakfast
244 E. Eighth St.
(231) 675-6709
oviatthouse.com

Park Place Hotel
300 E. State St.
(231) 946-5000
parkplace-hotel.com

Places to Eat in Northwest Michigan

BEAVER ISLAND

Dalwhinnie Bakery
38240 Michigan Ave.
(231) 448-2736
mcdonoughsmarket.com
Deli

Stoney Acre Grill & Donegal Danny's Pub
26420 Carlisle Rd.
(231) 448-2560
stoneyacre-donegaldannys.com
Bistro

BEULAH

Cherry Hut
211 N. Michigan Ave.
(231) 882-4431
cherryhut.com
American

BOYNE CITY

Red Mesa Grill
117 Water St.
(231) 582-0049
magnumhospitality.com
Tex-Mex

OTHER ATTRACTIONS

Benzie Area Historical Museum
6941 Traverse Ave.
Benzonia
(231) 882-5539
benziemuseum.org

Colonial Michilimackinac
102 W. Straits Ave.
Mackinaw City
(231) 436-8705
mackinacpark.com

Empire Area Museum
11544 S. Lacore St.
Empire
(231) 326-5568
empiremimuseum.org

Gaslight Shopping District
Petoskey
petoskeydowntown.com

Leelanau Historical Museum
203 Cedar St.
Leland
(231) 256-7475
leelanauhistory.org

Lighthouse Park
20500 Center Rd.
Old Mission Peninsula
(231) 223-7324
missionpointlighthouse.com

Sunset Park
101 E. Lake St.
Petoskey
(231) 347-2500
petoskey.us

CHARLEVOIX

Grey Gables Restaurant
308 Belvedere Ave.
(231) 547-9261
greygablesinn.com
Fine Dining

Stafford's Weathervane Restaurant
106 Pine River Ln.
(231) 547-4311
staffordsweathervane.com
American

Terry's of Charlevoix
101 Antrim St.
(231) 547-2799
terrysofcharlevoix.com
Seafood and Chops

ELK RAPIDS

Pearl's New Orleans Kitchen
617 Ames St.
(231) 264-0530
magnumhospitality.com
Cajun

Riverwalk Grill and Taproom
106 Ames St.
(231) 264-0377
rwgrillandtap.com
American

Siren Hall
151 River St.
(231) 264-6062
sirenhall.com
Fine Dining

ELLSWORTH

Rowe Inn Restaurant
6303 E. Jordan Rd.
(231) 588-7351
roweinn.com
Fine Dining

Tapawingo
9502 Lake St.
(866) 588-7881
amatteroftastemi.com
American

FRANKFORT

Chimney Corners Resort
1602 Crystal Dr.
(231) 352-7522
chimneycornersresort.com
American

Dinghy's Restaurant & Bar
415 Main St.
(231) 352-4702
dinghysrestaurant.com
American

The Fusion
300 Main St.
(231) 352-4114
the-fusion.com
Asian

Hotel Frankfort Restaurant
231 Main St.
(231) 352-8090
thehotelfrankfort.com
American

GAYLORD

Bearded Dogg Lounge
302 S. Otsego Ave.
(989) 619-0298
beardeddogglounge.com
American

Diana's Delights
138 W. Main St.
(989) 732-6564
dianasdelights.net
American

Iron Pig Smokehouse
143 W. Main St.
(989) 448-2065
theironpigsmokehouse.com
Barbecue

The Pine Squirrel Bar & Grill
1600 S. Otsego Ave.
(989) 448-2771
pinesquirrelgaylord.com
American

GRAYLING

Spike's Keg o' Nails
301 Cedar St.
(989) 348-7113
spikeskegonails.com
Tavern

HARBOR SPRINGS

New York Restaurant
101 State St.
(231) 526-1904
thenewyork.com
American

Pierson's Grille & Spirits
130 State St.
(231) 526-2967
piersonsgrille.com
American

Willow
129 E. Bay St.
(231) 412-6032
willowharborsprings.com
American

LAKE LEELANAU

Dick's Pour House
103 W. Phillip St.
(231) 256-9912
dickspourhouse.com
Pub

LELAND

Bluebird Restaurant & Tavern
102 E. River
(231) 256-9081
bluebirdleland.com
Seafood

The Cove
111 River St.
(231) 256-9834
thecoveleland.com
American

The Riverside Inn
302 E. River St.
(231) 256-9971
theriverside-inn.com
Fine Dining

MISSION PENINSULA

The Jolly Pumpkin Cafe & Brewery
13512 Peninsula Dr.
(231) 223-4333
jollypumpkin.com
American

Mission Table
13512 Peninsula Dr.
(231) 223-4222
missiontable.net
Fine Dining

Old Mission Tavern
17015 Center Rd.
(231) 223-7280
oldmissiontavern.com
American

PETOSKEY

Chandler's
215½ Howard St.
(231) 347-2981
chandlersrestaurant.com
Fine Dining

City Park Grill
432 E. Lake St.
(231) 347-0101
cityparkgrill.com
Eclectic

Palette Bistro
321 Bay St.
(231) 348-3321
palettebistropetoskey.com
Fine Dining

Roast & Toast
309 Lake St.
(231) 347-7767
roastandtoast.com
American

Thai Orchid Cuisine
433 E. Mitchell St.
(231) 487-9900
thaiorchidpetoskey.com
Thai

Vintage Chophouse & Wine Bar
3600 Village Harbor Dr.
(844) 717-2072
innatbayharbor.com
Steakhouse

TRAVERSE CITY

Alliance Restaurant
144 Hall St.
(231) 642-5545
foodforalliance.com
New American

Blue Tractor Barbecue
423 S. Union St.
(231) 922-9515
bluetractorcookshop.com
American

Don's Drive-In
2030 US 31 North
(231) 938-1860
donsdriveinmi.com
Burgers

North Peak Brewing Company
400 W. Front St.
(231) 941-7325
northpeak.net
Brewpub

Poppycock's
128 E. Front St.
(231) 941-7632
poppycockstc.com
Eclectic

Red Ginger
237 E. Front St.
(231) 944-1733
eatatginger.com
Asian

Eastern Upper Peninsula

The "Mighty Mac" sounds like a hamburger with the works, but to most Michiganders it's the Mackinac Bridge, the only link between the Lower and Upper Peninsulas and the third longest bridge in the country. Building a bridge was first considered in 1884, but the 5-mile span wasn't built until 1957, finally uniting a state that for its first 120 years was divided by a stretch of water known as the Straits of Mackinac.

Most travelers view the *Mackinac Bridge* as a very scenic drive. A trip across the Mighty Mac is a 360-degree panorama of shorelines, Great Lakes, and islands scattered everywhere, while below, the straits bustle with ferries, freighters, and fishing boats. The bridge is also the link between two worlds. Unlike industrialized southern Michigan, the Upper Peninsula's economy was based on lumbering and mining. After the majestic white pines were cut and the mines closed, this section of Michigan fell upon hard times, which in some ways continue today. Residents of the north, however, are quick to point out that the first permanent settlement in the state was not Detroit but Sault Ste. Marie and that their endurance proves their long history is not about to end anytime soon. Survival is a way of life in the U.P.

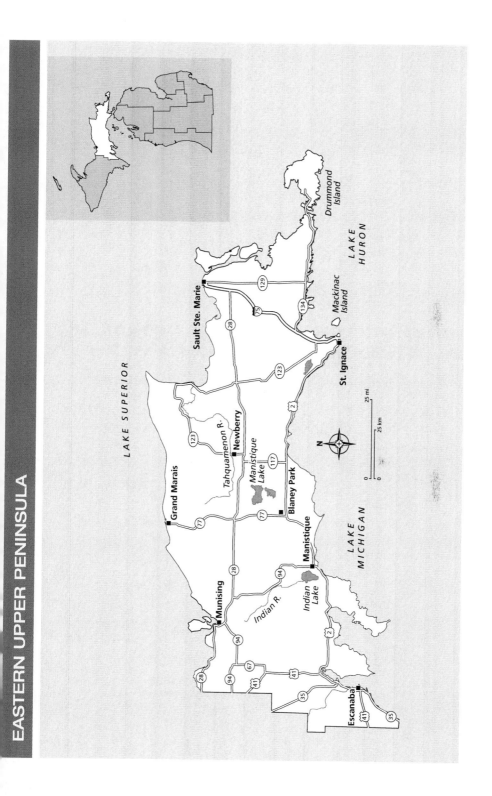

What travelers will quickly discover upon crossing the bridge is a place of remote beauty and unique character, where interstates are almost nonexistent, and motel chains and fast-food restaurants are few and far between. Almost every road in the U.P. is "off the beaten path," offering natural beauty, family-run inns and cafes, and outdoor opportunities that will satisfy any lover of pristine forests, lakes, and streams.

Mackinac County

Sometimes in our rush to see one place, we overlook another. Such is often the case of a place like *St. Ignace.* This historical town, the second oldest settlement in Michigan, has a scenic harbor and a main street full of shops and restaurants. Only who takes the time to look around when we're all racing through to catch the next boat to Mackinac Island?

AUTHOR'S TOP TEN PICKS

Fayette Historic State Park
4785 II Rd.
Garden
(906) 644-2603

Fort Mackinac
7127 Huron Rd.
Mackinac Island
(906) 847-3328
mackinacparks.com

Grand Hotel
286 Grand Ave.
Mackinac Island
(800) 334-7263
grandhotel.com

Great Lakes Shipwreck Museum
18335 N. Whitefish Point Rd.
Paradise
(906) 635-1742
shipwreckmuseum.com

Kitch-iti-kipi
8970 W. County Road 442
Manistique
(906) 341-2355
cityofmanistique.org

Peninsula Point Lighthouse
3722 County Road 513
Stonington
(906) 789-7862

Pictured Rocks Boat Cruises
100 City Park Dr.
Munising
(906) 387-2379
picturedrocks.com

Seney National Wildlife Refuge
1674 Refuge Entrance Rd.
Germfask
(906) 586-9851
fws.gov/refuge/seney

Soo Locks Park
329 W. Portage Ave.
Sault Ste. Marie
(906) 632-7020
saultstemarie.com

Tahquamenon Falls
41382 W. M 123
Paradise
(906) 492-3415

Slow down. St. Ignace is an intriguing city, and you don't have to go any farther than the **Museum of Ojibwa Culture** to discover why. The city-operated museum gives a vivid picture of the Straits of Mackinac in the 1600s and 1700s when the Ojibway, Huron, and Odawa Indians mingled with the French in what is now downtown St. Ignace. The museum is housed in a former Catholic church, and through video presentations and exhibits it focuses on the Woodland Indian culture and how these indigenous people survived the harsh winters of the Upper Peninsula. Outside there is a replica of a Huron longhouse that can be viewed.

michigantrivia

Labor Day is the only time of the year that people are allowed to walk across the Mackinac Bridge. More than 70,000 people trek across the 5-mile-long bridge that day, including most governors of Michigan and, in 1992, President George H. W. Bush. Walkers begin on the north side of the bridge and jump on free shuttle buses to return to their cars afterward.

The Museum of Ojibwa Culture (906-643-9161; museumofojibwaculture .net) is at 500 N. State St., next door to the St. Ignace Chamber of Commerce office. Hours are daily 10 a.m. to 6 p.m. Check the website for seasonal hours. Admission is by donation.

Next door to the museum is **Marquette Mission Park,** while across State Street is one end of the **Huron Boardwalk.** Together the small park and the 2-mile-long boardwalk take you back more than 300 years into the life of this town.

Marquette Mission Park features Father Marquette's grave and several outdoor exhibits that retrace the significance of this little plot of land. From the park you then cross the street to Huron Boardwalk, which winds south along the St. Ignace waterfront. The boardwalk features its own series of historical displays, which cover everything from "Nineteenth-Century St. Ignace" to the "Legacy of White Pine" in text and photos. Between the displays are benches, each with a million-dollar view of Mackinac Island, the ferries making high-speed runs to the resort island, and the rest of the bustling waterfront. To reach Marquette Mission Park and Huron Boardwalk from I-75 on the north side of the Mackinac Bridge, take exit 344A and follow Business Loop I-75 to State Street, which parallels the boardwalk.

There are numerous forts to visit in Michigan, but without a doubt the most famous and probably the most beloved is **Fort Mackinac** on **Mackinac Island** at 7127 Huron Rd. Built and first occupied by the British in 1779, the fort is part of **Mackinac Island State Park** and the scene of cannon firings and other living-history demonstrations throughout the summer. The Officer's

A Legitimate Tourist Trap

Before there was Mystery Spot and Sea Shell City with its "man-eating clam" or a minigolf course in the shape of Michigan, there was **Castle Rock.** In a region of the state lined with tourist traps and gift shops selling rubber tomahawks and "I Am a Yooper" refrigerator magnets, Castle Rock is the original. It is also one of the most affordable attractions on either side of the Mackinac Bridge and, right at exit 348 off I-75, a great leg stretcher after the long drive north.

What the heck, let's stop.

There is nothing phony about the rock itself. Castle Rock is a sea stack, one of a handful in and around St. Ignace, the result of limestone caves collapsing and waves eroding the remaining rock into pillars and arches more than 4,000 years ago. The most famous are Sugar Loaf and Arch Rock on Mackinac Island, while in downtown St. Ignace there's St. Anthony's Rock. At 183 feet, Castle Rock is not only the tallest one but also the only one you're allowed to climb.

The slick brochure promoting Castle Rock states it was used by Indians as a look-out and that Pontiac, the great Ojibway chief, was thought to have stood on it. Of course, it also says that the legendary giant Paul Bunyan and his blue ox Babe once sat at the base of it. Believe what you want.

We do know that historical photos show people climbing the rock as early as 1911 and in 1930 Clarence Eby purchased the rock and 80 acres around it. He built a souvenir stand at the base and a stairway to the top, and charged people 10 cents to climb it, enticing them with signs that read: "Stop and climb. Still only a dime!"

That's one of the most amazing things about Castle Rock—its admission fee. It remained 10 cents until 1979, when it was raised to 25 cents. Now, the fee is $1. Still, it's cheaper to climb Castle Rock than to cross the Mackinac Bridge.

To reach the sea stack, you first have to pass through Castle Rock Curios Shop, and this is where you might lose the kids. The large gift shop is stocked with thousands of souvenirs people expect you to bring home from the Upper Peninsula: polished agates, Mackinac Bridge playing cards, Daniel Boone raccoon caps, fake arrowheads, and a bald man's hairbrush (it has no bristles).

From the shop you head outside where there is a giant statue of Paul Bunyan and Babe (life-size?) and the stairway to the top of Castle Rock, a climb of 170 steps.

The climb is worth it as the view is magnificent. Spread out below you is St. Ignace, while offshore is Mackinac Island and in between them a handful of ferries hustling tourists back and forth. You can see Lake Huron, Lake Michigan, even the towers of the Mackinac Bridge. The view is so expansive that it's easy to envision Indians using Castle Rock as an observation post. But as for Paul Bunyan using it as a back-rest . . . that's still a stretch for this flatlander.

Castle Rock (906-643-8268; castlerockmi.com) is open May through Oct from 9 a.m. to 9 p.m. daily. It is located at N2690 Castle Rock Rd.

Stone Quarters, constructed of limestone in 1781, is the oldest building in Michigan. The scene of the white stockade looming above the island's downtown area is probably one of the most photographed in the state.

The fort is open daily from 9 a.m. to 5 p.m. from May through the first weekend in June, from 9:30 a.m. to 7 p.m. the second week of June to first week of Sept, and from 9:30 a.m. to 5 p.m. from the second week of Sept through the second week of Oct. Admission is $13.50 per adult, $8 children ages 5 to 12, which also covers 6 other interesting museums in the downtown area of Mackinac Island including Biddle House and Mackinac Art Museum.

Mackinac Island State Park actually covers 1,800 acres, or 83 percent of the island, and offers much more than just cannon demonstrations twice a day. There are 140 miles of roads and trails, open to use by hikers, cyclists, and equestrians, but not cars, which are not allowed on the island. The roads and trails loop through a surprisingly rugged and wooded terrain, past some of the most interesting natural formations in Michigan, including **Arch Rock,** the almost perfect 50-foot-wide limestone arch. The vast majority of visitors reach these attractions on a bicycle, which can either be brought to the island on the ferry or rented in the downtown area.

For more information contact Mackinac Island State Park (906-847-3328; mackinacparks.com). For information on the two ferry companies that provide transportation to the island, call **Shepler's Mackinac Island Ferry** (231-436-5023; sheplersferry.com) or **Star Line** (800-638-9892; mackinacferry.com).

When Mackinac Is Mackinaw

Let's see; there's Mackinac Island and Mackinaw City and Fort Michilimackinac and the mackinaw, which some people still wear. No wonder many out-of-staters are tongue-tied when they visit this region of Michigan.

The word *Mackinac*—or *Mackinaw*—is a shorter form of *Michinnimakinong,* which was the Native Americans' description of the area; *mishinnimakinong* or "great connecting place." That's a good description for the Straits of Mackinac, which connect Lake Michigan and Lake Huron. Thus on the north side you have Mackinac Island and Fort Mackinac, and on the south side there's Mackinaw City and Fort Michilimackinac. A mackinaw is also a regional cloth or coat made from thick woolen material.

To sound like a Yooper (somebody who lives in the Upper Peninsula), just make sure you always end any of those words in "awe" and never "ack." Mackinac should never rhyme with "bric-a-brac," but rather with "Saginaw." The only time you say "ack" is when you call the Mackinac Bridge by its nickname . . . the Big Mac.

Somewhere in Time Celebrated at Grand Hotel

On a whim, a young playwright from Chicago decides to take a trip and stay at the **Grand Hotel** (800-334-7263; grandhotel.com) on Mackinac Island. Although he is a success in his profession, Richard Collier feels lonely and unhappy. He has never found his special love.

Wandering around the historic hotel to pass the time, the writer steps into the Grand Hotel Hall of History. There he encounters the photo of an actress who appeared at the hotel in 1912. Drawn to the picture, the young man feels driven to will himself back in time to meet the beautiful actress, his destiny Elise McKenna. Somehow or other, he succeeds.

Of course, this is all a Hollywood movie. And it was made way back in 1980, for goodness' sake. But, if you visit the Grand Hotel on a special October weekend, you would never know the story wasn't true or that the tale was filmed decades ago. Ladies in long dresses and frilly hats will be enjoying tea in the hotel lobby, walking the beautiful grounds with dainty parasols to protect them from the sun, or watching the sunset from the world's longest front porch. Men in turn-of-the-20th-century suits and gentlemanly hats will be sipping fine wine, discussing the merits of strong steeds pulling the passing carriages or taking a turn on one of the island's many bicycles.

It will truly be like turning back the clock to *Somewhere in Time,* the 1980 movie that critics bashed but moviegoers loved. "I've never seen anything like it," says Bob Tagatz, historian at the Grand Hotel. "I've been here almost 20 years and there has not been a single day that someone has not asked me about the movie. The following of the movie borders on bizarre."

Starring Jane Seymour and Christopher Reeve, the classic movie featured the Grand Hotel as its backdrop. In fact, some folks swear the 1887 Victorian hotel is actually the scene stealer. Perched high over the Straits of Mackinac, the hotel seems to have gotten even more beautiful with the passing years.

The annual *Somewhere in Time* weekends officially started in 1991, but movie fans were staging their own impromptu tributes even before that. R.D. Musser, owner of the Grand Hotel, allowed the facility to be used by Universal Studios for free. All filming took place in the height of the season, with the hotel fully booked. The film company worked around the dining of paying guests, filming the dining room during the night.

Every setting required by the *Somewhere in Time* script was found on Mackinac Island. The movie was filmed entirely on the island, except for a few brief scenes shot in Chicago.

"It's just a beautiful movie," Tagatz says. "I am an historian so time travel is something I am very interested in. Then the theme of the movie that love transcends death is something I think everyone wants to believe in."

Hint: The two lovers are not destined to live happily ever after in 1912. But they eventually do find each other again—somewhere in time.

Scenic shoreline drives abound in Michigan, but it's hard to argue when someone says the most spectacular of all is the stretch of US 2 from St. Ignace to the hamlet of Naubinway. The views of Lake Michigan, beaches, dunes, and offshore island are rarely interrupted along this 42-mile segment. One of the places to spot for a panoramic view on this drive is **Cut River Gorge Roadside Park** on US 2, 26 miles west of St. Ignace.

Actually there are 3 parks on both sides of this stunning gorge that are connected by the impressive Cut River Bridge, a steel-arch cantilever structure that was built in 1948 and stands 147 feet above the river. You can walk across the bridge for an impressive view of Lake Michigan or follow one of 3 foot trails that wind down to the Cut River and then out to a beautiful beach on the Great Lake. By combining two of the trails with a walk across the bridge itself, you'll enjoy an interesting loop of between 1 and 1.3 miles.

michigantrivia

Mackinac Island was the site of one of the most celebrated moments in Michigan's history. After Americans took over Fort Mackinac diplomatically, the British recaptured it during the War of 1812 by secretly landing in the middle of the night and dragging a cannon up a bluff overlooking the fort. When the American garrison woke up the next morning and saw what was aimed at them, they gave up without firing a single shot.

A much less traveled but equally scenic route is east of the Mackinac Bridge on M 134. The road follows the U.P. shoreline along northern Lake Huron, passing the intriguing Les Cheneaux Islands and ending at De Tour, the departure point for remote Drummond Island, a haven of fishing resorts. The best stretch is the 24 miles from Cedarville in Mackinac County to De Tour in Chippewa County. This segment is one continuous view of the lake, the islands, and long stretches of sand where there are more than a dozen turnoffs and roadside parks, allowing everybody an uncrowded beach for a lazy afternoon in the sun.

Chippewa County

Sault Ste. Marie is synonymous with the Soo Locks, the world's largest and busiest locking system, the crucial link for freighters passing between Lake Superior and Lake Huron. The city of 14,253 is Michigan's oldest and has been an important center since the French Canadian voyagers in the 1700s portaged their long canoes and bales of furs around St. Mary's Rapids.

SS *Valley Camp* Showcases Life Aboard a Great Lakes Ship

A strange combination of wide-open spaces and tight cramped quarters, the Museum Ship *Valley Camp* is not for the claustrophobic. At 550 feet long, the boat stretches over a good chunk of water. But the crew's quarters—luxurious for a freighter—leave little room for movement.

The *Valley Camp* once housed a crew of 32 men. She is the most intact example of the classic Great Lakes ore carriers that once numbered in the hundreds. Only a few survive today.

Built in 1917 and originally named the *Louis W. Hill*, the steamship was launched in Lorain, Ohio, and hauled iron ore and coal for 38 years. In 1955, she was sold to the Wilson Marine Transit Co., renamed the *Valley Camp,* and carried an array of goods including grain and stone.

The boat changed hands again in 1959, when she was bought by the Republic Steel Corporation to move iron ore and coal to their mills in Buffalo, Cleveland, and Indiana Harbor, Indiana.

She sailed her last in 1967. The boat was retired not because of age but because her triple expansion engine was still being fed by coal-burning boilers.

She was going to be decommissioned and sold for scrap metal. Instead, she became a museum in 1972 so people can board an old freighter and see what life was like.

In her heyday, the *Valley Camp* was a frequent sight on the Great Lakes. She sailed more than 3 million miles over the Great Lakes.

Most of this colorful history of shipping can be appreciated by walking along Water Street, beginning at its east end, where the **SS *Valley Camp*** is docked next to the Chamber of Commerce Information Center at 326 E. Portage Ave. The 550-foot freighter was once owned and used by the Republic Steel Corporation and frequently passed through the locks. Today it has been turned into one of the largest Great Lakes marine museums and is listed as a National Historic Site. From the pilothouse and the 1,800-horsepower steam engine to the captain's quarters and the galley, visitors are free to roam the ship for a close-up look at life aboard an ore carrier, where a crew of almost 30 worked, slept, and ate. Down below, in its massive cargo holds, are models and displays of Great Lakes vessels, aquariums of the freshwater fish that abound nearby, and a room devoted to the wreck of the *Edmund Fitzgerald*, the ore carrier that sank in raging Lake Superior in 1975, taking its captain and crew of 28 with it.

The SS *Valley Camp* (888-744-7867) is open 10 a.m. to 5 p.m. Mon through Sat and 11 a.m. to 5 p.m. Sun mid-May through June, 9 a.m. to 6 p.m. in July

Although the *Valley Camp* seems huge, the boat is small compared to the thousand-footers that now ply the Great Lakes. Newer vessels are four times as large as the *Valley Camp*.

When the boat was initially opened as a museum, the *Valley Camp* was moored in water. But now the boat is only partially immersed.

She cannot move at all now. She is grounded, although the back third of the boat is still floating and you can still feel things moving around. She was entirely floating in 1972 but that shows how much the water level has fluctuated.

Considered the world's largest Great Lakes maritime museum, the *Valley Camp* allows visitors to explore crew sleeping quarters, dining areas, engine room, and pilothouse.

The *Valley Camp* also features more than 100 exhibits in the boat's cargo holds. Showcased are shipwrecks, lighthouses, models, photographs, artifacts, and local history. Four 1,200-gallon aquariums are home to trout, walleyes, perch, pike, and more.

One huge space offers a display on the *Edmund Fitzgerald*, the huge freighter that disappeared suddenly with 29 crew members aboard.

A trailing freighter lost sight of the *Fitzgerald* in the disastrous November 1975 storm. After Coast Guard searches and dives by the Whitefish Point Shipwreck Museum, it's still not clear whether the ship split in two by hitting bottom or on the surface or whether the tragedy was caused by not closing all the hatches.

The *Fitzgerald*'s two torn lifeboats were among only a few remnants of the wreck to surface. Showcased at the *Valley Camp*, the lifeboats are a sad reminder of the tragic *Fitzgerald*.

and Aug but 10 a.m. to 5 p.m. on Sun, and 11 a.m. to 5 p.m. from Sept through mid-Oct. Admission is $14.50 for adults and $7.25 for children ages 5 to 17.

Another interesting stop in any tour of the city is the ***River of History Museum.*** Through the use of 8 exhibit galleries and a state-of-the-art audio system, the museum takes you on an 8,000-year journey along the shores of St. Mary's River. You begin with the sounds of ice melting and the rapids roaring as a glacier carves out the river valley. You move on to the sprawling Indian camp that was once here and then see the first French explorers paddling ashore in 1662.

The River of History Museum (906-632-1999; riverofhistory.org) is at 531 Ashmun St. It's open May through mid-Oct from 11 a.m. to 5 p.m. Mon through Sat. Admission is $7 for adults and $3.50 for children ages 5 to 17.

To reach the locks to the north, return to and follow Water Street, which in 1982 was renovated into the ***Locks Park Walkway,*** providing an excellent overview of the city's 350-year past. The walkway is marked by blue symbols of freighters, and interpretive plaques explain the history of various areas and renovated buildings. Along the way you'll pass the Baraga House, the 1864 home of Bishop Frederic Baraga, a missionary and historian known as the "Snowshoe Priest" who was the first bishop of the U.P. Nearby is the Johnston House, which was constructed in 1794 for an Irish fur trader, making it the oldest surviving home in Michigan. The walkway also passes the site of Fort Brady, built by the Americans in 1823 and the spot where in 1820 General Lewis Cass lowered and removed the last British flag to fly over US soil.

Water Street ends at *Soo Locks Park* in the heart of downtown Sault Ste. Marie. The US Army Corps of Engineers maintains the park and visitor center, and next to the locks it has built a raised viewing platform that provides an excellent view of ships being raised and lowered to the various lake levels. Your chances of seeing this take place are quite good; some 12,000 vessels

Feasting on Mackinac Island

Dinner began downtown, near Huron Street, where daytime visitors, with a rubber tomahawk under one arm and a 1-pound box of fudge under the other, were scurrying toward the ferries to get off this historical island before dark. We went in the other direction.

We signaled for a horse-drawn taxi and then settled back in the cushioned carriage seats as it clip-clopped its way past the Grand Hotel, up a steep hill, and finally into the island's wooded interior. Some 15 minutes later we emerged from the trees at the impressive Stonecliffe Mansion, home of the **Woods Restaurant** (906-847-3699; grandhotel.com).

Built in 1905, it was once the site of several religious and educational institutions. The interior is a cross between a hunting lodge and a Bavarian mountain retreat with clunky wooden chairs, a huge stone fireplace, and enough stuffed animals on the walls to make any hunter feel at home.

We feasted on Wiener schnitzel, Austrian steak soup, and wild mushroom stew, and then enjoyed a second bottle of wine, not worrying about drinking and driving because, as our waiter pointed out, "there are no cars on the island to drive." We topped off the evening with another carriage ride back to our hotel.

And you thought the only thing to eat on Mackinac Island was fudge.

There is more to dining at this summer retreat than its legendary candy shops. Dozens of restaurants, cafes, and pubs cater to thousands of tourists each summer, satisfying even those with the most finicky taste buds. But the key to a memorable dining experience is to stick around after the last ferry has pulled out, to book a room in a hotel or a bed-and-breakfast, and then indulge in that time-honored tradition of a late and leisurely dinner, enjoyed long after the daytime crowds have vanished.

Reserve a room by first calling the **Mackinac Island Tourism Bureau** (906-847-3783;

pass through the locks annually. During the summer an average of 30 freighters pass through each day.

The interesting visitor center was doubled in size in 1995 and tells the history of the locks, beginning with the construction of the first American lock in 1853. Exhibits include a short video and a working model of a lock. The ***Soo Locks Visitor Center*** (906-253-9290) is open mid-May through mid-Oct from 9 a.m. to 9 p.m. There is no admission fee. The park and observation platform are open daily from 6 a.m. until midnight.

You can also experience the locks directly through ***Soo Locks Boat Tours,*** which offers a 2-hour cruise up and down St. Mary's River, first passing through an American lock and then returning through the Canadian one. Boats depart daily from mid-May through mid-Oct, beginning at 10 a.m. and ending with the last cruise at 4:30 p.m. Soo Locks Boat Tours (800-432-6301; soolocks

mackinacisland.org) for a list of accommodations. Then hop on the first ferry leaving the mainland and take a gastronomic romp around the island:

Horn's Gaslight Bar & Restaurant: In the 1920s Ed Horn was working for the Life-Saving Service at the Round Island Lighthouse when he and his wife opened up a pool hall and snack shop on Huron Street. After Prohibition, Horn acquired one of Michigan's first liquor licenses, and his pool hall became Horn's Gaslight Bar in 1933. It still is, and the interior includes the original tin roof, historical photos on the walls, a long polished bar, and, of course, a honky-tonk piano player. Try the tequila prawns, oversize shrimp sautéed in tequila, lime, and garlic. Horn's is located at 7200 Main St. (906-847-6154; hornsbar.com).

Grand Hotel Main Dining Room: Everybody knows there is a $10 fee during the day to stroll along the world's longest porch if you're not a guest. Few people realize you can have dinner at the hotel's main dining room without either booking a room or paying that fee. And everybody should, at least once. Dinner at the Grand Hotel (800-33-GRAND; grandhotel.com) is an experience, not a meal. You begin by strolling through the middle of the huge, 760-seat dining room along the carpeted runway affectionately known as "Peacock Alley." Go ahead, strut a little on the way to your table.

An army of 55 waiters will tend to your needs as you indulge in such entrees as broiled whitefish and trout scaloppine, sliced veal loin with sweetbreads, or herb-roasted prime rib of beef. Afterward you can enjoy a fine cigar and a snifter of brandy on the porch.

Fort Mackinac Tea Room: There's more to this fort than just the musket and cannon demonstrations. The Tea Room Restaurant (906-847-6327; grandhotel.com) in the Officer's Stone Quarters is a string of yellow-canopy tables overlooking the island's bustling harbor, the Mackinac Bridge, the two Great Lakes that meet there, and so on.

Thus at the fort they boast that you can enjoy sandwiches, soups, and salads in the oldest building on Mackinac Island (1781) with the best view in the state.

.com) maintains 2 docks, both on Portage Avenue south of the SS *Valley Camp*. Tickets are $29 for adults and $12 for children ages 5 to 12 (4 and under free). Soo Locks Boat Tours also offers several other cruises including dinner and lunch cruises, lighthouse cruises, fireworks cruises, and charter cruises.

As well known to locals as the locks is **The Antlers Restaurant,** an Irish bar and restaurant at 804 E. Portage Ave. The exterior of the simple stone building that houses the eatery is misleading. Inside, the decor is a museum of collectibles (or, some say, junk) including hundreds of mounted animals on the walls, a birch-bark canoe hanging from the ceiling, and a 15-foot boa constrictor overlooking the bar. No wall is left bare. Hockey great Gordie Howe (whose picture also adorns the walls) was a frequent patron of the restaurant, which is known for its steaks and "Paul Bunyan" hamburgers. The Antlers (906-253-1728; saultantlers.com) is open daily from 11 a.m., and dinner prices range from $15 to $30.

One of the more interesting drives in the U.P. follows Whitefish Bay, beginning at Brimley (reached from M 28) and ending at desolate Whitefish Point. At Brimley follow Lake Shore Drive to the west as it hugs the shoreline, with frequent views of beaches and Lake Superior. In 7.5 miles, you'll come to the **Point Iroquois Lighthouse** at 12942 W. Lakeshore Dr. The classic lighthouse was built in 1870 and operated until 1963, when sophisticated radar made it obsolete. The Coast Guard turned it over to the US Forest Service, which worked with local historical societies to open it to the public in 1984. It has since been added to the National Register of Historic Places and features a few displays and artifacts in 3 rooms of the lightkeeper's house. This lighthouse is mainly popular for its curved staircase of 70 steps that leads to the top of the tower and a view of the surrounding area. The panorama, needless to say, is impressive, as you can see almost the entire coastline of Whitefish Bay and miles out into Lake Superior, including any freighter that happens to be passing by. The lighthouse (906-437-5272) is open May 15 through Oct 15 from 9 a.m. to 5 p.m. daily.

michigantrivia

More than 82 million tons of cargo pass through the Soo Locks annually, with more than half of it iron ore from mines in the Upper Peninsula and Minnesota. Coal being shipped north accounts for 15 million tons, and Minnesota wheat being shipped east, 9 million tons.

Lakeshore Drive, with its numerous turnoffs and scenic beaches, ends at M 123. The state road is well traveled as it first heads north along Whitefish Bay and then swings west at Paradise to head inland to Tahquamenon Falls. Though the popular falls, second in size only to Niagara Falls east of the Mississippi River, is the destination for most travelers, there is a good reason to continue heading north on Whitefish Point Road. At the very end, at the very tip of the remote peninsula that juts out into Lake Superior, is the ***Great Lakes Shipwreck Museum.*** at 18335 N. Whitefish Point Rd. Whitefish Point is a combination of sandy beach, small dunes, and thunderous Lake Superior waves crashing along the shoreline. It also marks the eastern end of an 80-mile stretch that sailors knew as the Graveyard of the Great Lakes. Raging northwest storms, built up over 200 miles of open water, have caused 350 recorded shipwrecks in which 320 seamen have died along this section of shoreline.

michigantrivia

The only Michigan highway not used by cars or trucks is M 185, the 8-mile blacktopped road that circles Mackinac Island. Except for emergency vehicles—fire trucks and ambulances—travel on M 185 is restricted to pedestrians, bicyclists, and horses.

The Great Lakes Shipwreck Historical Society, a group of divers researching the wrecks, opened the museum in 1986 in abandoned buildings of the Coast Guard station, whose light, beaming since 1849, is the oldest active one on Lake Superior. In the main museum, each display is devoted to a different shipwreck. Visitors see a drawing or photograph of the vessel and artifacts that divers have collected, and read the story of its fatal voyage. The ships range from sailing schooners of the early 1800s to the *Edmund Fitzgerald*, the latest and largest shipwreck, which continues to fascinate residents of the U.P. A darkened interior with theatrical lights, soft music, and special sound effects of seagulls and foghorns sends tingles down the spines of most people.

Another building has been turned into a theater where underwater films of the wrecks are shown, and the lightkeeper's house has been restored. The newest addition at the museum is lodging for those who want to spend a night

International Bridge Walk

The International Bridge that connects Sault Ste. Marie in Michigan with Ontario's Sault Ste. Marie is a 2-mile-long toll bridge that was built in 1962 and financed by both the American and Canadian governments. The bridge rises to 124 feet above the St. Mary's River, and from the middle of it, you can see the famous St. Mary's Rapids and the Soo Locks, which ships use to bypass them. In June Sault Ste. Marie stages an International Bridge Walk that is similar to, but shorter than, the well-known Mackinac Bridge Walk on Labor Day. Call the Sault Ste. Marie Convention and Visitors Bureau (800-647-2858; saultstemarie.com) for dates and details.

Legend of *Edmund Fitzgerald* Lives on at Shipwreck Museum

"The legend lives on from the Chippewa on down
Of the big lake they called Gitche Gummee
Superior, they said, never gives up her dead
When the gales of November come early."

—Gordon Lightfoot

The SS *Edmund Fitzgerald* left port on a sunny Sunday afternoon with only ripples on the lake. The largest vessel then operating on the Great Lakes, "The Big Fitz" was loaded with iron ore.

Anticipating bad weather, the boat's captain, Ernest McSorley, set a course hugging the sheltered Minnesota North Shore. But it was clear that the approaching storm was growing in intensity well beyond the initial forecast.

The *Fitzgerald* entered the eye of the storm in the northeastern corner of Lake Superior. As the vessel headed for shelter, rising wind and waves came out of the north. Heavy seas swamped the freighter.

In less than 10 minutes, the *Fitzgerald* had disappeared from the surface without a distress call being heard by anyone. On Nov. 10, 1975, the *Edmund Fitzgerald* sank with 29 crewmen aboard. No survivors, no bodies were ever found.

On this beautiful sunny day in Michigan, visitors are standing on the beach at Whitefish Point at the **Great Lakes Shipwreck Museum** looking solemnly out over the lake.

"The *Edmund Fitzgerald* went down just 17 miles off the coast here," said our tour guide.

at the lightstation. The 1923 Coast Guard Lifeboat Station Crews Quarters is now a bed-and-breakfast, offering 5 rooms with private baths and televisions, yet possessing the historic charm of the lighthouse era. Lodging is available Apr to late Nov, and the double rooms are $150 per night and include admission to the museum.

The Great Lakes Shipwreck Museum (888-492-3747; shipwreckmuseum .com) is open from May through Oct daily from 10 a.m. to 6 p.m. Admission is $13 for adults, $9 for children ages 5 to 17, or $40 for a family.

Most of the point is a state wildlife sanctuary, renowned for the variety of birds that pass through. The Michigan Audubon Society has established the **Whitefish Point Bird Observatory** at 16914 Whitefish Point Rd. across from the Point Iroquois Lightstation, where a small information room tells birders the species to be watching for as they hike along the point's network of trails. The point is best known for hawks, as up to 25,000 have been sighted in a

People often stand at the water's side to pay their respects to the lost seamen.

The *Fitzgerald* and her crew now rest in a 535-foot watery grave. The catastrophe remains a mystery. Controversy about exactly how and why the *Fitzgerald* sank lives on.

"No one is really sure but there were three rogue waves that caught up to the *Fitzgerald* that night and that might be what put her under," said the guide. Called the "Three Sisters," the rogue waves were reported to be a towering 30 feet high.

Lake Superior has been called the most dangerous body of water in the world. It is an inland teakettle in which any tempest can turn deadly. When a cold Canadian northwestern weather front hits the warmer lake, it can gather strength across 200 miles of open water and whip toward Michigan's Whitefish Bay with waves that, swirling around the narrowing lake, can twist a boat in two.

It is little wonder that the bottom of Lake Superior is littered with the skeletons of no less than 350 ships, most of them falling victim to the temperamental November gales.

At the front of the museum is the bell from the sunken ship. The bell had sat in total darkness and silence for 20 years until it was recovered on July 4, 1995.

"We brought it up because the families of the *Fitzgerald*'s crew wanted us to and we made a replica to leave on the ship that is engraved with the names of the lost sailors and their position on the ship," said our guide.

As the 200-pound bronze bell was being removed from the deep, those bringing it up said it tolled softly. The bell is now sounded at 7:10 p.m. each Nov. 10 in memory of the lost crew. It is tolled 29 times for the crew members of the *Fitzgerald* and a 30th time in memory of the 6,000 other ships that have gone down on the Great Lakes and the 30,000 people who have died in shipwrecks.

season, while in April and May, as many as 7,000 loons will pass by. Other species seen include bald eagles, peregrine falcons, and a variety of songbirds. The observatory (906-492-3596; wpbo.org) is open from 10 a.m. to 4 p.m. daily from mid-Apr through mid-Oct.

Luce County

The county that lies between Chippewa and Alger is probably best known for the Two Hearted River, used by Ernest Hemingway as the title for one of his most famous short stories. Today it remains a favorite for anglers and canoers, who enjoy the solitude of this remote wilderness river that empties into Lake Superior.

The best place to soak in this wilderness setting is ***Tahquamenon Falls State Park,*** the second largest state park in the Upper Peninsula. Split

TOP ANNUAL EVENTS

JUNE

International Bridge Walk
Sault Ste. Marie
(906) 632-3366

Lilac Festival
Mackinac Island
(906) 847-3783
mackinacisland.org

Straits Area Antique Auto Show
St. Ignace
(800) 338-6660
stignace.com

AUGUST

Les Cheneaux Antique Wooden Boat Show
Hessel
(906) 484-2821
lciboatshow.com

Upper Peninsula State Fair
2401 12th Ave. N.
Escanaba
(906) 786-4011
upstatefair.org

SEPTEMBER

Labor Day Bridge Walk
St. Ignace
(906) 643-7600
mightymac.org

between Luce and Chippewa Counties, the 38,496-acre park includes *Upper Tahquamenon Falls,* which spans 200 feet across the Tahquamenon River and descends 50 feet into a sea of mist and foam. You can hear the thunder of the falls the minute you step out of the car.

East of the Mississippi River, only Niagara Falls in New York and Cumberland Falls in Kentucky have longer drops than Tahquamenon.

The falls is a day-use area 21 miles from Newberry on M 123. From the parking lot, it's a quarter-mile walk to the bluffs overlooking the Upper Falls. The best views, however, are obtained by descending the long staircase into the gorge.

Four miles downriver is *Lower Tahquamenon Falls.* While not as impressive as the Upper Falls, this series of cascades is much more fun because it is best viewed by combining a short paddle across the river with a walk around a small island.

The adventure begins by renting a rowboat from the park concession and then shoving off into the brown waters, which are stained by tamarack trees, of the Tahquamenon River. At the island there is a large dock at which to tie up your boat while a wooden stairway leads to the start of the trail. Step-for-step this is one of the most beautiful footpaths in the state, only there are not a lot of steps. It's a loop of less than a mile that skirts the outside of the island, passing one display of tumbling water after another. Along the way parents and kids kick their shoes off, wade out onto the ledge of one of the many drops, and let the river cascade across their legs.

Lower Tahquamenon Falls (906-492-3415) is at 41382 W. M 123, 12 miles west of Paradise and 23 miles northeast of Newberry. A vehicle entry permit is required for the state park, and there is a small fee to rent the rowboats.

For travelers in Luce County who want to spend their nights in comfort at a historic inn, they should book a room at **Chamberlin's Ole Forest Inn** right on H 33 at N9450 Manistique Lakes Rd., a mile north of the blinker light to Curtis. Built in the late 1800s, it was originally a railroad hotel near the Curtis depot. The railroad stopped service in 1909, and 15 years later the building was moved to its present location on a high bluff overlooking Manistique Lake.

The classic 19th-century hotel features a wraparound veranda overlooking the lake; a sprawling lobby complete with wicker chairs, deep sofas, and a 6-foot stone fireplace; and 12 rooms with a unique turn-of-the-20th-century decor. Room rates for the Ole Forest Inn (906-586-6000; chamberlinsinn.com) range from $95 to $140 per night and include a full breakfast in the morning.

Another pleasant spot in Luce County to spend a night is **Muskallonge Lake State Park** at the north end of County Road H 37 in the northwest corner of the county at 30042 CR 407. The park is actually a strip of land between

Frozen Falls

The *Upper Tahquamenon Falls,* a stunning sight in the summer, is equally beautiful in the winter when the Upper Peninsula's frigid temperatures turn the tumbling water into sculpted ice. There is no need to pack snowshoes. The falls is such a popular sight with snowmobilers that the park staff plows the parking lot and keeps the short path and stairs to the viewing decks open.

During most winters the river above the falls remains open and flows to the brink of the cascade where the water in the middle tumbles down across large ice formations. Downriver everything is frozen white, and along the rocky bluffs that enclose the falls are gigantic icy stalactites and stalagmites, some of them 10 to 15 feet long.

The walk in is short. Within a quarter mile from the parking lot, you're standing at the first overlook, viewing the falls from a distance. The best view, however, is reached by descending the 94 steps into the gorge to a platform right above the cascade where you can lean against the railing for a close-up of the ice formations that grow larger with every splash of water heading downstream.

The formations are so varied and intriguing that you could study them for hours. But most winter visitors are scurrying back up the stairs after 10 or 15 minutes before their toes and fingers turn into stalagmites and stalactites, too.

Muskallonge Lake, known for its pike, perch, and smallmouth bass fishing, and Lake Superior. You can camp on a site overlooking the small lake and then wander over to Lake Superior to enjoy its seemingly endless sandy shoreline. There is a vehicle fee to enter Muskallonge Lake State Park (906-658-3338) and an overnight fee of $25 for peak season and $20 for off-season for one of its 159 modern campsites.

Alger County

Grand Marais, a booming lumber town of 2,500 at the turn of the 20th century, is a sleepy hamlet of about 500 today and the gateway for the eastern half of Pictured Rocks National Lakeshore.

One spot to see within the national lakeshore is the *Grand Sable Banks and Dunes.* To reach the sandy hills, follow County Road H 58 west of town, first passing the parking lot and short side trail to Sable Falls and then the Grand Sable Visitor Center. From both places there are half-mile trails that lead to the Grand Sable Dunes. Or you can continue following the county road a mile past the visitor center. On one side of the road are the picnic area and beach of Grand Sable Lake, and on the other side is a huge dune. No more than 50 yards separate the lake and this mountain of sand. Visitors first tackle the heart-pounding scramble up the dune, where the top offers a magnificent view of the windswept sand, Grand Sable Lake, and Lake Superior off in the distance. Then it's a mad dash down the steep bank of sand and usually right into the lake to cool off.

The dunes are a 4-square-mile area of sandy hills about half as high as Sleeping Bear Dunes in the Lower Peninsula, but no less impressive. They end with the Grand Sable Banks, steep sandy bluffs some 300 feet tall that tower right above the Lake Superior shoreline. The best view is obtained by turning off H 58 onto a marked side road for the *Log Slide* 8 miles west of Grand Marais. A short boardwalk leads to a breathtaking overlook 300 feet above Lake Superior, where Au Sable Point Lighthouse to the west is silhouetted against the water and the banks to the east curve 5 miles back toward Grand Marais. Down below is the 500-foot wooden slide that loggers used in the 1800s to send trees into Lake Superior on their way to town.

To see shipwrecks without swimming in frigid Lake Superior, continue along County Road H 58 to Hurricane River Campground. East of the campground, Lakeshore Trail becomes an old access road to *Au Sable Light Station* (906-387-3700; nps.gov) at E18850 County Road H 58, and near its trailhead is a shipwrecks sign pointing down to the beach. These ruins lie in the water and are hard to spot when the lake is choppy. But walk another 1.5 miles up the trail, and you'll see a second shipwreck sign that directs you to 3 sets of ruins half-buried in the sandy beach.

The lighthouse, which was built in 1874, has been renovated by the National Park Service as a museum and historic site and makes a perfect place to lunch before heading back to the campground. The 40-minute tours are led by park rangers and include climbing the 100 steps to the top of the tower for

Michigan's Most Beautiful Hike

The Lakeshore Trail in Pictured Rocks National Lakeshore is one of Michigan's most popular backpacking treks, a 42.8-mile hike from Grand Marais to Munising with most of it strung along Lake Superior. But if you don't have four days to spare or the desire to haul a backpack for that long, the *Chapel Loop* is the perfect alternative.

This hike begins and ends at Chapel parking lot, 14 miles east of Munising via County Road H 58 and then north on Chapel Road. The entire loop is a 10.2-mile walk over generally level terrain, making it a long day hike, but there are many ways to shorten it.

The first leg of the loop is hiking to Lake Superior along Chapel Falls Trail, an old road that heads north into the woods and in 1.4 miles reaches *Chapel Falls,* one of the most impressive in the park. Two observation decks provide a good view of the 60-foot waterfall that hurls itself over the sharp edge of a cliff into a steep-sided canyon.

In another quarter mile you reach Lake Superior and Chapel Rock, a striking pair of sandstone pillars with a large pine growing on the top of them. Just to the west is Chapel Beach, a half mile of wide, sandy shoreline framed in at one end by colorful sandstone cliffs and at the other by a waterfall where Chapel Creek leaps into Lake Superior.

At this point most people return to the parking lot, following the Chapel Lake Trail for a 6.1-mile loop. Big mistake.

By heading east on Lakeshore Trail, you'll see the most impressive scenery of the day. For the next 4.5 miles, the trail skirts Lake Superior and passes numerous overlooks of the promontories and formations that make up the Grand Portal cliffs. There is no shoreline in Michigan more beautiful than this stretch, where the orange-reddish sandstone contrasts vividly with the deep blue of Lake Superior.

The most interesting spot is a sandy beach just past Grand Portal Point, 4.6 miles into the loop. Only this beach is on top of the cliffs, almost 200 feet above the cold waters of Lake Superior.

From Grand Portal Point you continue along Lake Superior, passing more views of the Pictured Rocks and breaking out at another clifftop beach, before arriving at Mosquito River. Mosquito Falls Trail, one of the newest trails in the park, will return you to the parking lot in 2.7 miles and along the way pass several waterfalls.

a stunning view of Lake Superior. Tours are given from 11 a.m. to 4:30 p.m. Wed through Sun from early June to Labor Day. Admission is $3 per person ages 6 and older. Note that exact amount is required as no change is provided.

You could continue along H 58, although only about half of it is paved, and end up in *Munising.* The scenic town is the gateway to the *Pictured Rocks,* sandstone cliffs that rise 50 to 200 feet above Lake Superior and stretch for 15 miles to the east. They are one of the top attractions in the U.P., and a *Pictured Rocks Boat Cruise* is the best way to view them.

The 3-hour cruises depart from Munising City Harbor, swing past Grand Island, and then skirt the most impressive stretch of Pictured Rocks. Along the way you view such noted formations as Miner's Castle, Battleship Rock, Indian Head, Rainbow Cave, and the Colors Caves, along with waterfalls that leap into Lake Superior and kayakers bobbing in and out of sea arches.

Pictured Rocks Boat Cruises (906-387-2379; picturedrocks.com) offers daily trips at 10 a.m. and 1 p.m. Memorial Day through June and Sept through mid-Oct, and daily trips at 10 a.m. noon, 1, 2, and 3 p.m. and a sunset cruise at various times between 5 p.m. and 7:30 p.m., depending on the sunset, from the last week of May through mid-Oct. The best time for a trip is in late afternoon or early evening when the sun setting in the west makes the cliffs even more colorful. The cost is $38 for anyone age 12 or older, $10 for children ages 6 to 12, and $1 for kids age 5 or younger. For a closer and more adventurous way to view the Pictured Rocks, contact *Northern Waters* (906-387-2323; northernwaters.com). The Munising outfitter offers a guided day paddle on Lake Superior that begins with the drive out to Miners Beach in the national lakeshore where they stage a half-hour kayak lesson. You then hop in your kayak and head east for an intimate view of the towering sandstone cliffs not possible on the boat cruises.

No previous kayaking experience is required and the 3-hour paddle is broken up with a shoreline lunch. The cost is $169 per adult and $149 per child ages 8 to 11 and includes all equipment, kayaks, transportation from Munising, and guides. Check the website for other tours.

Michigan's Smallest State Park

The smallest unit of the Michigan State Park system is *Wagner Falls Scenic Site.* The day-use park is only 22 acres and consists of a small parking area along M 94, 2 miles south of Munising, and a 200-yard trail that ends at an observation deck. The park is small but beautiful as the deck overlooks Wagner Falls, a 20-foot cascade that splashes down several rock ledges.

A Diner in the U.P.

Grand Marais at the end of M 77 is a peaceful oasis of unexpected delights. Officially the town serves as the eastern gateway to Pictured Rocks National Lakeshore, but it is also home to several museums, the most unusual being the **Pickle Barrel House.** The highly unusual summer home with its peek-a-boo windows belonged to William Donahey, creator of the **Teenie Weenies** in the 1920s, which was the longest running cartoon series continuously drawn by the same artist. The home was originally located on Sable Lake but has since been moved downtown to Lake and Randolph Streets and is open 1 to 4 p.m. daily in July and Aug and run by the Grand Marais Historical Society.

Along with a house that looks like a giant pickle barrel, Grand Marais is also the unlikely site of a 1949-vintage diner. The diner was once located in Pennsylvania and hosted such notables as John F. Kennedy and heavyweight champ Floyd Patterson. Eventually it was moved to New Jersey, New York, and finally a vacant field north of Grand Rapids before Rick Guth and Ellen Airgood transported it across the Mackinac Bridge in 1997 and renovated it into **West Bay Diner.** The atmosphere is retro and food is excellent: hamburgers on homemade onion rolls, hand-tossed pizza, classic malts, and Airgood's deep-dish cherry pie. The West Bay Diner (906-494-2607) is at the corner of Woodruff and Veterans Streets at E21825 Veteran St. and hours are "open to close." That's as committed as anybody gets in Grand Marais.

Waterfalls abound in the Munising area, some right on the edge of town. One of them is **Munising Falls.** From H 58 head up Sand Point Road a short way to the National Park Visitor Center, where a quarter-mile path takes you into the woods and up a shaded sandstone canyon. The first viewing platform provides a fine overview of the 50-foot cascade that tumbles straight down a sandstone cliff; a nearby stairway lets you walk up to the falls for a most unusual view of the falling water.

Munising is also on the edge of another park, the **Alger Underwater Preserve,** a graveyard of shipwrecks that date to the 1800s and early 1900s. The 113-square-mile preserve also includes underwater sea caves hollowed out of the Pictured Rocks cliffs by waves, and between the wrecks and the caves this slice of Lake Superior has become a popular destination with scuba divers.

Not a diver? Not a problem. Nondivers and even nonswimmers can enjoy the treasures of Lake Superior through **Glass Bottom Shipwreck Tours.** The company uses a 42-foot vessel with a specially designed hull glass viewing area to let passengers see wrecks in Lake Superior. The 2-hour tours depart from Munising daily during the summer and glide over 3 wrecks as well as sail past the historic lighthouse and the intriguing rock formations of Grand Island.

Tasty Trenary Toast

Finnish culture has heavily influenced the Upper Peninsula, from their winter sports like the luge and ski jumping to what they nibble for breakfast, *Trenary Toast*. A carryover from the Finnish cinnamon treat called *korpu*, Trenary Toast is slices of bread covered with a layer of cinnamon and sugar, then toasted.

The result is a hard, sweet, and very long-lasting slice of bread. Even without any preservatives, Trenary Toast has a shelf life of at least six months and longer if you keep it in a cool, dry place. During a long, cold U.P. winter that's important. When you don't have the energy to battle a raging snowstorm outside, you just reach for the Trenary Toast to sustain you until warmer days arrive.

And Yoopers do. **Trenary Home Bakery,** the sole producer of the famous toast, has 18 employees who make between 3,000 and 4,000 bags a week, most of it consumed in the U.P. If passing through the hamlet of Trenary, you can stop to visit Trenary Home Bakery (906-446-3330; trenaryhomebakery.com) at E. 2914 State Forest Campround Rd. and purchase a bag of cinnamon Trenary Toast for only $4.75. Don't worry, it will still be good by the time you get home.

The most intriguing wreck is the *Bermuda*. The wooden schooner was loaded with 488 tons of iron ore when it left Marquette in 1870 and sank in Grand Harbor during a fierce storm. In 1884 a Canadian salvage company raised the ship, removed its cargo, and resank it in Grand Island's Murray Bay. The *Bermuda* lies only 10 feet below the surface, and in the clear, protective waters of the bay, you can glide right over it and view an entire 19th-century ship.

"Everything is still there," says one guide, "everything except the sails and the crew."

Glass Bottom Shipwreck Tours (906-387-4477; shipwrecktours.com) departs from the Munising Dock 1.5 miles west of downtown off M 28. Tours are offered at 10 a.m. and 1 p.m. daily from Memorial Day weekend through Oct 9. During the summer, there are also 12:30 p.m. and 3:30 p.m. tours, weather permitting. Check the website for exact tour times. The cost is $35 for adults and $12 for children ages 6 to 12 (5 and under are $1).

Schoolcraft County

Blaney Park is the town that refuses to die. It's been foreclosed on, boarded up, even auctioned off building by building, but today the village is surging back as a quiet resort with an ideal location for touring the Upper Peninsula. No more than 90 minutes from this one-road hamlet are the U.P.'s most popular attractions: Tahquamenon Falls, Pictured Rocks, the historic town site of Fayette, and miles of Lake Michigan's sandy shoreline.

Originally a logging camp, Blaney and the area around it were logged out by 1926, so its owners searched for another endeavor for the town's residents. With all the lakes and sandy beach nearby, recreation was the answer, and soon Blaney became Blaney Park. Tourists began arriving from all over the Midwest to spend their vacations on the Upper Peninsula. The resort featured a 9-hole golf course, tennis courts, riding stables, daily excursions to Lake Michigan beaches, and a lighted swimming pool for those who preferred to stay close to their cottages. A lumber baron's mansion was renamed Celibeth and was described in one brochure as "a beautiful club-type hotel." The boardinghouse where loggers had lived was turned into a 21-room lodge, and in 1934 the Blaney Inn was built, a huge dining facility that featured stone fireplaces, walls paneled in knotty pine, and seating for 400.

Improved roads in the Upper Peninsula were Blaney Park's downfall. The family that owned the town tried twice to sell it, only to end up with it again when the buyers defaulted on their payments. The last tourist season was in 1972, after which many of the buildings were boarded up, and Blaney Park finally was auctioned off in 1985.

Today Blaney Park has come back to life again as a tourist destination. It can be reached from the Mackinac Bridge by following US 2 west for 66 miles and then north on M 77 for 1 mile.

The 22-room **Celibeth** at 4446N M 77 is a beautiful bed-and-breakfast with 7 rooms decorated in antiques and furnishings from the resort era of the 1920s. There is an enclosed porch that overlooks the front lawn and features a row of rocking chairs and a sunroom in the back where breakfast is served. The bed-and-breakfast (906-283-3409; celibethhousebnb.com) is open from May through Oct, and the rooms range from $80 to $125 per night.

The heart of Schoolcraft County, some 96,000 acres, has been preserved as the largest wildlife refuge east of the Mississippi River. The **Seney National Wildlife Refuge** was established in 1935 by the US Fish and Wildlife Service to provide a habitat for wildlife, primarily waterfowl migrating to nesting grounds in Canada. The refuge surrounds the Great Manistique Swamp, which endured rough treatment beginning in the 1870s when loggers were intent on stripping every tree from the area. Fires were then set deliberately to clear away the debris of the lumbering operation, preventing new forests from taking root. Finally a land development company came through, drained acre after acre of the swamp, and sold the land to farmers for agriculture in 1911. The farmers lasted about a year before discovering they had been swindled—the soil would grow little.

Seney was a wasteland that nobody wanted. The state ended up with it, and during the Great Depression, deeded it to the federal government with the recommendation that it be turned into a refuge. Civilian Conservation Corps workers came in and built dikes, dug ditches, and used other water-control devices to impound 7,000 acres of water in 21 major ponds, almost miraculously restoring the marsh. Seney again became a habitat for waterfowl when 332 Canada geese were released in 1936 and established its present nesting flocks. Still more geese and other species of birds depend on the area as an important rest stop on their long migration to and from nesting sites in Canada.

Other wildlife—timber wolves, deer, black bears, moose, and coyotes—live in the refuge, but the Canada goose has clearly become the symbol of Seney's return to wilderness. You will see the "honkers" the minute you drive into the parking lot of the visitor center, as a few tame ones are always around looking for a handout from softhearted tourists. The center overlooks one of the many ponds in the refuge, and a telescope at its large viewing window lets you search the marsh area for some of the more than 200 species of birds that can be found here. The center has displays, a children's touch table, and an auditorium that hosts nature movies and slide programs each hour. It is open from mid-May through mid-Oct from 9 a.m. to 5 p.m. daily.

michigantrivia

Manistique boasts a bridge "below the level of the river." Built in 1919, the 300-foot-long Siphon Bridge crosses the Manistique River and is actually below the river because water is atmospherically forced under it. The bridge became famous when it was featured in the *Ripley's Believe It or Not* newspaper series. The bridge is on M 94 at the north end of the downtown area.

The best way to view the wildlife is to follow the 7-mile **Marshland Wildlife Drive** in your car as it winds its way among the ponds, starting near the center and ending at M 77 just south of the refuge entrance. Pick up a free guide that points out items of interest at a number of marked stops, including an active bald eagle nest that can be seen clearly from the drive. Timing is important for spotting wildlife, and it is best to follow the drive either in early morning or at dusk when the animals are most active. Often during the peak of the tourist season, the refuge will stage guided evening tours that depart around 6 p.m. and last for almost 2 hours. Call the visitor center (906-586-9851) for information about the auto tours.

Another unique way to view remoter areas of the refuge is to paddle the handful of rivers that flow through it. **Northland Outfitters** (906-586-9801; northoutfitters.com), located in nearby Germfask at 8174 M 77, offers canoe rentals for the area. It will supply canoes, paddles, life jackets, and transportation to the Manistique River, which runs through the southeast corner of Seney. The trips are self-guided, last either 2 or 4 hours, and offer the possibility of spotting beavers, deer, otters, and a variety of birds or of fishing for walleye or pike in the river.

On the opposite scale of parks is **Palms Book,** a state park of only 388 acres located 12 miles northwest of Manistique on M 149. The park may be small, but it's equally intriguing because of **Kitch-iti-kipi,** Michigan's largest spring. The natural spring pours out more than 10,000 gallons of water per minute from fissures in the underlying limestone, and has created a crystal clear pool 200 feet wide and 40 feet deep. Visitors board a wooden raft with observation holes in the middle and pull themselves across the spring to get a good view of the fantasy world below. Between the swirls of sand and ghostly bubbles rising up, you can view ancient trees with branches encrusted in limestone, huge brown trout slipping silently by, and colors and shapes that challenge the imagination. The spring is especially enchanting in the early morning,

A Hemlock Cathedral

When we entered the cathedral, it was quiet, a little dark, and almost spiritual. It was a place to ponder, maybe even meditate, but this was no church. It was a stand of hemlocks that somehow survived the logging era Michigan experienced at the turn of the 20th century.

Today the **Hemlock Cathedral** is part of the **Little Bay de Noc Recreation Area,** and it's where you go to see what a 300-year-old tree looks like. Trees that old are so tall you can't see the tops of them, so big that two people can't link arms around them, so rare that all that's left are pockets scattered across a state that was once blanketed by them.

In Escanaba residents could see the giant hemlocks on the other side of Little Bay de Noc, and by the late 1800s the spot was a popular weekend retreat known as Maywood. When a small resort hotel was built there in 1904, this pocket of old growth was preserved from the loggers advancing down the Stonington Peninsula.

Today the Hemlock Cathedral in the Little Bay de Noc Recreation Area is as quiet and impressive as it was a century ago. The virgin hemlocks are seen by hiking the Maywood History Trail, an easy half-mile loop that includes almost a dozen interpretive plaques.

The recreation area also includes a sandy beach, picnic area, 36 rustic campsites, and 2 other trails. The Hiawatha National Forest facility is on County Road 513, 7 miles south of US 2 on the Stonington Peninsula. There is a vehicle entry fee and a nightly fee for camping. For more information call the Rapid River Ranger Station at (906) 474-6442.

when a mist lies over the water and the trout rise to the surface. Palms Book has a picnic area but no campsites, and there is a vehicle fee to enter. The raft is free.

Delta County

In the mid-1800s iron ore was shipped from the Upper Peninsula mines to foundries in the lower Great Lakes area at a tremendous cost to companies. The high price of shipping was due to the inefficient method of transportation coupled with the nearly 40 percent waste the ore contained. Fayette Brown, general manager of the Jackson Iron Company, studied the problem and decided the solution was to build a company-owned furnace not far from the mine, where the ore could be smelted into pig iron before it was shipped to the steelmaking centers. The town he planned to build at the smelter had to be a reasonable distance from the Escanaba ore docks, possess a natural harbor, and be near large amounts of limestone and hardwood forests to smelt the iron ore. In 1866 Brown chose a spot on the Garden Peninsula overlooking Big Bay de Noc, and the town of *Fayette* was born.

A year later work began on the furnace and charcoal kiln, and by Christmas the first iron from Fayette was cast. Quickly a town emerged. There were the superintendent's house on a bluff overlooking the harbor, a company office, 9 frame dwellings for the engineers and skilled workers, and 40 log cabins for the laborers. Eventually Fayette featured a machine shop, a small railroad, barns, a blacksmith shop, a hotel, and even an opera house. It was a total community that in 1884 had a population of almost 1,000 and turned out 16,875 tons of iron. Toward the end of that decade, however, Fayette's fate was sealed. The price of pig iron fell, and newly developed coke blast furnaces produced a higher-quality iron at a much cheaper cost. In 1891 the company closed down the furnaces, and within a few years Fayette became a ghost town.

Fayette changed hands several times; at last the state of Michigan obtained the area in 1959 and turned it into *Fayette Historic State Park.* The town booms again now as a scenic ghost town overlooking Snail Shell Harbor, with its towering white cliffs. The 365-acre park is reached from US 2 on County Road 483 and contains an interpretive museum with information, guide maps, and a scale model of Fayette during its heyday. From there you leisurely wander among 22 existing buildings, of which 9 are open. The renovated structures, which are furnished, include the company office, the hotel, the opera house, and a home of one of the skilled employees. More will be opened up in the future.

Fayette Historic State Park (906-644-2603) also has 80 campsites, a beach and picnic area, and boat-launching facilities. The museum is open daily mid-May through June and Sept to mid-Oct from 9 a.m. to 5 p.m. and in July and Aug from 9 a.m. to 8 p.m. There is a vehicle fee to enter the park and a per-night fee to camp.

Another spot worth searching out on the Garden Peninsula is ***Portage Bay State Campground,*** which is reached from County Road 483 (before the state park) by turning off on County Road 08 and carefully following the signs. Getting to the rustic campground (no electricity, pit toilets) is a bumpy 5-mile ride along dirt roads, but the camping area is worth it: You pitch your tent or park your trailer among the pine trees that border the sandy beach of the bay. You can stroll along the beach, follow the hiking trails in the area, or take a dip in the clear water of Lake Michigan.

A delightful picnic area in Delta County is ***Peninsula Point Lighthouse,*** the guiding light at the very tip of the Stonington Peninsula that was built in 1865. Congress authorized the funds the year before, because the wooden sailing ships hauling lumber, iron ore, and fish from Escanaba and Fayette were no match for the treacherous shoals and reefs that separated Big Bay de Noc from Little Bay de Noc. The light went out for the last time in 1936, and the house portion of the lighthouse burned to the ground in 1959. But the view from the point was so spectacular that the Forest Service made it into a public picnic area in 1937.

Climb the 40 steps to the top of the square brick tower and you're greeted with a 360-degree panorama that includes the Escanaba waterfront to the west, the limestone bluffs of Fayette State Park to the east, and the length of Lake Michigan in front of you. You can either hike to it or drive in. The 1.5-mile hike is a scenic walk, while the final mile to the 19th-century light is a narrow, winding, and very bumpy one-lane road not recommended for vehicles more than 16 feet long or 8 feet high.

To reach the lighthouse from Rapid River, head east on US 2 to the Stonington exit. Go south 19 miles on County Road 513 to Stonington, and then take Forest Road 2204. The RV parking area and trailhead are reached before the forest road turns into a narrow, one-lane road in the final mile.

Places to Stay in the Eastern Upper Peninsula

AU TRAIN

Au Train Lake B & B
N 6925
(510) 919-0688
paulsonhouse.com

Pinewood Lodge Estate
E4836 M 28
(906) 420-6098
pinewoodlodgeestate.com

BLANEY PARK

Celibeth House Bed & Breakfast
4446 N M 77
(906) 283-3409
celibethhousebnb.com

ESCANABA

The DeGrand House
1925 Fifth Ave. South
(906) 786-6420
degrandhouse.com

Sandy Shores Cottages
E4717 M 35
(906) 786-3625
sandyshorescottages.com

Terrace Bay Hotel
7146 P. Rd.
(906) 786-7554
terracebayhotel.com

GRAND MARAIS

Bally House Bed & Breakfast
121 E. Third St.
(218) 387-5099
ballyhousebnb.com

MacArthur House Bed & Breakfast
520 W. Second St.
(218) 260-6390
macarthurhouse.net

Pincushion Trails Inn Bed & Breakfast
968 Gunflint Trail
(218) 387-2009
pincushiontrailsinn.com

Sunset Cabins
E22424 County Road H 58
(906) 494-2693
sunsetcabinsmi.net

MACKINAC ISLAND

Chippewa Hotel Waterfront
7221 Main St.
(800) 241-3341
chippewahotel.com

Cottage Inn of Mackinac Island
7267 Market St.
(906) 847-4000
cottageinnofmackinac.com

Grand Hotel
1 Grand Ave.
(800) 334-7263
grandhotel.com

Lilac Tree Suites & Spa
7372 Main St.
(866) 847-6575
lilactree.com

Metivier Inn
7466 Market St.
(906) 847-6234
metivierinn.com

Mission Point Resort
One Lakeshore Dr.
(231) 715-4900
missionpoint.com

Pine Cottage
1427 Bogan Ln.
(906) 847-3820
pinecottagemackinac.com

MANISTIQUE

Northshore Motel
801 E. Lakeshore Dr.
(906) 341-4151
up-northshoremotel.com

Quality Inn & Suites
905 E. Lakeshore Dr.
(906) 341-3777
choicehotels.com

MUNISING

Cherrywood Lodge of Munising
10160 M28
(855) 255-1901
cherrywoodlodgemunising.com

Magnuson Hotel Pictured Rocks Munising
County Road H 13 and M 28
(906) 387-2466

Pictured Rocks Bed & Breakfast
1464 Washington St.
(906) 202-2502
picturedrocksbedandbreakfast.com

NEWBERRY

The Knollwood Inn
13467 M 28
(906) 293-8111
knollwoodinn.com

Quality Inn & Suites
13954 State Hwy M 28
(906) 293-3218
newberrymichigan.net

PARADISE

Magnuson Grand Hotel Lakefront Paradise
8112 N. M 123
(906) 492-3770
magnusongrandlakefront
.com

Tahquamenon Suites Lodging
7967 M 123
(906) 492-3752
tahquamenonsuites.com

SAULT STE. MARIE

Comfort Inn
4404 I-75 Business Loop
(906) 635-1118
choicehotels.com

Kewadin Casino Hotel
2186 Shunk Rd.
(800) 539-2346
kewadin.com

Ramada Plaza Ojibway
240 W. Portage
(906) 632-4100
wyndhamhotels.com

ST. IGNACE

Bavarian Haus Lakefront Inn
1067 N. State St.
(800) 732-9746
bavarianhauslakefront.com

Colonial House Inn
90 N. State St.
(906) 643-6900
colonial-house-inn.com

K Royale Lakefront Inn
1037 N. State St.
(906) 643-7737
(800) 882-7122
kroyale.com

Places to Eat in the Eastern Upper Peninsula

AU TRAIN

Brownstone Inn
E 4635 M 28
(906) 892-8332
brownstoneinnup.com
American

BRIMLEY

Wilcox's Fish House
1232 S. Wilcox Ln.
(906) 437-5407
Seafood

SELECTED CHAMBERS OF COMMERCE & TOURISM BUREAUS

Mackinac Island Tourism Bureau
7274 Main St.
Mackinac Island 49757
(800) 454-5227
mackinacisland.org

Newberry Area Tourism Association
4947 Twin Lakes Rd.
Newberry 49868
(800) 831-7292
newberrytourism.com

Sault Ste. Marie Convention and Visitors Bureau
225 E. Portage Ave.
Sault Ste. Marie 49783
(800) 647-2858
saultstemarie.com

St. Ignace Visitors Bureau
6 Spring St.
St. Ignace 49781
(800) 338-6660
stignace.com

Visit Escanaba
1001 N. Lincoln Rd.
Escanaba 49829
(800) 533-4386
visitescanaba.com

OTHER ATTRACTIONS

Grand Island Recreation Area
N8016 Grand Island Landing Rd. I
Munising
(906) 387-3503
grandislandup.com

Mackinac Island Butterfly House
6750 McGulpin St.
Mackinac Island
(906) 847-3972
originalbutterflyhouse.com

Mackinac Island Carriage Tours
7396 Market St.
Mackinac Island
(906) 847-3307
mict.com

Sand Point Lighthouse
Escanaba

Seul Choix Point Lighthouse
Gulliver
(906) 283-3183
greatlakelighthouse.com

Tahquamenon Logging Museum
Newberry
(906) 293-3700
tahquamenonloggingmuseum.org

ESCANABA

Crispigna's Restaurant
1213 Ludington St.
(906) 786-1213
crispignas.com
Italian

The Family Inn
6380 N. Eleventh St.
(906) 786-6774
thefamilyinn.com
American

Hereford & Hops
624 Ludington Ave.
(906) 789-1945
herefordandhops.com
Brewpub

Stonehouse Restaurant & Lounge
2223 Ludington St.
(906) 786-5003
stonehouseescanaba.com
Steaks & Seafood

GRAND MARAIS

Lake Superior Brewing Company
14283 Lake Ave.
(906) 494-2337
Brewpub

The West Bay Diner
E. 21825 Veterans St.
(906) 494-2607
Breakfast & Sandwiches

MACKINAC ISLAND

Carriage House
Hotel Iroquois
7485 Main St.
(906) 847-3321
iroquoishotel.com
Fine Dining

The Gate House
1547 Cadotte Ave.
(906) 847-3772
grandhotel.com
American

Mary's Bistro
7463 Main St.
(906) 847-9911
marysbistromackinacisland.com
Brewpub

Pink Pony
7221 Main St.
(906) 847-3341
pinkponymackinac.com
American

Woods Restaurant
8655 Cudahy Cir.
(906) 847-3699
grandhotel.com
American & European

MUNISING

Camel Riders
5609 N. Camel Rider Dr.
Wetmore
(906) 573-2319
American

Muldoon's Pasties
1246 M 28
(906) 387-5880
muldoonspasties.com
Pasties

Tracey's
815 W. Munising Ave.
(906) 387-8000
roam-inn.com
American

NEWBERRY

Pickelman's Pantry
14045 County Road 460
(906) 293-3777
American

Woodland Grill
5073 M 123 South
(906) 293-8422
newberrycountryclub.com
American

PARADISE

Brown Fisheries Fish House
32638 M 123
(906) 492-3901
American

The Inn Gastropub & Smokehouse
8112 M 123
(906) 492-3529
theinngetsome.com

Tahquamenon Falls Brewery
Tahquamenon Falls State Park
24019 Upper Falls Dr.
(906) 492-3300
tahquamenonfallsbrewery
.com
Brewpub

SAULT STE. MARIE

The Antlers Restaurant
804 E. Portage Ave.
(906) 253-1728
saultantlers.com
American

Freighters
Ojibway Hotel
240 W. Portage Ave.
(906) 632-4100
ojibwayhotel.com
Fine Dining

Karl's Cuisine, Winery and Brewery
447 W. Portage Ave.
(906) 253-1900
karlscuisine.com
American

Lockview Restaurant
329 W. Portage Ave.
(906) 632-2772
thelockviewrestaurant.net
American

The Wicked Sister
716 Ashmun St.
(906) 259-1086
wickedsistersault.com
Pub

ST. IGNACE

Hillside House Restaurant
1040 N. State St.
(906) 643-8228
American

Village Inn
250 N. State St.
(906) 643-9511
viofmackinac.com
American

Western Upper Peninsula

Michigan's remotest and most rustic region is the rugged western Upper Peninsula. Two small ranges located here constitute the only true mountains in any of the Great Lakes states; between Baraga and Marquette lie the Huron Mountains, and along the Lake Superior shoreline, from west of Ontonagon to Copper Harbor, is the Copper Range. Within these rugged hills are Mount Arvon, the highest point in Michigan at 1,979 feet above sea level, and the Porcupine Mountains, between whose ridges and peaks lies the stunning Lake of the Clouds.

It was in these hills of the western U.P. that the great iron and copper mines flourished from the 1800s to the 1940s, bringing boatloads of immigrants from Norway, Finland, and Italy to work in the shafts. Today the remnants of the mining era are ghost towns, abandoned mines, and communities with strong ethnic heritage and pride.

For most Michigan residents, this region of the state is a remote, distant place; driving to Copper Harbor from Detroit is the same distance as traveling to Washington, DC. But once it is "discovered," travelers marvel at the western U.P.'s natural wonders. More than for its mines, pasty shops, and historical museums, you come to this region of Michigan for the beauty

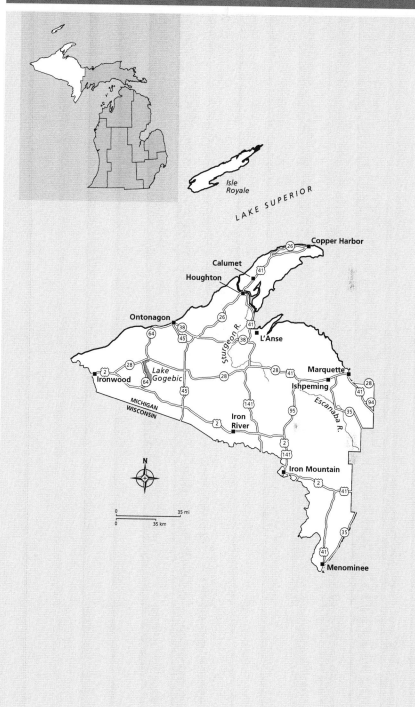

Isle
Royale

LAKE SUPERIOR

Copper Harbor

Calumet

Houghton

Ontonagon

L'Anse

Sturgeon R.

Ironwood

Lake
Gogebic

Marquette

Ishpeming

MICHIGAN
WISCONSIN

Escanaba R.

Iron
River

Iron Mountain

Menominee

N

0   35 mi
0   35 km

of nature's handiwork: cascading waterfalls, panoramas of forested wilderness, a lake set in a sea of reds, yellows, and oranges painted by autumn leaves.

Marquette County

The largest county in Michigan consists of 1,873 square miles, 1,800 lakes, 73 miles of Lake Superior shoreline, and *Marquette,* the largest (and, some say, only) city in the Upper Peninsula. The city of 20,680 became a spot on the map with a post office in 1849, and it bloomed the following decade as the port and shipping center for the nearby iron mines and logging camps. The lumber and mining barons graced the streets of Marquette with mansions, many still standing today. From Front Street turn east onto Ridge Street and you'll head toward Lake Superior, passing one late-Victorian home after another until you end up in the parking lot of the *Marquette Maritime Museum* on the waterfront.

The museum is housed in the red sandstone Old Water Works Building at 300 Lake Shore Blvd. and features displays on shipwrecks, antique outboard

AUTHOR'S TOP TEN PICKS

Black River Harbor Drive
Bessemer
(906) 667-0261

Canyon Falls and Gorge
L'Anse
(906) 524-7444

Fort Wilkins
15223 US 41
Copper Harbor
(906) 289-4215

Hanka Homestead Museum
13249 Hanka
Askel
(906) 334-2575
hankahomesteadmuseum.org

Iron County Historical Museum
100 Brady Ave.
Caspian
(906) 265-2617

Lake of the Clouds
Silver City
(906) 884-2047
porcupineup.com

Michigan Iron Industry Museum
73 Forge Rd.
Negaunee
(906) 475-7857

Piers Gorge Nature Trail
Norway
(906) 774-2002

Quincy Mine
49750 US 41
Hancock
(906) 482-3101
quincymine.com

US National Ski and Snowboard Hall of Fame
610 Palms Ave.
Ishpeming
(906) 485-6323
skihall.com

motors and boats, 3 Fresnel lenses, commercial fishermen who worked the area, and other facets of the city's maritime days, which fed many and made some (from the look of their homes) incredibly wealthy. The museum (906-226-2006; mqtmaritimemuseum.com) is open from mid-May through mid-Oct Tues to Sun from 11 a.m. to 4 p.m. Admission to the museum and lighthouse is $12 for adults and $5 for children 12 and under.

The largest and most interesting structures on Marquette's waterfront are the iron ore docks that load the rock into Great Lakes freighters for a journey south. The Lake Superior and Ishpeming Railroad docks are still operating today, and the best vantage point is *Presque Isle Park.* The 328-acre city park is not an island but a peninsula that juts out into Lake Superior on the north side of Marquette. A road circles the park shoreline, beginning on the south side, where you can see the ore docks and, if your timing is right, watch a freighter take on its load (1 to 3 times a week).

The drive continues and passes the steep red cliffs of Lookout Point and then the view at Sunset Point, where residents gather to watch the end of another day. The park also has an outdoor band shell with weekly events, a small zoo, a beach and bathhouse, picnic areas, and bicycle paths. Hiking trails crisscross the forested interior of Presque Isle and become a favorite spot for Nordic skiers during the winter. The park is open daily from 7 a.m. to 11 p.m., and perhaps the best time of year to visit it is the last weekend in July during its Art on the Rocks Festival, when local artists gather to display and

michigantrivia

The Superior Dome on the Northern Michigan University campus is the largest wooden dome in the world. Dedicated in 1991, it is 150 feet high and covers 272,330 square feet. It contains more than 100 miles of Douglas fir tongue-and-groove decking.

sell their work in this picturesque setting. For the days and times to watch iron ore boats being loaded, call the Michigan Department of Transportation Welcome Center (906-249-9066) in Marquette.

In Marquette's Lower Harbor are the Old Ore Docks, no longer operating, which have been designated a state historic site. An excellent place to view the docks is from a table in the *Vierling Restaurant* at 119 S. Front St. The saloon was opened in 1883 by Martin Vierling, an art lover and saloonkeeper who headed north with his paintings after running an establishment in Detroit. Later the art lover's bar became just another cafe during Prohibition, but the present proprietors, Terry and Christi Doyle, have turned back the clock by renovating the interior and returning the building to its original function as a saloon, brewpub, and fine restaurant. The brick walls inside once again feature paintings and prints, as the owners exhibit the works of a different artist every month. There are also old photographs and artifacts of early Marquette, and the large windows in the rear of the restaurant overlook the iron ore docks. A pair of binoculars hangs on the back wall for anyone wanting a closer look at the massive structure.

The fare is "fresh and homemade," and the dinner menu features whitefish, shrimp, and chicken entrees, but its most popular requests are for the baked French onion soup and the home-brewed blueberry wheat beer. In December 1995, the Vierling became one of Michigan's first brewpubs with the addition of a 5-barrel microbrewing system. The brew equipment, direct from Budapest, Hungary, is configured to produce some of the finest ales and lagers in 155-gallon hand-crafted batches. The relatively small-size batches of beer ensure a fast product turnover, which enables the Vierling to serve the freshest beer possible with a multitude of varieties. The Vierling Restaurant (906-228-3533; thevierling.com) is open daily except Sun from 11 a.m. to 10 p.m. Dinner is served after 4 p.m., and prices range from $30 to $40.

A Cabin in the Woods

The most unusual lodging accommodations in Marquette County come without a flush toilet, a shower, or any plumbing, for that matter. There are no mattresses, telephones, or televisions with HBO. Heat is a stack of logs and a wood-burning stove. Hopefully you brought some matches.

But what a view!

From the porch of Cabin No. 3 in the **Little Presque Isle State Forest Recreation Area,** you can watch the rays of an early morning sun spread across Harlow Lake. In the background is the rocky crown of Hogsback Mountain, and when the rising sun paints it in a light shade of pink, it's the closest thing we have to alpenglow in Michigan.

Built in 1996, the 6 rustic cabins are scattered in Little Presque Isle, a 3,040-acre tract 5 miles northwest of Marquette and split in the middle by County Road 550. You can't drive to them, but the walk in is not far. Cabins No. 1, 2, and 3 are a mere 200 yards from where you park the car. Cabin No. 5, the farthest from the trailhead, is only a half mile away.

Yet for the price of a little boot leather and the $74-per-night rental fee, you're ensured of solitude and peace of mind in one of the most picturesque settings in the Upper Peninsula. To reserve the cabins or obtain a brochure on Little Presque Isle State Forest Recreation Area, call the Department of Natural Resources office in Marquette at (906) 339-4461 or (800) 447-2757.

For an excellent view of all of Marquette, head north of town on County Road 550 for a few miles and turn into the dirt parking lot marked by the large SUGAR LOAF sign. This is the start of the **Sugar Loaf Recreation Trail,** a wide and easy path that winds 0.6 mile up the peak of the same name. You actually climb 315 feet through forest and over granite ridges by a series of steps until you reach the rocky knob marked by a stone monument. The view is spectacular on a clear day, a 360-degree panorama that includes the city, Lake Superior, the rough coastline, and the many offshore islands.

By continuing north on County Road 550 for another 26 miles, you reach its end in the small village of Big Bay on the shores of Lake Independence. Big Bay is best known as a place where scenes for the 1959 film *Anatomy of a Murder,* starring Jimmy Stewart and Lee Remick, were shot. The story is true, with the murder taking place at the **Lumberjack Tavern** (906-345-9912), a classic north woods bar at 202 Bensinger St. that was used for one scene in the movie. You can still see the famed bullet hole in the wall of the tavern and visit other movie location sites with the help of an *Anatomy of a Murder* self-guided tour brochure available free online from the **Marquette County Convention and Visitors Bureau** (800-544-4321; travelmarquettemichigan.com) at 117 W. Washington St.

An interesting place to stay in Big Bay, in fact one of the most interesting bed-and-breakfasts in the U.P., is the **Big Bay Point Lighthouse,** the secluded retreat 3.5 miles north of town on Lighthouse Road. The light at Big Bay was built and put into service in 1896 and included a 2-story, redbrick dwelling with 18 rooms. The house was divided in half, with the lightkeeper living in one half and his assistant in the other. The Coast Guard automated the light in 1941 and then sold the structure in 1961 after building a new steel tower nearby.

In 1986 the lighthouse became a unique bed-and-breakfast offering guests the rare opportunity to stay overnight in one of its 6 bedrooms. The lights stand high above Lake Superior on a rocky point in the middle of 40 wooded acres that include 2 miles of trails. You can climb the narrow staircase to the top of the tower for a splendid view of the area, catching a sunrise over Lake Superior at daybreak, a sunset over the Huron Mountains at dusk, or possibly the northern lights at night. The interior has been completely renovated and refinished, showing its natural wood and brick, and the various rooms include a delightful sauna.

The lighthouse is open year-round, with special rates for the off-season, weekdays, and package stays. The basic rate for the summer ranges from $149 to $239 for rooms that sleep from 2 to 4 people. For reservations contact Big Bay Lighthouse (906-345-9957; bigbaylighthouse.com).

One of the most unusual Michigan historical museums is tucked away in the woods near Negaunee and is probably passed up by many visitors. That's a shame. The *Michigan Iron Industry Museum* is an interesting stop that lets you leisurely explore the history of the Upper Peninsula's iron industry. The museum lies in the forested ravines of the Marquette Iron Range and overlooks the Carp River, where the first iron forge in the Lake Superior region was built in 1848. The U.P.'s iron deposits had been discovered 4 years earlier when William Burt, leader of a US Geological Survey party near the area, noticed the magnetic needle of his compass jumping wildly about. He instructed his men to search the ground, and they immediately turned up outcroppings of almost pure iron among the roots of pine trees. The iron era of the U.P. had begun, and in 1846 the Jackson Mine, the first operation in the U.P., was opened near Negaunee.

Upper Peninsula Cuisine

The Upper Peninsula's finest cuisine has been hooked, picked, or includes, among other things, rutabaga. If traveling the U.P. here are three specialties to try:

Pasties: These pies combine ground beef, potatoes, onions, and rutabaga in a flaky crust, baked until golden brown. Cornish immigrants are credited for introducing them to the U.P. while miners made them a staple because they are incredibly filling and practical to carry.

You can purchase pasties in almost any town in the U.P., but three places that stand out are *Muldoon's Pasties* (1246 W. M 28; 906-387-5880; muldoonspasties.com) in Munising, *Jean Kay's Pasties* (1635 Presque Isle Ave.; 906-228-5310; jeankayspasties.com) in Marquette, and *Joe's Pasty Shop* (116 W. Aurora St.; 906-932-4412; joespastyshop.com) in Ironwood.

Smoked Fish: You'll see small shops and fish houses selling a variety of smoked fish, ranging from lake trout to herring, and most of it caught locally. Start with whitefish, which has the most delicate flavor and is not as greasy as lake trout.

Wilcox's Fish House (Lakeshore Drive; 906-437-5407) near Bay Mills sells a delicious smoked fish spread and whitefish sandwiches as well as a variety of smoked fillets.

Thimbleberry Jam: A thimbleberry looks like an overgrown raspberry but is found only in the Keweenaw Peninsula and the western U.P. The jam it makes is divine but hard to find, the reason it usually costs $8 to $10 for a half-pint jar.

The Jampot (6500 M 26; societystjohn.com/store), 3 miles east of Eagle River and operated by the Society of St. John monks, is renowned for its wild thimbleberry jam.

TOP ANNUAL EVENTS

JANUARY

Noquemenon Ski Marathon
Marquette
(866) 370-7223
noquemenon.com

FEBRUARY

Pine Mountain Classic
Iron Mountain
(800) 236-2447

Snowburst
Porcupine Mountains Wilderness
State Park
(906) 885-5209
porcupinemountains.com

U.P. 200 Sled Dog Race
Marquette
(800) 544-4321
up200.org

Winter Carnival
Houghton
(800) 338-7982
mtu.edu/carnival

JUNE

PastyFest
Calumet
mainstreetcalumet.com

Pine Mountain Music Festival
Iron Mountain
(906) 482-1542
pmmf.org

JULY

Art on the Rocks
Marquette
(906) 250-6156
marquetteartontherocks.com

U.P. Championship Rodeo
Iron River
(906) 265-9938
upprorodeo.com

AUGUST

Ore to Shore Mountain Bike Epic
Ishpeming
(906) 486-4841
oretoshore.com

The museum at 73 Forge Rd. does an excellent job of leading you through the history of iron, from its beginnings to its most robust era to the decline of the industry in the 1960s. Inside are several levels of displays, a reconstructed mine shaft to walk through, and an auditorium that presents a short introductory program. Outside are more artifacts, including a mine locomotive, and trails leading to the old forge site on the Carp River. Expanded by 4,000 square feet in 2006, the Michigan Iron Industry Museum (906-475-7857; michigan.gov/ironindustrymuseum) is open year-round. Hours from May 1 through Oct 31 are daily from 9:30 a.m. to 4:30 p.m.; Nov 1 to Apr 30 they are from Wed to Fri from 9:30 a.m. to 4 p.m. and the first Sat of each month from 9:30 a.m. to 4 p.m.

The museum is reached from US 41 by turning onto County Road 492 about 3 miles east of Negaunee, and admission is free. From the state mining museum it's only a short drive to more mining history at *Cliffs Shaft Mine Museum* in Ishpeming. Cliffs Shaft Mine was opened in 1879 by the Iron Cliffs

Co. and became the nation's largest producer of hard, spectacular hematite, a type of iron ore. When it closed in 1967, Cliffs Shaft was the last operating mine in Ishpeming and included 3 shafts that reached depths of 1,358 feet and more than 65 miles of tunnels running under most of the town.

Chilling Tales at the Ski Museum

With a baby strapped to his chest, the brave skier headed out in the coldest, darkest, most dangerous time of the year. By his side was another of the village's skilled skiers. Their mission seemed impossible. They were the original *Birkebeiners.* They were the people who spirited out to safety the crown prince of Norway during the Norwegian Civil War.

Peasants and fierce warriors, the Birkebeiners (Birch Legs) got their name because they were so poor they had to tie bark from birch trees around their legs as footwear. Their enemies, the Baglers, were a rich, powerful dynasty who needed to get rid of the baby—the king's son—and then all of Norway would belong to them.

Of course, the Birkebeiners succeeded or there probably wouldn't be a display honoring them at the *US National Ski and Snowboard Hall of Fame and Museum.* In 1206, the Birkebeiners saved the child who went on to become King Haakon Hakonsson IV. As king, he ended Norway's civil wars and brought stability to the country.

Another display spotlights the development of the chairlifts to carry skiers up mountains, instead of skiers having to climb the steep slopes. Getting people to the top of the hill is very important. Before the creation of chairlifts, would-be skiers had to climb to the top of the mountain and had to be tough to do it. The chairlifts made it easier for more people to enjoy the sport.

Installed in 1936 in Sun Valley, Idaho, the world's first known chairlifts were based on a system for loading bunches of bananas onto boats. Instead of hooks for the bananas, the design called for chairs for skiers to sit on while wearing skis. The chairs were suspended from a single cable running above the chair.

The Modern Ski Warfare exhibit honors the American 10th Mountain Division troops of World War II. The division started as an experiment to train skiers and climbers to fight in the most difficult mountain terrain in Europe. The 10th Division was deployed to the mountains of northern Italy, where for six months the Germans had stymied the US Army atop a dangerously high mountain. On February 18, 1945, when night fell, the steep mountain was covered in snow and ice. The Germans didn't even bother to post a guard, believing that no American unit could climb such a difficult ridge. They were wrong. The soldiers of the 10th climbed silently to the top and secured Riva Ridge. The next day's assault on the mountain proved victorious for the American soldiers. But the victors paid a high cost. They lost 1,000 men in the process. After the war, veterans of the 10th Division created most of the first generation of US ski resorts. Contact the Ski Hall of Fame at (906) 485-6323; skihall.com.

The museum opened its doors in 2002 with former miners guiding visitors through the Dry Building, where workers used to change into their work clothes, the Shop Building, which houses historic equipment, and across the grounds. Among the displays is the Ishpeming Rock and Mineral Club room with its extensive mineral collection and model of the sprawling mine complex from the 1960s.

The Cliffs Shaft Mine Museum (906-485-1882; michigan.org) is at 501 W. Euclid St. and can be reached from US 41/M 28 in Ishpeming by heading south on Lakeshore Drive. The museum is open from noon to 5 p.m. Tues through Sat, May to Oct. There is a small admission.

Though it might surprise a few people, especially avid skiers, Ishpeming is home of the **US National Ski and Snowboard Hall of Fame.** The hall was established here in 1954 because the Ishpeming Ski Club is "the oldest active ski club in the country."

Formed in 1887, the club was founded by Scandinavians who had emigrated to the U.P. to work the Marquette Range iron mines and brought their love of skiing with them. They were soon hosting ski jumping tournaments and in 1926 moved their ramps and competition site to a large bowl owned by Cleveland-Cliffs, Inc. When a skier badly injured himself in practice that first year, a local reporter dubbed the area "Suicide Hill" and the name stuck, much to the alarm of club officials who were trying to promote the new jumps.

In the early 1990s the Hall of Fame was relocated to a new building in Ishpeming that features an impressive roofline in the shape of a ski jump. Inside are exhibits and displays that detail the history of skiing from medieval times to the latest Winter Olympics. All three forms of skiing are included—Nordic, Alpine, and ski jumping—and many visitors are amazed to learn that Alpine skiing is a relatively new version of the sport.

The Ski Hall of Fame (906-485-6323; skihall.com) is on US 41 between Second and Third Streets at 610 Palms Ave. and is open from 10 a.m. to 5 p.m. Mon through Sat. Admission is free.

Baraga County

Most roadside rest areas in the Upper Peninsula consist of little more than picnic tables, a pair of pit toilets, and a hand pump for water. Then there is the one on US 41, 8 miles south of L'Anse. It consists of picnic tables, a pair of pit toilets, a hand pump for water, and one of the most beautiful canyons in Michigan. The state's Department of Transportation maintains the tables and the toilets, but it was forestry students from Michigan Technological University who built the wooden boardwalks and observation platforms that make **Canyon Falls and Gorge** such a pleasant stop.

From the large display map in the rest area, the path departs into the woods, crosses a bridge over Bacco Stream, and within a half mile comes to the impressive Canyon Falls formed by the Sturgeon River. The falls mark the beginning of the canyon by thundering over a rock ledge to the river 30 feet below. Handrails have been erected here, and you can lean over the top of the cascade to listen to its roar or to feel the mist the falling water creates.

At this point there is a TRAIL ENDS sign, but the best part of the area, the gorge itself, can be seen only by following the original path, which snakes around a huge rock face. This path hugs the half-mile-long canyon and lets you view the Sturgeon River, a stretch of roiling whitewater that rushes through sheer rock walls 50 feet high. All visitors, especially families with young children, should be extremely careful if they choose to continue to the end of the old trail, a mile-long one-way hike. The original log handrails are still up, but they're flimsy and weak in places, and after they end there is nothing between you and the sharp edge of the gorge.

To reach the roof of the state, you have to find **Mount Arvon** in the Upper Peninsula, which at 1,979 feet is 21 feet short of being a true "mountain" but still the highest point in Michigan. The outing involves following unmarked logging roads in a remote section of Baraga County and hoping you can find your way back. Once on top, there is no majestic view, just a yellow box in a forest with a register book inside.

But enough people undertake this adventure that the **Baraga County Convention & Visitors Bureau** (800-743-4908; baragacounty.org) publishes a map and a set of detailed directions to the high point. The association visitor center is right off US 41 as you enter L'Anse from the east at 755 E. Broad St. and is open 9 a.m. to 5 p.m. Mon through Fri.

Although serious research on the subject has never been done, many say the largest and best sweet rolls in the state are found at the **Hilltop Restaurant,** on US 41 just south of L'Anse at 18047 US Hwy. 41. One roll is an ample breakfast for most people since it measures more than 5 inches across and 3 inches thick and arrives filled with cinnamon and dripping in glaze. The restaurant has been baking the sweet rolls for more than 60 years and on a good weekend will serve more than 1,000. On a typical busy weekend, the Hilltop will use about 3,000 pounds of flour and 150 pounds of sugar, plus other ingredients, to make the famous sweet rolls. The record so far is 204 dozen sweet rolls baked in the kitchen in the course of one long day. The eatery also has other items on its menu (including good pastries), but who has room for anything else after devouring its sticky specialty with a cup of fresh-brewed coffee? The Hilltop (906-524-7858; sweetroll.com) is open from 7 a.m. to 8 p.m. daily from June through Oct. Winter hours from Nov to May are Sun through Thurs 7 a.m. to 7 p.m., Fri and Sat 7 a.m. to 8 p.m.

One of Baraga County's most interesting attractions is the ***Hanka Homestead Museum,*** a "living outdoor museum" where visitors learn about and see the lifestyle of the early Finnish farmers who immigrated to what was then a remote and isolated region of the state. The farm dates back to 1896, when the Hanka family applied for a homestead on two 40-acre parcels along the military road to Fort Wilkins at the tip of the Keweenaw Peninsula. The first thing Herman Hanka built was an 18- by 24-foot log house. But he was Finnish, so the second thing he constructed was his *savu*, or smoke sauna. Eventually he added barns, a self-cooling milk house that straddles a small spring, a horse stable, a blacksmith shop, and a granary.

The amazing thing about the farm is that it's never been wired for electricity, even though the youngest son, Jalmer Hanka, lived there until 1966. It was added to the National Register of Historic Places in 1984 and opened to the public the next year. Today there are 10 buildings and a root cellar to explore, each filled with the Hanka possessions. From US 41 in L'Anse, head north

Strange as it Sounds

Highpointers are a group of adventurers whose mission in life is to stand on the highest point in all 50 states. They used to come to L'Anse from every corner of the country looking for **Mount Curwood,** which for two decades was thought to be Michigan's highest point at 1,996.4 feet. They would fly to Marquette, drive to Baraga County, and then search out some local for detailed directions on how to follow a maze of logging roads to the top of the peak.

Imagine their shock when the Department of the Interior conducted a survey in 1982 and concluded that Mount Curwood is really only 1,978.34 feet in elevation and actually the second highest spot in the state. Michigan's loftiest peak is nearby **Mount Arvon,** which at 1,979.238 feet above sea level is 11 inches higher than Curwood.

Many highpointers, who had climbed Mount Curwood 15 or 20 years earlier, were forced to return to Michigan and climb Mount Arvon. And when they finally reached the peak, what did they see? Most of the time nothing more than the trees at the top. The exception is in late fall after the leaves have dropped and a view through the trees is possible.

What there is on the summit of Arvon is a USGS brass marker verifying the elevation. There is also a small yellow mailbox containing a logbook so you can document your achievement of not getting lost as well as noting how many other highpoints you have reached.

toward Houghton, and in 12 miles turn west on Arnheim Road. Follow the small museum signs to 13249 Hanka. If you pass Otter Lake, you've gone too far west. The homestead (906-334-2601; hankahomesteadmuseum.org) is open Tues, Thurs, Sat, and Sun from noon to 4 p.m. from Memorial Day to Labor Day. At other times, visitors are welcome to take a brochure for self-guided tours of the grounds. Admission is $3 per person.

Houghton County

One of the most spectacular areas of the U.P.'s interior is relatively unknown to travelers who are hesitant to leave paved roads. The **Sturgeon River Gorge Area** is located just inside Houghton County along its border with Baraga County south of M 3838. The wilderness area includes the gorge cut by the Sturgeon River, which in some places is more than 400 feet deep, making it the largest and deepest in the Great Lakes states. For the best view of it, follow M 3838 west of Baraga and turn south onto Prickett Dam Road (also called Forest Road 193), marked by a NATIONAL FOREST sign. Within 11 miles the road merges into Sturgeon Gorge Road (Forest Road 191), and a few hundred yards to the right there is a sharp 90-degree curve. At this bend an extremely rough jeep trail leads west to the edge of the gorge. It is best to walk the quarter mile that ends at one of the most beautiful panoramas in the U.P. You see the deep gorge below and miles of forested ridges and hills to the west.

Before reaching Sturgeon Gorge Road, you will pass a directional sign for **Silver Mountain.** Located on the edge of the Sturgeon River Gorge Wilderness in Houghton County, Silver Mountain is a 1,312-foot peak, once the site of a fire tower. At a small parking lot, you'll find a long stairway—long as in 250 steps—but once on top you'll see the foundation of the old fire tower, two USGS markers, and a view that includes miles of the rugged Sturgeon River Gorge Wilderness.

There are a handful of mine tours in the Upper Peninsula, but the best one is at the **Quincy Mine.** The Quincy Mining Company was organized in 1846 and for almost 100 years it mined the Pewabic copper lode located just north of Hancock. It was such a moneymaker that the

michigantrivia

In Laurium, where Tamarack Street joins M 28, is the George Gipp Memorial. Better known as "the Gipper," Laurium's most famous son went on to become a football star at Notre Dame University. Legend has it that from his death-bed, he uttered the famous line to coach Knute Rockne, "Tell the boys to win one for the Gipper." The part of the Gipper and the deathbed scene gave Ronald Reagan his most memorable movie role.

Toledo for the Upper Peninsula

By 1835 Michigan had grown sufficiently to qualify for statehood, but Congress held it up because of a boundary controversy with Ohio over a sliver of land that included Toledo. The so-called Toledo War resulted in both states' calling out their militias but, fortunately, no bloodshed. When Michigan gave up claims to the city, it was awarded the Upper Peninsula and statehood, becoming the 26th state in 1837.

mine was nicknamed Old Reliable, and today it is part of the new Keweenaw National Historical Park.

The 2-hour tour begins with the world's largest steam hoist, a giant spool that holds 13,200 feet of cable and lowered workers into Shaft No. 2 of the underground mine to a depth of 9,200 feet. You then board a cog tram for a journey down the steep Quincy Hill to the entrance of Shaft No. 5. Here tractor-drawn wagons take you a half mile into a horizontal tunnel 400 feet below the surface. Exhibits and videos in the hoist house round out a visit to the mine at 49750 WS 41. The Quincy Mine (906-482-3101; quincymine.com) is open from the end of Apr to the first week of June, and full tours are $40 for adults and $20 for children ages 6 to 12. Winter hours are 9:30 a.m. to 5 p.m. on Fri, Sat, and Sun.

In nearby Lake Linden, right downtown at 300 Calumet St., is *Lindell's Chocolate Shoppe.* Joseph Bosch had the building erected in 1893 for his Bosch Brewing Company, but in 1918 it was refurbished with wooden ceiling fans, 20 high-backed oak booths, a nickelodeon, leaded-glass windows, and a 6-foot-long marble food preparation table that took 4 people to lift. It became the Chocolate Shop, and though the entire building was moved down the street in 1928, little of the interior has changed since then.

The menu has, however, but the shop still makes some of the best home-made ice cream in the U.P. The 1943 ice cream maker is still proudly displayed in the front window. Lindell's Chocolate Shoppe (906-296-8083) is also a restaurant and bar with a full menu, but unquestionably it is the ice cream and the malts, milkshakes, sundaes, and banana splits that are its most popular items. The shop is open Mon through Thurs 6 a.m. to 4 p.m., Fri and Sat 6 a.m. to 8 p.m., and Sun 6 a.m. to 2 p.m.

Keweenaw County

Under the forceful will of President Andrew Jackson, Michigan became a state in 1837, when it grudgingly accepted the entire U.P. in exchange for surrendering Toledo to Ohio. In only six years, this "worthless wilderness" became a land of incredible wealth after Douglas Houghton, the first state geologist, explored the Keweenaw Peninsula and reported finding chunks of pure copper. Miners began arriving by 1841, and within two years there was a lively copper rush to this small section of the U.P., forcing the US Army to build Fort Wilkins in Copper Harbor (today a state historical park) to maintain law and order. As in all stampedes for a precious metal, many mines quickly died, and thousands of miners went home disillusioned and broke. Nevertheless, substantial lodes of copper were uncovered, and by the 1860s this area was producing 15 million pounds annually, or almost 90 percent of the national total. Two of the most profitable mines were Calumet and Hecla, and near them sprang up the town of Red Jacket. Later renamed *Calumet,* this city of 66,000 in 1898 had wealth, importance (it was considered as a new site for the state capital), and a peculiar problem.

Because of large contributions to the city budget from the mines, the council found itself with a surplus of funds. Already the community had paved streets, electric lights, and telephones, so the town decided to build an opera house, the grandest theater in the Midwest, one that would rival the stages of the East Coast. The *Calumet Opera House* was built in 1899 at Sixth and Elm Streets, and no expense was spared. It was designed in an Italian Renaissance style and inside featured two balconies, private viewing chambers along the walls, and rococo plaster ornamentation of gilt, cream, and crimson. The acoustics were nearly perfect: An actor could whisper on the stage and be heard in the last row of the top balcony.

On March 20, 1900, the first performance was given to a packed house of 1,100 and was described by the *Copper Country Evening News* as "the greatest social event ever known in the copperdome's metropolis." A string of legendary performers arrived at the famed opera house, including John Philip Sousa, Sarah Bernhardt, Douglas Fairbanks, and Lillian Russell. Eventually the theater, like the town, fell upon hard times. The local mines, the last to operate in the Keweenaw Peninsula, were closed for good because of a labor strike in 1968; by then Calumet's population had dwindled to 1,000. Today, the population of Calumet is 727.

The mines are still closed, but the opera house has reopened. Declared a National Historic Site in 1974, it was fully restored, and its opulence can be viewed on a guided tour from mid-July through Aug. The tours are offered at 1, 2, 3, and 4 p.m. on Wed. Admission is $6 for a peek into Calumet's past. The building has also returned to live theater after a stint showing motion pictures of the 1920s and 1930s. Contact the Opera House at 340 Sixth St. (906-337-2610; calumettheatre.com) for information.

At one time or another in the late 1800s, there were 14 active copper mines in the Keweenaw Peninsula, and today a number of them have been preserved, offering a glimpse of the underground world of the miners. The least promoted but perhaps the most intriguing is the *Delaware Mine* on US 41 between Calumet and Copper Harbor at 7804 Delaware Rd. To reach it you pass through Delaware, a ghost town of a few abandoned buildings and a sobering reminder that when the copper ran out, so did the lifeblood for boomtowns throughout the peninsula.

Interest in the copper at Delaware began in 1845 and involved one early investor by the name of Horace Greeley. The famous newspaper editor actually made a trip to the Keweenaw Peninsula but never traveled much farther than Eagle River. A mining company was organized in 1848, and actual mining began the following year. From 1849 to 1851 the mine produced 522,541 pounds of copper, but the Northwest Copper Mining Company lost almost $100,000 on the operation. The mine was sold again and again to new investors, with one company building a huge hoist house in 1870 to pull the cars out of the deep shafts that were being dug. Despite all efforts, the Delaware never really turned a profit, and the shafts were sealed for good in 1887. The town of Delaware, which in 1879 had 300 residents, also disappeared.

Now a tourist attraction, the Delaware offers 2 different tours during the summer. A 40-minute tour takes you down a 100-foot staircase into Shaft No. 1 to the first level. The top level is 900 feet of tunnel from which other passages, shafts, and a huge cavern can be viewed. The Rustic Lantern Tour goes deeper into Shaft No. 3—without the aid of a staircase—and usually lasts 90 minutes. There is still plenty of copper lying around in this level, and in the information center visitors are told how to recognize and search for it in the mine. They are also given tips afterward on cleaning any metal they find.

The Delaware Mine (906-289-4688; delawarecopperminetours.com) is open 10 a.m. to 5 p.m. daily mid-May through mid-Oct. Admission is $12 per adult, $7 for children ages 6 through 12.

The men who actually worked the mines were often immigrants from the Cornwall area of England or from Finland or Norway, and they brought to Copper Country their strong ethnic heritages. Traces of that heritage can be seen in the Cornish pasties that are sold throughout the U.P. and in the

michigantrivia

Lake Superior is the largest and deepest of the Great Lakes, and its 31,700 square miles make up the largest surface area of any body of freshwater in the world. Measuring 383 miles long and 160 miles wide, Superior holds half of all the water in the Great Lakes.

Copper Country Cruising

Locals love to refer to the Keweenaw Peninsula as Copper Island because it is surrounded by water: Portage Canal on one side and Lake Superior on the rest. And departing from this "island" are numerous scenic cruises.

Docked at Copper Harbor is the 100-foot-long *Isle Royale Queen IV,* best known for its trips to Lake Superior's largest island, Isle Royale National Park. But from July 4 through Labor Day the **Isle Royale Queen** (906-289-4437; isleroyale.com) also departs between 7:30 and 8:30 p.m. (depending on when the sun sets) Tues, Wed, Thurs, and Sat, weather permitting, for a sunset cruise in which the passengers are treated to the sun melting into the Great Lake on one side of the boat and the rugged Keweenaw shoreline on the other. The fare for the 1.5-hour cruise is $25 for adults, $20 for seniors, and $15 for children ages 5 to 14 years.

popularity of Finnish saunas. For years the sauna took the place of bathtubs and showers in homes, as early settlers would build their sauna huts first and worry about their cabins later. A good sauna begins with a shower to open up the pores, followed by a stay in a cedar-paneled room where a small pile of rocks is heated. As water is tossed on the rocks, a dry heat emerges that makes the body perspire profusely, flushing out dirt and grime from the skin. The temperature ranges from 160 to 180 degrees, and the old miners used wicker sticks to beat their backs to get the blood moving. The entire ordeal ends with a cold shower to close the pores.

The copper rush of the Keweenaw Peninsula began in 1843, and Copper Harbor quickly became the center of exploration parties, newly formed mining companies, and a "rough population of enterprising prospectors, miners, and speculators." Because of the seedy nature of the miners and the constant threat of Chippewa Indians wanting to reclaim their lost land, Secretary of War William Wilkins dispatched two companies of infantry to the remote region of Michigan. They arrived in late May of 1844, and by November **Fort Wilkins** was built.

The threat of Indian hostilities never materialized, and the troops discovered the Upper Peninsula winters were long and cold. Isolated from the rest of the world with little more than duty and drill to occupy their time, the garrison of 105 men ran into problems of boredom, low morale, and illegal whiskey. The following year half the troops were transferred to Texas in preparation for the Mexican War, and in 1846, less than two years after it was built, Fort Wilkins was abandoned. In 1921 Fort Wilkins was recognized as a historic landmark by the state, and in 1923 it was designated a state park. Today the structure is noted for being one of the few surviving wooden forts east of the Mississippi River.

Although the fort was insignificant militarily, it's an outstanding example of a mid-19th-century frontier outpost, with 12 of its 16 buildings from the original structure. You can wander through the fort year-round, even ski through it in the winter, but the buildings are open mid-May through mid-Oct. Ranging from kitchen and mess room to the bakery, company barracks, and hospital, many contain restored furnishings and artifacts depicting the rough life troops endured here. From mid-June through Labor Day, interpreters in period dress give tours daily from 9 a.m. to 5 p.m., adding a touch of realism to the fort.

michigantrivia

The Porcupine Mountains and the Huron Mountains to the east are the only ranges in Michigan formed by volcanic activity.

The main entrance to the park and the fort is a mile east of Copper Harbor on US 41. A vehicle pass is required to enter the park and the fort. For more information on Fort Wilkins or on camping in the state park, call (906) 289-4215.

Keweenaw is the smallest county in the U.P., but it has more than its share of scenic drives, where every curve reveals another striking view. The most famous is the ***Brockway Mountain Drive,*** a 10-mile stretch to Copper Harbor that is the highest above-sea-level drive between the Rockies and the Alleghenies. Less traveled but almost as scenic in its own way is the ***Sand Dune Drive*** between Eagle River and Eagle Harbor. From Eagle River this portion of M 26 heads west along the Lake Superior shoreline, climbing high above the water along sandy bluffs. The road provides sweeping views of the Great Lake on the horizon and the sandy shoreline below, and the best turnoff looms above Great Sand Bay. The road returns to the lake level at Cat Harbor, a delightful beach for sunning and swimming if you can handle Superior's chilly waters, and then swings through Eagle Harbor, passing the picturesque ***Eagle Harbor Lighthouse,*** which is now a museum open to the public.

Built in 1871, the lighthouse and the lightkeeper's residence have been renovated and furnished to reflect an early-20th-century lightstation. Next door is a small museum that contains, among other things, a display on Keweenaw's prehistoric copper culture. Signs from M 26 lead you to the lighthouse at 670 Lighthouse Rd. (906-289-4990; keweenawhistory.org), which is open daily from noon to 5 p.m. mid-June through early Oct. Admission is $5 for adults and free for children.

From Eagle Harbor M 26 continues east, first passing the junction to Brockway Mountain Drive and then returning to the edge of Lake Superior, whose shoreline becomes a rugged mass of red sandstone gracefully carved by the pounding waves. Along this segment you will pass ***Devil's Wash Tub,*** a huge depression in the shoreline that echoes the waves crashing in and out of it.

Ontonagon County

Three miles west of Silver City is ***Porcupine Mountains Wilderness State Park,*** a preserve of 58,000 acres of primitive forests, secluded lakes, and the rugged "Porkies." For most visitors, this state park is a quick drive to the end of M 107, where they follow a short wooded path to the escarpment overlooking ***Lake of the Clouds,*** a watery gem between the peaks and ridges of the mountains. Those willing to don a pair of hiking boots can enjoy some of the most unusual accommodations found in the U.P. with a night in one of the park's rustic cabins.

Copper Peak Adventure Rides

North of Bessemer along Black River Harbor Drive is *Copper Peak,* a mountain that's impossible to miss because it's crowned by a ski ramp.

Built in 1969, the 469-foot slide rises 241 feet above the summit and is so immense they needed 300 tons of steel grids to support the ramp, the reason it's dubbed "the Eiffel Tower of the U.P." Despite being the world's largest ski jump, Copper Peak has always been used more in the fall by leaf peepers, who have no intention of leaving the ramp, than in the winter by daredevil skiers, who do.

You begin with a chairlift ride to the summit and then step into an 18-story elevator to continue the upward journey. When the cage door swings open, you walk still higher, to the top of the ramp, to almost 1,800 feet in elevation, where the wind blows in sudden gusts and the faint-of-heart, who had to be coaxed out of the elevator, are clutching the railing in a death grip.

But from Sept through mid-Oct the ski ramp is a $22 ticket to a million-dollar view. From the top there is a 360-degree panorama that includes Minnesota, Wisconsin, Canada, even Isle Royale National Park. What isn't the deep blue of Lake Superior is foliage painted in a palette of fall colors, from crimson reds to dazzling golds. This is autumn at its best: dramatic and colorful.

Copper Peak Adventure Rides (906-932-3500; copperpeak.net) are offered 10 a.m. to 4:30 p.m. Tues through Sun from mid-June to Labor Day; Sat and Sun from Sept to mid-Oct. Admission is $22 for adults and $8 for children age 14 and under.

Camping in Michigan

With more than 14,000 campsites, the Michigan State Park system ranks third in the country for total number of sites. Add almost 5,000 more sites in its national and state forests, and it's easy to understand why camping holidays are a time-honored tradition here, especially in the Upper Peninsula.

I prefer rustic campgrounds because they are smaller and remoter. For a list of and directions to all public campgrounds in the U.P., pick up a copy of the U.P. Travel and Recreation Association's Four Season Travel Planner. It's free and can be obtained by calling the association at (800) 562-7134; uptravel.com. Here are my favorite rustic campgrounds in the U.P.

Big Eric's Bridge State Forest Campground, Baraga County

Big Knob State Forest Campground, Mackinac County

Gene's Pond State Forest Campground, Dickinson County

Kingston Lake State Forest Campground, Alger County

Mouth of Two-Hearted River State Forest Campground, Luce County

Norway Lake National Forest Campground, Iron County

Within the Porkies is a trail network of more than 85 miles, and scattered along the footpaths are 16 wilderness cabins, each located in a scenic setting along a stream or lake or on the shore of Lake Superior. You can reach them only on foot, and some take an all-day hike while others lie only 30 or 40 minutes from the nearest parking lot. The cabins have no electricity, running water, or toilets that flush. Modern conveniences are replaced by candles, woodstoves, and an outhouse up the hill—ideal for anybody who wants to spend a night in the woods without having to "rough it" in a tent, sleeping on the ground.

The cabins provide bunks, mattresses, cooking utensils, and for those on an inland lake, a small rowboat. You must provide a sleeping bag, clothing, and food. The park rents the cabins, which hold from 4 to 8 people, from Apr through Nov at $35 to $65 per night. Stop at the park visitor center (906-885-5275) just off S. Boundary Road (open daily from 10 a.m. to 6 p.m. from mid-May through mid-Oct) for maps and a list of open cabins. You can reserve the cabins up to a year in advance through the *Michigan Campground Central Reservation System* (800-447-2757; midnrreservations.com).

Thanks to a rich history of loggers and miners, Michigan is blessed (cursed?) with a scattering of ghost towns throughout the state. Fayette is the most famous and most visited, but *Old Victoria* can be an equally interesting

Black River Drive—The Waterfall Road

Departing from Bessemer, **Black River Drive** (also labeled CR 513) heads north for 15 miles to end at Black River Harbor, one of the few access points to Lake Superior and the site of a national forest campground. It's a scenic drive past 5 waterfalls all a short walk from the road.

The cascades are linked together by a portion of the North Country Trail, which hikers can walk from Copper Peak Ski Flying Hill to the campground, a 5.5-mile trip. But it's more convenient if you drive the road, stopping at the trailhead of each individual falls. The hikes are short, the longest being a 1.5-mile round-trip, but do include a number of long staircases.

The first cascade, Great Conglomerate Falls, is reached 12 miles north of Bessemer and is followed by Potawatomi Falls, Gorge Falls, Sandstone Falls, and Rainbow Falls. The drive to view the falls makes an excellent side trip at any time of the year, even in the winter, but autumn, especially from late September through early October, is by far the most spectacular time to go.

stop. The Ontonagon County town was originally named Cushin and established in 1849 after the discovery of an ancient miner's pit that still contained a mass of copper. In 1858, a new group of investors came in and renamed the mine town Victoria, and the company town grew to more than 2,000 residents.

Victoria became a ghost town when the copper ran out. Most of the buildings date to the late 19th century. There are classic hand-hewn log cabins, ruins of a rock house, and mining equipment lying all over the place. Old Victoria (906-886-2617; exploringthenorth.com) is located 4 miles west of Rockland in Ontonagon County, with an entrance road that is clearly posted on US 45 at 25401 Victoria Dam Rd. Historical tours are given from Memorial Day through fall colors in Oct daily from 11 a.m. to 5 p.m.

Upper Tahquamenon Falls in Luce County is the largest waterfall in the state, but many cascade connoisseurs think **Bond Falls** in southern Ontonagon County near Paulding is much more beautiful. The cascade is a drop of more than 50 feet where the Middle Branch of the Ontonagon River fans out and leaps down a series of steplike rocks and around a small island of large boulders in the middle. It's the constantly tumbling water that makes Bond Falls so alluring.

From US 45 in Paulding turn east onto Bond Falls Road and in 3.2 miles you'll come to the trailhead to the cascade and a small parking area. The falls are a half-mile hike that includes numerous stairways, some steep, and boardwalks. Nearby are a picnic area, beach, and campground.

Gogebic County

Waterfalls of every type and description are the gems of the Upper Peninsula, and there are more than 150 of them scattered across this region of Michigan. **Black River Harbor Drive** (also known as Black River Road and County Road 513) in Gogebic County is virtually a parkway of whitewater splendor. The 15-mile road departs from Bessemer on US 2 and enters Ottawa National Forest, ending at scenic Black River Recreation Area on Lake Superior. Heading north you first pass **Copper Peak Ski Flying Hill,** the largest artificial ski slide in the world and the site of 500-foot jumps during the winter.

From Copper Peak, Black River Road enters the heart of the national forest and winds near 5 waterfalls, each lying at the end of a trail from a marked turn-off. Gorge and Potawatomi Falls are among the most spectacular and easiest to reach. The 2 falls are within 800 feet of each other and only a 5-minute walk from the parking lot. Potawatomi is the larger, with a 130-foot-wide cascade that drops 30 feet into the Black River. Gorge, smaller with a 24-foot drop, is encased in a steep and narrow red rock canyon—a spectacular setting. A well-marked path with stairs and observation decks leads you past both falls.

At the end of the road, you can camp at Black River Harbor Recreation Area, or those who want a little more luxury can rent a log cabin at **Bear Track Cabins** nearby. The small resort has been around since the 1930s, when it catered to lumbermen and commercial fishermen. Its name came from a hungry bear who wandered in one night while the main cabin was being built and walked in the wet cement of the front steps. The name stuck, and the tracks can still be seen today. The inn has only 3 cabins for rent, but 2 are authentic log structures, and all 3 feature natural wood interiors, woodstoves and stone fireplaces, and kitchen facilities. The large cabin can sleep 10, the others hold 4 people each, and during the summer the rates range from $90 to $180 per night for double occupancy. For reservations call the inn at (906) 932-2144 or write Bear Track Inn, 15325 Black River Rd., Ironwood 49938.

The most famous statue in Ironwood is **Hiawatha,** the world's tallest and largest Indian that overlooks the downtown area at the end of Burma Road. At 50 feet high and 16,000 pounds, this Indian can withstand winds of up to 140 mph. But this city's newest statue is equally out of proportion; a red **Stormy Kromer** cap along US 2 that is 6 feet tall and 8 feet wide. A hat so big it would fit Paul Bunyan.

Why a Stormy Kromer?

This distinctive cap with its quirky, Elmer Fudd-like six-panel design is as much a part of the Upper Peninsula as pasties and deer hunting. It has been an indispensable part of the Yooper wardrobe since 1903 when George "Stormy"

Kromer, a semipro baseball player turned railroad engineer, asked his wife to fix his baseball cap so it would stay on his head better and keep his ears warm. That's when the famous cap with earflaps and slightly downward visor was born.

Since then the **Stormy Kromer Mercantile** has grown from a northern Wisconsin mom-and-pop operation producing a North Country favorite to a national company with a 30,000-square-foot facility in Ironwood, manufacturing more than 50,000 Stormy Kromer caps per year in 6 styles and 12 colors, including blaze orange for hunters, a green and gold cap for Green Bay Packers fans, and a Lil' Kromer for infants and toddlers.

At Stormy Kromer Mercantile (888-455-2253; stormykromer.com) at 1238 Wall St. east of Ironwood along US 2 you can hear the history of the hat during a free factory tour that is offered at 1:30 p.m. Mon through Fri. The store is open Mon through Fri 8 a.m. to 5 p.m. and Sat 9 a.m. to noon. Or skip the tour and just shop for a new Stormy Kromer. You'll fit in with the locals and your ears will never be cold again.

Pine Mountain Ski Jump

Known as the King of Hills, **Pine Mountain Ski Jump** is an awesome sight. Built in 1938 as a Works Progress Administration project and upgraded several times since, the 90-meter ski ramp features a 186-foot-high scaffold and a 381-foot slide. It sits majestically on top of a landing hill with a vertical drop of another 349 feet. Add it all up and you have a 1,440-foot run that sends skiers through the air at speeds of 55 to 65 miles an hour. In Iron Mountain they tell you it's like jumping off a 29-story building, of which there are none in the U.P.

Jumpers use skis that are wide, heavy, and often 265 centimeters or longer. Both their boots and bindings are much more closely related to Nordic skiing than Alpine, especially with the ability to lift the heels off the skis.

The jumpers are able to defy gravity by basically turning themselves into airplane wings when they lift out of the back of their bindings on takeoff and lean forward until their bodies are almost parallel to the skis. In 1994, an Austrian set a US record at Pine Mountain when he leaped 400 feet.

If you're around Iron Mountain in mid-February, you can see the jumpers in action during the annual Pine Mountain Classic, which draws almost 20,000 spectators. In the summer you can climb the 280 steps to the top of the jump and be rewarded with a panoramic view that includes seven lakes.

To reach the ski jump from US 2, turn west on Kent Street and follow it past the Cornish Pump Engine and Mining Museum. Turn north on Upper Pine Mountain Road, which will wind to the ski ramp at the top of the hill.

Going Underground in the Upper Peninsula

Mining has had a long and colorful history in the Upper Peninsula, and there are many places where you can experience from a miner's point of view what it was like to go underground. Some of the following mines are covered in greater detail in this chapter:

Iron Mountain Iron Mine: Guided tours that begin on a rail tram (miner's train) take you through 2,600 feet of underground drifts and tunnels in this iron mine at W4852 US 2 in Vulcan, east of Iron Mountain; (906) 563-8077; ironmountainmine.wixsite .com.

Adventure Mine: This mine near Greenland, just off M 38 at 200 Adventure Ave., was operated from 1850 to 1920 by the same board that oversaw the highly profitable Quincy Mining Company. Although at one point the copper mine consisted of five shafts, including Shaft No. 3 that contained 13 levels and extended down 1,300 feet into the ore body, it was never profitable. Today Adventure Mine offers a variety of tours, ranging from a 45-minute walk through Shaft No. 2 (adults $18, children $8) to the 3-hour Miners Underground Tour that includes rappelling down a mine shaft in darkness ($65 per adult; children not permitted). For $125 per adult (children under age 13 not permitted), the Captain's Underground Tour includes a 5- to 6-hour tour plus a pasty lunch underground; (906) 883-3371; adventureminetours.com.

Delaware Mine: Located in Keweenaw County east of Mohawk at 7804 Delaware Rd., this is the only mine offering a self-guided tour into its shafts. You descend 110 feet into the mine and then follow a horizontal shaft where you can look for nuggets of pure copper. Find any and they're yours; (906) 289-4688; keweenawheritagesites .org.

Quincy Mine: This is the best mine tour in the Upper Peninsula. The Houghton County copper mine is just a mile north of Hancock at 49750 US 41 and includes an underground tour 400 feet into the No. Two Shafthouse and a scenic ride on a rail tram; (906) 482-3101; quincymine.com.

Iron County

Perhaps the U.P.'s largest and least-known historical complex is the *Iron County Historical Museum,* located in the village of Caspian on County Road 424 at 100 Brady Ave., 2 miles south of US 2 at Iron River. The grounds include almost 20 buildings, many a century old, in a Greenfield Village–like setting that lacks some of the polish of the famous Dearborn attraction but is no less interesting. The park occupies the site of the Caspian Iron Mine, and the head frame that hoisted cars out of the mine in the 1920s still towers over the complex. The main museum is the former engine house, which has been considerably enlarged and today is a maze of displays and three-dimensional exhibits. The favorite is the iron ore mining model that, for a nickel, will automatically run through the process of the rocks being rinsed from the mine and loaded into railroad cars above ground. Other interesting exhibits are the renovated saloon, blacksmith shop, schoolroom, and a hand-carved model of a logging camp that fills an 80-foot display case with hundreds of figures and pieces.

Outside you can wander through one historic building after another: a logging camp bunkhouse with a table set for supper and mackinaw shirts (made of a heavy plaid wool) still hanging up near the door, a barn filled with plows and threshers of the 1800s, a completely furnished homesteaders' cabin, and many other exhibits. You could easily spend an entire day exploring this fascinating folk-life complex. The Iron County Historical Museum (906-265-2617; ironcountyhistoricalmuseum.org) is open from mid-May to Sept from 10 a.m. to 4 p.m. Mon through Sat; Sept hours are Mon through Sat noon to 4 p.m. Admission is $10 for adults and $5 for children ages 5 through 18.

Dickinson County

As in the copper fields, many workers in the iron mines were immigrants from Europe. At Iron Mountain, many Italians came to work the Chapin Mine, which opened in 1879 and went on to become the second leading ore producer in the U.P. You can learn about the miners' life and work at the **Menominee Range Historical Museum** and see the huge water pump that was built for the exceptionally wet mine at the **Cornish Pump Engine and Mining Museum.**

The pump engine was built for the Chapin Mine, and while Chapin led iron ore production in the Menominee Range, it was also one of the wettest mines ever worked. To dry things out, the E.P. Allis Company of Milwaukee was commissioned in 1889 to build a pumping system for the excess water. The centerpiece of the museum is the 725-ton steeple compound condensing engine that rises 54 feet from the floor and features a 40-foot flywheel. It has been documented as the largest steam-driven pumping engine in the United States.

There are also photos and exhibits on the underground mining days of Iron Mountain and an intriguing exhibit on Henry Ford's World War II gliders, which were manufactured in the area and used to secretly deploy troops behind enemy lines. The museum (906-774-1086) is in downtown Iron Mountain at 300 E. Ludington St., 1 block west of US 2 on Kent Street. Hours are 9 a.m. to 5 p.m. Mon through Sat and noon to 4 p.m. Sun from mid-May to mid-Oct. Admission is $5 for adults and $4.50 for children ages 10 to 18; a ticket that includes the Menominee Range Historical Museum, the Glider Museum, and the Cornish Pump Museum is $15 for adults and $6 for children ages 10 to 18 (906-774-4276; menomineemuseum.com).

The Menominee River forms almost half of the border between Wisconsin and Michigan's Upper Peninsula, beginning west of Iron Mountain and extending to its mouth on Green Bay. Two miles south of Norway, the river flows through Piers Gorge, a whitewater area of large falls, holes, and swirls as the river tumbles through a scenic forested canyon. The gorge picked up its name in the 1840s when loggers built piers along this section of the river to slow the current and prevent logs from jamming and splitting on the jagged rocks. You can view this spectacular stretch of wild water by heading south of Norway on US 8; just before its bridge across the Menominee, turn left onto Piers Gorge Road. The paved road quickly turns into a dirt one, and then after 0.6 mile it ends at **Piers Gorge Nature Trail.** The trail is a round-trip of 3 miles but swings past a series of viewing points above the falls.

During the summer you can also experience the gorge and what many rafters call the "Midwest's premier whitewater river" through **Kosir's Rapid Raft.** The company offers a 3-hour raft trip that takes you through Piers Gorge and over its falls. On Sat and Sun, the rafters meet nearby and then proceed to the river with their large inflated rafts. It's a wild ride, one that will leave you soaking wet but exhilarated. The company provides the rafts, guides, helmets, life jackets, and a paddle for each passenger.

Kosir's Rapid Raft (715-757-3431; kosirs.com) is based in Wisconsin. The raft trips, which also can be set up during the week by advance reservation, cost $45 per person on weekends and holidays or $40 per person Mon through Thurs.

Menominee County

One of the products of Michigan's white pine era was hardwood floors by the IXL Company of Hermansville. Established by C. J. Meyer in the 1870s as part of his Wisconsin Land and Lumber Company, IXL became world-renowned for its floors after machines were invented in Hermansville that could precision-manufacture tongue-and-groove hardwood flooring in one operation. By the early 1900s IXL had the largest such plant in the country, and its flooring could be seen (and walked on) in the main lodge at Yellowstone National Park and the Mormon Temple in Salt Lake City.

In 1881 Meyer erected a huge office building to manage his sprawling lumber operation, and today it's one of the most intriguing museums in the Upper Peninsula. The **IXL Historical Museum** is literally a step into a 19th-century business office. On the first floor visitors wander through the payroll and accounting departments as well as the private offices of the company executives. All are fully furnished and appear as if the workers had just stepped out for lunch. In one room are dictaphones, mimeographs, typewriters, and other machines complete with instruction booklets, while across the hall beautiful rolltop desks and an ornate walk-in vault can be seen. On the second floor several rooms are devoted to the machinery and equipment used in the flooring industry, and on the third floor visitors can still flip through original payroll records and see what a worker earned each week (along with deductions) in the 1890s.

The museum is located in the heart of Hermansville, a small town on US 2, 26 miles west of Escanaba and 30 miles east of Iron Mountain at 5551 River St. N. The museum (906-498-2181; ixlmuseum.com) is open from Memorial Day through Labor Day from 12:30 to 4 p.m. daily. Admission is by donation.

Places to Stay in the Western Upper Peninsula

BIG BAY

Big Bay Depot Motel
301 Depot Rd.
(906) 345-9350

Big Bay Point Lighthouse Bed & Breakfast
4674 County Rd. KCB
(906) 345-9957
bigbaylighthouse.com

Thunder Bay Inn
400 Bensinger
(906) 345-9220
thunderbayinn.net

BLACK HARBOR

Bear Track Cabins
15325 Black River Rd.
(906) 932-2144

CALUMET/LAURIUM

Americinn
56925 S. Sixth St.
(906) 337-6463
wyndhamhotels.com

Laurium Manor Inn Bed and Breakfast
320 Tamarack St.
(906) 337-2549
laurium.info

Victorian Hall Bed & Breakfast
305 Tamarack St.
(906) 337-2549
laurium.info/victorianhall

COPPER HARBOR

Brockway Inn
840 Gratiot St.
(906) 289-4588
brockwayinn.com

Keweenaw Mountain Lodge
14252 US 41
(906) 289-4403
keweenawmountainlodge.com

Mariner North Resort
245 Gratiot St.
(906) 289-4637
manorth.com

EAGLE RIVER

Fitzgerald's Hotel
5033 Front St.
(906) 337-0666
fitzgeralds-mi.com

HOUGHTON

Hampton Inn Hilton
820 Shelden Ave.
(888) 487-1700
travelhoughton.com

Sheridan on the Lake
47026 Sheridan Pl.
(906) 482-7079
sheridanonthelake.com

Travelodge Houghton
215 Shelden Ave.
(906) 482-1400
travelodgeofhoughton.com

IRON MOUNTAIN

Comfort Inn
1565 N. Stephenson Ave.
(906) 774-5505
choicehotels.com

Edgewater Resort Cabins
N4128 US 2
(800) 236-6244
edgewaterresortmi.com

Woodlands Motel
N3957 US 2
(906) 774-6106
exploringthenorth.com

IRONWOOD

Classic Motor Inn
1200 E. Cloverland Dr.
(906) 932-2000
westernup.com

Quality Inn
210 E. Cloverland Dr.
(906) 932-2224
choicehotels.com

ISHPEMING

Jasper Ridge Inn
1000 River Pkwy.
(906) 485-2378
magnusonhotels.com

Magnuson Hotel Country Inn
850 US 41
(906) 485-6345
magnusonhotels.com

MARQUETTE

Blueberry Ridge Bed & Breakfast
193 Oakridge Dr.
(906) 249-9246
blueberryridgebedand
breakfastmqt.com

Cedar Motor Inn
2523 US 41
(906) 228-2280
cedarmi.com

SELECTED CHAMBERS OF COMMERCE & TOURISM BUREAUS

Baraga County Convention & Visitors Bureau
755 E. Broad St.
L'Anse 49946
(800) 743-4908
baragacounty.org

Dickinson Area Chamber Alliance
600 S. Stephenson Ave.
Iron Mountain 49801
(906) 774-2002
dickinsonchamber.com

Keweenaw Convention and Visitors Bureau
56638 Calumet Ave.
Calumet 49913
(800) 338-7982
keweenaw.info

Marquette County Convention and Visitors Bureau
117 W. Washington St.
Marquette 49855
(800) 544-4321
travelmarquettemichigan.com

Upper Peninsula Travel and Recreation Association
1050 Pyle Dr.
Kingsford 49802
(800) 562-7134
uptravel.com

Western U.P. Convention and Visitor's Bureau
648 W. Cloverland Dr.
Ironwood 49938
(800) 522-5657
explorewesternup.com

Landmark Inn
230 N. Front St.
(888) 752-6362
thelandmarkinn.com

Nestledown Bed & Breakfast
975 N. Lakeshore Blvd.
(906) 273-0996
nestledownmarquette.com

SILVER CITY

Americinn
120 Lincoln Ave.
(906) 662-9111
wyndhamhotels.com

Mountain View Lodges
34042 M 107
(906) 885-5256
mountainviewlodges.com

WATERSMEET

Forest Gardens Getaway
E23493 Twist Lake Rd.
(906) 544-2664
forestgardensgetaway.com

The Guest House on Majestic Point
3428 White Birch Rd.
(630) 986-0948
majesticpoint.com

Vacationland Resort
E 19636 Hebert Rd.
(906) 358-4380
vacationlandresort.com

Places to Eat in the Western Upper Peninsula

CALUMET/LAURIUM

Café Rosetta
102 Fifth St.
(906) 337-5500
caferosetta.com
Cafe

Carmelitas
618 Oak St.
(906) 337-4025
carmelitassouthwestern
grille.com
Southwestern

Michigan House Café and Brew Pub
300 Sixth St.
(906) 337-1910
michiganhousecafe.com
American

Toni's Country Kitchen
79 Third St.
(906) 337-0611
American

COPPER HARBOR

Brickside Brewery
64 Gratiot St.
(906) 289-4772
bricksidebrewery.com
Brewpub

Harbor Haus Restaurant
77 Brockway Ave.
(906) 289-4502
harborhaus.com
German/Austrian

Keweenaw Mountain Lodge
14252 US 41
(906) 289-4403
keweenawmountainlodge
.com
Fine Dining

Pines Restaurant
174 Gratiot Ave.
(906) 289-4222
copperharborpines.com
American

Tamarack Inn Restaurant
571 Gratiot St.
(906) 289-4522
American

EAGLE RIVER

Fitzgerald's Restaurant
Eagle River Inn
5033 Front St.
(906) 337-0666
fitzgeralds-mi.com
Lakeview Dining

HOUGHTON

Ambassador Restaurant
126 Shelden Ave.
(906) 482-5054
theambassadorhoughton
.com
Pizza & Pasta

Joey's Seafood & Grill
304 Shelden Ave.
(906) 483-0500
joeys-grill.com
Seafood

Keweenaw Brewing Company
408 Shelden Ave.
(906) 482-5596
kbc.beer
Microbrewery

OTHER ATTRACTIONS

Bishop Baraga Shrine
17570 US 41
L'Anse
(906) 524-7021
exploringthenorth.com

Marquette Regional History Center
145 W. Spring St.
Marquette
(906) 226-3571
marquettecohistory.org

Houghton County Historical Museum
53102 M 26
Lake Linden
(906) 296-4121
houghtonhistory.org

Menominee Heritage Museum
904 11th Ave.
Menominee
(906) 863-9000
menomineehistory.org

Ironwood Historic Depot & Museum
150 N. Lowell St.
Ironwood
(906) 932-0287
ironwoodareahistoricalsociety.com

Upper Peninsula Children's Museum
123 W. Baraga Ave.
Marquette
(906) 226-3911
upchildrensmuseum.org

Library Restaurant
62 Isle Royale St.
(906) 481-2665
thelibraryhoughton.com
Brewpub

Suomi Home Bakery & Restaurant
54 Huron St.
(906) 482-3220
Finnish

IRON MOUNTAIN

Spiro's Downtown Restaurant
427 S. Stephenson Ave.
(906) 774-3499
spirosironmountain.com
Seafood

IRON RIVER

Alice's Supper Club
402 W. Adams St.
(906) 265-4764
alicesironriver.com
Italian

Mr. T's Family Restaurant
3599 US 2
(906) 265-4741
mrtsfamily.com
American

Outer Limits Bar & Grill
101 W. Genesee St.
(906) 265-3663
outerlimitsbarandgrillonline
.com
American

IRONWOOD

Elk & Hound Restaurant
200 Country Club Rd.
(906) 932-3742
American

Joe's Pasty Shop
116 W. Aurora St.
(906) 932-4412
joespastyshopironwood
.com
Pasties

Manny's
316 E. Houk St.
(906) 932-0999
Italian

Mike's
106 E. Cloverland Dr.
(906) 932-0555
mikesironwood.com
American

ISHPEMING

Jasper Ridge Brewery
1075 Country Ln.
(906) 485-6017
jasperridgebrewery.com
Brewpub

Mama Mia's Italian Restaurant
207 E. Pearl St.
(906) 485-5813
mamamiasishpeming.com
Italian

Ralph's Italian Delicatessen
601 Palms Ave.
(906) 485-4557
ralphsitaliandeli.com
Italian

L'ANSE

Hilltop Restaurant
18047 US 41
(906) 524-7858
sweetroll.com
American

MARQUETTE

Bodega
517 N. Third St.
(906) 226-7009
cafebodegamqt.com
Bakery & Cafe

Donckers
137 W. Washington St.
(906) 226-6110
donckersonline.com
Soda Fountain & Sandwiches

Jean Kay's Pasties
1635 Presque Isle
(906) 228-5310
jeankayspasties.com
Pasties

Lagniappe Cajun Creole Eatery
145 Washington St.
(906) 226-8200
marquettecajun.com
Cajun Creole

Landmark Inn Capers
230 N. Front St.
(888) 752-6362
thelandmarkinn.com
Fine Dining

Steinhaus
102 W. Washington St.
(906) 273-1531
steinhausmqt.com
German

The Vierling Restaurant
119 S. Front St.
(906) 228-3533
thevierling.com
Brewpub

Index